SOCIETY FOR NEW TESTAMENT STUDIES
MONOGRAPH SERIES

GENERAL EDITOR
MATTHEW BLACK, D.D., F.B.A.

ASSOCIATE EDITOR
R. McL. WILSON

33

REDACTIONAL STYLE IN THE MARCAN GOSPEL

REDACTIONAL STYLE IN THE MARCAN GOSPEL

A Study of Syntax and Vocabulary
as guides to Redaction in Mark

E. J. Pryke

*Rector of Offord D'Arcy and Offord Cluny with Great Paxton
Cambridgeshire (former Recognized Teacher of London University
and Senior Lecturer of St Mark and St John, Plymouth)*

CAMBRIDGE UNIVERSITY PRESS

CAMBRIDGE

LONDON · NEW YORK · MELBOURNE

Published by the Syndics of the Cambridge University Press
The Pitt Building, Trumpington Street, Cambridge CB2 1RP
Bentley House, 200 Euston Road, London NW1 2DB
32 East 57th Street, New York, NY 10022, USA
296 Beaconsfield Parade, Middle Park, Melbourne 3206, Australia

First published 1978

Printed in Great Britain at the
University Press, Cambridge

Library of Congress cataloguing in publication data

Pryke, E. J. 1920–
Redactional style in the Marcan Gospel.

(Monograph series – Society for New Testament Studies; 33)
Bibliography: p.
Includes index
I. Bible. N.T. Mark – Language, style. I. Title.
II. Series: Studiorum Novi Testamenti Societas.
Monograph series; 33

BS2585.3. P78   226'.3' 06   76–52184

ISBN 0 521 21430 0

CONTENTS

v

CONTENTS

ACKNOWLEDGEMENTS

First, and foremost, I am grateful to my supervisor, the Reverend Professor C. F. Evans, King's College, London, for his criticism, encouragement, and counsel during the six years of my study for the London Ph.D. degree. I am also obliged to him for the translation of Sundwall and Wellhausen. The other German translations are by my former colleague, Mr J. Jefferey, while the French are my own.

I also place on record my indebtedness to the Revd Professor E. Best, the Revd Dr T. F. Glasson, Prof. M. Hooker, and the Revd Dr N. Turner for constructive criticisms and suggestions. A former pupil, A. Pierce, helped me check back the Greek vocabularies, while my wife and several pupils have been generous in reading back the typist's manuscript.

I recall in gratitude the friendship shown to me by the late Professor R. H. Lightfoot, and the instructive seminars on the text of Mark which I enjoyed under the Revd Professor G. D. Kilpatrick.

I also acknowledge my thanks to London University for their award of the degree of Doctor of Philosophy in the Faculty of Theology in 1971, and also for my recognition as a Teacher of the University in the Faculty of Education in 1968.

LIST OF ABBREVIATIONS

Allen = W. C. Allen, *The Gospel according to Saint Mark* (London, 1915)

Best = E. Best, *The Temptation and the Passion: The Markan Soteriology* (Cambridge, 1965)

Black = M. Black, *An Aramaic Approach to the Gospels and Acts*, 3rd ed. (Oxford, 1967)

Blass–Debrunner = F. Blass and A. Debrunner, *A Greek Grammar of the New Testament*. Trans. and revision by R. W. Funk of 9th–10th German ed. (Cambridge and Chicago, 1961).

Bultmann = R. Bultmann, *The History of the Synoptic Tradition*, 2nd ed. (Oxford, 1968). Trans. by J. Marsh of *Theologie des Neuen Testaments* (Tübingen, 1953).

Burkill = T. A. Burkill, *Mysterious Revelation, An Examination of the Philosophy of St. Mark's Gospel* (Cornell, U.S.A., 1963).

Cranfield = C. E. B. Cranfield, *The Gospel according to Saint Mark* (Cambridge, 1959)

Dibelius = M. Dibelius, *From Tradition to Gospel*, trans. B. L. Woolf (London, 1971).

Doudna = J. C. Doudna, *The Greek of the Gospel of Mark*, *J.B.L.* Monograph Series 12 (Philadelphia, 1961)

Hawkins = J. C. Hawkins, *Horae Synopticae* (Oxford, 1899)

Horstmann = M. Horstmann, *Studien zur Markinischen Christologie* (Münster, 1969)

J.B.L. = *Journal of Biblical Literature*

J.T.S. = *Journal of Theological Studies*

Kertelge = K. Kertelge, *Die Wunder Jesu im Markusevangelium* (München, 1970)

Kuhn = H. W. Kuhn, *Ältere Sammlungen im Markusevangelium* (Göttingen, 1971)

Lagrange = M. J. Lagrange, *Évangile selon Saint Marc* (Paris, 1929)

Lambrecht = J. Lambrecht, *Die Redaktion der Markus-Apokalypse*, Analecta Biblica 28 (Rome, 1967)

Lightfoot = R. H. Lighfoot, *History and Interpretation in the Gospels* (London, 1935)

Marxsen = W. Marxsen, *Der Evangelist Markus* (Göttingen, 1959)

Moule = C. F. D. Moule, *An Idiom Book of New Testament Greek* (Cambridge, 1953)

Moulton = J. H. Moulton, *Grammar of New Testament Greek*, vols 1, 2, 3

Neirynck=F. Neirynck, *Duality in Mark, Contributions to the Study of Markan Redaction*, Bibliotheca Ephemeridum Theologicarum Lovaniensium XXXI (Leuven, 1972)

N.T.=Novum Testamentum

N.T.S.=New Testament Studies

Pesch=R. Pesch, *Naherwartungen: Tradition und Redaktion in Mk 13* (Düsseldorf, 1968)

Rawlinson=E. J. Rawlinson, *The Gospel according to St. Mark* (London, 1925)

Reploh=K. G. Reploh, *Markus – Lehrer der Gemeinde: Eine redaktionsgeschichtliche Studie zu den Jüngerperikopen des Markus-Evangeliums* (Stuttgart, 1969)

Schreiber=J. Schreiber, *Theologie des Vertrauens: Eine redaktionsgeschichtliche Untersuchung des Markusevangeliums* (Hamburg, 1967)

Schweizer=E. Schweizer, *The Good News according to Mark*, trans. D. H. Madvig (London, 1971)

Sundwall=J. Sundwall, 'Die Zusammensetzung des Markusevangeliums' in *Acta Academiae Aboensis, Humaniora IX* (Abo, 1934), pp. 1–86

Swete=H. B. Swete, *The Gospel according to St. Mark*, 2nd ed. (London, 1908)

Taylor=V. Taylor, *The Gospel according to St. Mark* (London, 1952)

Trocmé=E. Trocmé, *La Formation de l'Évangile selon Marc*, Études d'Histoire et de Philosophie Religieuses, no. 57 (Paris, 1963)

Turner=C. H. Turner, series of articles on 'Marcan Usage', *J.T.S.* (1924–8)

Zerwick=M. Zerwick, *Biblical Greek*, trans. J. Smith (Rome, 1963)

Further Abbreviations

h.p.=historic present

M.L.C.=Marcan Literary Construction

m.v.=main verb

part.=participle

Q.Z.D.=Qumran Scrolls Zadokite Documents

R=redactional

S=source

S.S.P.—Summary Statement of Progress

vocab.=vocabulary

V.S.O.=verb, subject, object order of the sentence

see also p. 24

INTRODUCTION

One of the results of the acceptance of the priority of Mark's Gospel has been that extensive and minute examinations of this Gospel have been conducted on its linguistic side, with a view to discovering by this method, if possible, what kind of a person the author was, what was his cultural and religious milieu, and what were his intentions and purposes in writing.

Outstanding in this field was the very notable series of articles on Marcan linguistic usage by C. H. Turner.[1] Though it followed on from the previous work of Sir John Hawkins,[2] it was in many ways a pioneer work. Turner investigated with the greatest care and detail the linguistic features of the Gospel. drawing particular attention to some of the most notable, such as the use of εὐθύς, the impersonal verb, the historic present etc. In this type of investigation he has had his successors, principally Prof. G. D. Kilpatrick,[3] Dr Nigel Turner,[4] and Dr Vincent Taylor,[5] while the work of Père Lagrange should not be forgotten.[6]

There is a certain objectivity about these studies, and their linguistic findings remain valid whatever literary-critical or theological view is taken of the Gospel. Not that they necessarily remain purely linguistic or without further application. In more than one instance, C. H. Turner made linguistics the basis of a judgement on Mark as a writer, as when he says that the evangelist's use of εὐθύς was determined by his desire to impart a liveliness of style to his narrative, or when, in analysing parenthetical clauses he compares Mark 8¹⁵ to an 'obtrusive reference' or footnote.[7] Kilpatrick has drawn attention to the way in which Turner used his conclusions on Marcan linguistic

[1] C. H. Turner, articles on 'Marcan Usage' in *J.T.S.* 25–9 (1924–8).

[2] Hawkins, pp. 9ff., 92ff.

[3] G. D. Kilpatrick, articles mainly on textual criticism; cf. Bibliography p. 181.   [4] Moulton, vol. 3.

[5] Taylor, both in the main body of the commentary and in its introduction, pp. 55ff.

[6] Lagrange, pp. lxviiiff.

[7] C. H. Turner, *J.T.S.* 26 (January 1925), 150.

usage to decide between variant readings in the sphere of textual criticism,[1] and he has himself followed the same procedure.[2] Further, in his essay on 'The Gentile Mission in Mark and Mark 13.9–11', he argued on grounds of Marcan linguistic usage for a certain punctuation of the text which has considerable bearing on the exegesis of the Gospel.[3] In one particular instance Turner linked his linguistic analysis to a literary-critical judgement, when he deduced from Mark's frequent use of impersonal verbs that immediately behind the repeated 'they' of Mark's text lay the 'we' and 'us' of Peter's diary.[4] Normally, however, Turner assumes that there is only one style in the Gospel, that of the evangelist.

With the further stage in the critical analysis of the Synoptic Gospels marked by the advent of form-criticism, the situation was changed even for purely linguistic studies. This may be seen in Dr Matthew Black's comment on Turner's explanation of the impersonal verbs mentioned above. He points out that such an explanation is not the only nor even the most likely one. In view of the impersonal nature of the oral tradition upon which form-criticism concentrates attention, to which Black cites parallels from rabbinic writings, and the imprecision typical of colloquialisms found in folk-literature of a religious kind, it might be better to look in this direction for the explanation of such a phenomenon.[5] For if the general assumption of form-criticism is correct, the evangelist composed his Gospel from originally independent pericopes, which had already to some extent been shaped in the oral period of tradition. In this case we can no longer proceed on the assumption that there will be a uniform style throughout the Gospel, and that the style of the evangelist himself.[6] The question how far in investi-

---

[1] E.g. in his edition of the British and Foreign Bible Society's edition of the Greek New Testament (London, 1958), p. xxiii, n. 1.

[2] 'Western Text and original text in the Gospels and Acts', *J.T.S.* 44 (January 1943), 24–36.

[3] In D. E. Nineham (ed.), *Studies in the Gospels: Essays in Memory of R. H. Lightfoot* (Oxford, 1955), pp. 145–58.

[4] C. H. Turner, *J.T.S.* 26 (April 1925), 225–8.   [5] Black, p. 127.

[6] Kilpatrick, 'Western Text', pp. 24–5: 'Sometimes his [CHT] decision was based upon the documentary hypothesis, but the more important side of his work was that in which he indicated that the reading of the Western text on occasion accorded best with the language and style of Mark.' See

gating the Gospel we are studying the linguistic usage of the evangelist, or the linguistic usage of the tradition before and behind him, becomes inescapable. The issue is well illustrated by Dr A. M. Farrer's thesis. He insists that the modes of expression in the Marcan Gospel are due to the inspiration of the evangelist's mind, and that in studying his grammar and syntax as well as his arrangement we are attempting to follow the traces of one man's prophetic inspiration. Farrer is only able to maintain this, however, because he explicitly rejects the form-critical account of things, and would have us see Mark as the creator of his own pericopes.[1] If, however, Farrer's rejection of form-criticism is itself rejected on good grounds, then a distinction may have to be drawn, however difficult it may be to draw it, between what the evangelist has supplied as an editor, and the material which he had edited.

Such a distinction is drawn by Dr Rudolf Bultmann in his work on form-criticism. The greater part of this work is concerned with the analysis of the tradition in its oral stage, and with delineating the original pericopes, but he has a final section concerned with the editing of the traditional material at two stages, that of the editing of the spoken word, and that of the editing of the narrative material and the composition of the Gospels.[2] In this section he devotes several pages to the editorial characteristics of Mark, whom he regards as the inventor of the literary type 'Gospel'. As Bultmann observes, 'There is no definable boundary between the oral and written tradition.'[3] He admits that the analysis of Mark along these lines cannot always be carried out with certainty, since 'the original situation-indicators are often so closely tied up with the editorial introductions and postscripts that it is no longer possible to make a clear division between them... It is uncertain which editorial links belong to Mark himself and which to some earlier stage of the tradition.'[4] Nevertheless Bultmann attempts such an analysis. How this approach could be built on and carried

also p. 31: 'An outstanding example of this kind of work [use of language and style] is provided in C. H. Turner's articles, already mentioned, on Marcan usage.'

[1] A. M. Farrer, *A Study in St. Mark* (London, 1951), pp. 4ff.
[2] Bultmann, Ch. 3, 'The Editing of the Traditional Material', pp. 321–67.
[3] *Ibid.*, p. 321.   [4] *Ibid.*, p. 338.

further can be seen in the study of J. Sundwall, which is a detailed and sustained attempt to answer the question – so much easier in the case of Matthew and Luke – what would be the methods and sources of a writer such as Mark. Sundwall places great emphasis on the 'catchword' principle as employed by the evangelist in linking together not only the material from his sources, but also his own redactional verses. He suggests that phrases like καὶ εὐθύς and the repetition of words and expressions at the redactional end of a pericope and at the opening of the following pericope betray not only the hand of Mark the redactor, but also the influence of his sources upon his own style. Obviously at this point the matter becomes exceedingly intricate and complicated. He also finds evidence of the redactor's hand in the placing of the material, e.g. in the cyclic repetition of the feeding miracles, and in the preparatory scenery of 'boat', 'crowd' and 'lake', which are redactional devices to give meaningful background to the parables and to the general plan of the Gospel.

Already with reference to Bultmann and Sundwall it has been necessary to use the word 'redaction', since these two writers start from the form-critical analysis of the Gospel, and inquire into the processes by which the independent pericopes were chosen and put together by an evangelist who in this respect was a redactor–editor. These two writers form a bridge to the more recent avowedly redactional studies of Mark. The same may be said of Taylor's commentary, with its insights into the literary structure of the Gospel as a whole, and into the literary and linguistic characteristics of the evangelist as an editor, though a certain reserve over form-criticism, and a certain conservatism of approach, prevent him from following his critical acumen and linguistic observations to their logical conclusions. It is only more recently, however, that redaction-history has emerged as a full-scale study of the Gospels, and as the next stage on from form-criticism.[1] At this stage the evangelists are examined not simply as collectors and transmitters of tradition, but as authors in their own right, from whose selection, arrangement and editorial methods inferences may be drawn as to the author, his community, and his con-

[1] See J. Rohde, *Rediscovering the Teaching of the Evangelists*, trans. D. M. Barton (London, 1968).

4

ception of the Gospel. In this type of investigation linguistics, literary analysis and theological interpretation are inevitably drawn closely together and can hardly proceed apart.

Outstanding here with respect to Mark has been W. Marxsen's study, in which an assessment of Mark's theological situation and purpose goes along with, and at times arises out of, a detailed examination of language and arrangement. Somewhat different in method, though similar in general approach, is E. Trocmé's analysis, in which an investigation of the evangelist's sources, and of his predilections and antipathies, is accompanied by inquiry into his vocabulary, and leads to a hypothesis of a proto-Mark (1–13), followed by a second edition (1–16[8]). Dr E. Best's study of the soteriology of the Marcan Gospel proceeds by way not only of Mark's particular selection of material, but also of a detailed examination of the Marcan 'seams', since 'the most obvious place to look for Mark's hand is in the words, phrases (and) sentences which join together the various incidents of the Gospel... But we do not confine our attention to them alone; we need also to take into account any relevant editing of the material itself.'[1]

Finally, along these lines Dr E. Schweizer, mainly on the basis of the placing of the source material and of the most frequent redactional words and expressions, has attempted to reconstruct a 'redactional' theology of Mark himself.[2]

The intention of this book is to pursue this line of research into Marcan usage, and, it is hoped, to refine it at certain points by a more detailed, at times statistical, study of linguistic usage both in the 'source' material (S) and the 'redactional' material (R), having particularly in mind its possible bearing on the theology of the evangelist. It starts from the general principles of form-criticism, and accepts in particular the pericopal structure of the Gospel. The literary structure of the Gospel then becomes easier to delineate. When we analyse the separate units into paradigms, miracle stories, etc., we are enabled to see the evangelist at work upon his source material, and to

[1] Best, p. 63.

[2] E. Schweizer, 'Anmerkungen zur Theologie des Markus' in *Supplements to Novum Testamentum*, vol. 6, 'Neotestamentica et Patristica' (Leiden, 1962), pp. 35–46.

decide with greater probability, though often by no means with certainty, what is 'redaction' as distinct from tradition. The study of Mark's work as an editor becomes a logical outcome. Major bridge passages such as 1^{14-15} and $3^{7ff.}$ are clearly redactional, and whether they are completely so is not so difficult to decide as might be imagined. The scenery and background verses are from the evangelist, developed by him either out of the tradition itself or out of his imagination. What are recognised as major features of the Gospel are not just present in the source material, but are extended into the redaction with considerable skill by a writer who in the main is utilising oral traditions, but who needs linking passages and background details to give his Gospel coherence and a goal.

Since redaction-history is concerned with the linking passages of a redactor–editor who pulls his sources into a logical and coherent form, purely linguistic features may also provide criteria by which the accuracy of the literary delineation may be tested or rejected. Thus the detailed and systematic studies of Hawkins and Turner should be of service, when these are applied to the entire material in the Gospel, first to those sections which have on literary grounds been earmarked as R, and then to the residual source passages to see if any of these too might be converted from S to R. To illustrate the method, some eighteen marked features of Marcan usage, pioneered by Turner and others, are tested to see if what was thought previously to be characteristic of the whole Gospel and evidence of a homogeneous style throughout might in fact be due to the redaction of the editor when he linked up the oral or written sources. Two aims are combined together here: (a) a careful and thorough investigation is attempted to justify or qualify statements made from time to time about the personal style or predilections of the author, such as his preference for πάλιν, the historic present, ἄρχομαι + infinitive, and (b) an attempt is made to see if linguistics might on their own be employed to confirm or pull into the redactional net verses which might otherwise be forgotten or missed. Here the vocabulary test (part B III) is of great help, inasmuch as it also can be an additional and independent way of approaching the problem of finding where exactly the author's special vocabulary, and therefore his redaction, is to be found.

In part B III the total Gospel vocabulary of words used five times and over is analysed in frequency order to try to discern the special vocabulary of the author, while not forgetting those words which are used only once. Here the importance which such an author as Mark attaches to the Old Testament must not be ignored, and therefore those words which are used by him only once among New Testament writers and can be found also in the Septuagint are included in redactional vocabulary. When the linguistic method is employed on its own, the syntax and R vocabulary often are found to confirm the selection of redactional verses made on literary-critical and linguistic grounds and sometimes draw our attention to other passages which on first reckoning might have been thought to belong to S rather than R.

The linguistic features selected from 'Marcan usage' have been those which might be regarded as essential to anyone who wished to be a translator into, and writer of, the Greek language. Thus the participle, the genitive absolute, the conjunctions, the main verb, the openings and conclusions of sentences, the chiastic placing of indirect speech have been examined in order to try to see where an author, who has been regarded as a 'paste and scissors writer', would most likely have shown his hand. Even when he is probably translating or paraphrasing from his sources we cannot leave it at that, for it is in the nuances of translation, and in the emphasis with which he underlines certain words and concepts, that we may arrive at the re-dactional theology which is the ultimate goal of the thesis. We have continually to bear in mind that our redactor is employing either written or oral sources which have been demarcated for us by the form-critical method, but even in his reduced parataxis, or preference for certain verbal forms like the periphrastic tenses and εὐθύς, we may well come to deduce criteria of a linguistic kind which will enable us to observe him in the editorial work in which, on literary arguments and form-critical hypotheses, scholars have already judged that his hand is to be discovered.

It is sometimes argued that the style of the Gospel is homogeneous. If at the same time we come to the conclusion that the author was really inspired to write the whole of the Gospel (as Farrer), then such a view is logical. But if we are convinced that what goes for Matthew and Luke also follows for Mark, i.e. that the author employed sources which he changed and modified to suit his form or plan when shaping the material, then surely there ought to be some evidence for redaction – and linguistic criteria at that. Even if the author is responsible for some of the sources, and works over rather heavily those which he has borrowed, there should be some repetition, clichés or mannerisms which betray his editorial work.

And so it is. We see him as working in a bi-lingual situation, Greek being perhaps his second language. As a collector of the pericopal sources he presented his Church's theology in a rough but nevertheless expressive and lively Greek. He operated in an area where the Christian faith had passed over from the Semitic to the Hellenistic world. The Septuagint was his Bible, and also his only book of style. The author shows respect for his sources, even if oral, and the lack of continuity or coherence sometimes displayed is probably to be explained by these factors and not by his illiteracy. Although we cannot say that he is a Demosthenes or even a Josephus, the fact remains that his Gospel is livelier and more interesting than Matthew's or Luke's, not simply because it is the first, but because of its intrinsic worth. He uses in a telling way the methods and principles he has learnt from the oral stages of transmission, and he has arranged his material in an overall pattern which is thematic and theological, as J. H. Ropes[1] and R. H. Lightfoot[2] suggested. He is neither the scribe of Peter, as Turner supposed, nor totally under divine inspiration, as Farrer maintained. He is limited by his respect for tradition; an excessive individuality does not appear, so that his plan can sometimes be apparent and sometimes fade.

While such a trait as parenthesis may be a purely literary convention designed to assist the Hellenistic reader of the Gospel, other traits of Marcan usage may be relics of the oral stage of tradition, or his own, so that just as his theology is that of his Church as well as his own, so even his style may have been so much part of his training within the tradition that he can effectively use it in his own literary creation of his Gospel. In the redactional vocabulary a preference is shown for such words as 'gospel', 'teach', and 'disciple', and from this some of the evangelist's own preferences and prejudices emerge, as well, perhaps, as something of his local situation.

[1] J. H. Ropes, *The Synoptic Gospels*, 2nd impression (London, 1960).
[2] R. H. Lightfoot, *The Gospel Message of St. Mark* (Oxford, 1950).

Thus by the use of literary criteria and by linguistic analysis arising out of the pericopal nature of the oral tradition, we may be able to some extent to observe the evangelist at work in handling his traditions, and perhaps detect something of his own unique contribution to the formation of his Gospel. When he is called a redactor it is not suggested that he seriously tampers with the tradition, for often the tradition can be seen to hamper his intentions. He is restrained in method and faithful to the local Christianity in which he has been nurtured, but this should not prevent us from saluting him as a creative worker of a high order, for he has made his Gospel out of limited resources, both collective and personal. Such a redactor has at one and the same time to integrate and yet to be conservative. Although he has no great literary pretensions, he has to make a unified work out of oral and disparate sources, but most of all he has to create a format for himself, since none seems to have been available. It has taken many centuries to recognise his genius in this. This book attempts to penetrate a little further into this matter along literary and linguistic lines.

A. REDACTIONAL VERSES LISTED
AND CLASSIFIED

1^{1-4} Best, pp. 63, 114; Bultmann, pp. 245ff., 347; Marxsen, pp. 32ff.; Neirynck, pp. 97, 101, 107; Schmidt, pp. 18–19; Schreiber, pp. 169, 193ff.; Schweizer, p. 29; Sundwall, p. 6; Trocmé, pp. 44–5.

1^6; 1^8 Bultmann, pp. 111; Neirynck, pp. 77, 115; Schreiber, p. 175; Schweizer, p. 14; Sundwall, p. 7; Taylor, p. 157; Trocmé, pp. 44–5.

1^{9a} Best, n. 1, p. 175; Bultmann, p. 247; Marxsen, p. 33; Schreiber, pp. 125–6; Sundwall, p. 7; Taylor, p. 159.

1^{10}; 1^{11a} Best, pp. 148–9; Horstmann, p. 120; Neirynck, p. 85; Schreiber, p. 168; Sundwall, p. 7; Taylor, p. 161.

1^{12} Best, p. 15; Bultmann, pp. 253ff.; Marxsen, pp. 32, 42; Schreiber, pp. 194ff., 202; Sundwall, p. 7; Taylor, p. 163.

1^{14-15} Best, p. 64; Bultmann, p. 341: 'Mk. 1^{15} is a summary of the Christian message of salvation', p. 118; Horstmann, p. 132; Marxsen, pp. 32ff.; Neirynck, pp. 70, 82, 122; Reploh, p. 14; Schreiber, pp. 125, 172–3; Schweizer, p. 44; Sundwall, p. 8; Taylor, p. 165.

1^{16ac} Bultmann, pp. 57, 64; Burkill, p. 33; Neirynck, pp. 75, 108, 114, 135; Pesch, p. 58; Schreiber, pp. 172, 208; Sundwall, p. 8; Taylor, p. 168.

1^{18}; 1^{20a} Bultmann, pp. 57, 64; Pesch, p. 58; Reploh, pp. 29ff.; Sundwall, p. 9; Taylor, p. 170.

1^{21-2} Best, p. 71; Burkill, pp. 33ff.; Bultmann, pp. 65, 209; Horstmann, p. 119; Dibelius, p. 237; Kertelge, pp. 50–1, n. 527, p. 130 considers 21b–22 R, but 21a S; Kuhn, n. 42, p. 225; Neirynck, pp. 52, 135; Reploh, p. 31; Schreiber, pp. 101–2; 163; Schweizer, p. 50; Sundwall, p. 9; Trocmé, p. 128.

1^{23a} M. Black, *Aramaic Approach to the Gospels*, p. 109; Kertelge, p. 51; M. J. Lagrange, *Marc*, pp. xcviiif. speaks of the quasi-literary character of εὐθύς; Neirynck, p. 85; Schreiber, p. 75; Schweizer, p. 54; Sundwall, p. 9.

1^{26-8} Best, p. 71; Bultmann, p. 209; Burkill, p. 34; Kertelge, p. 51; E. Lohmeyer, *Das Evangelium des Markus*, p. 38; Marxsen, p. 60; Neirynck, pp. 50, 94, 114; Pesch, p. 58; Schreiber, pp. 112, 172; Schweizer, p. 50; Sundwall, p. 9.

1^{29a} Bultmann, p. 345; Burkill, p. 36; Kertelge, p. 60; Kuhn, p. 20; Reploh, p. 33; Neirynck, p. 75; Schreiber, p. 314; Sundwall, p. 9; Taylor, p. 178.

1^{30b}; 1^{31a}; 1^{32-4} Best, p. 116; Bultmann, p. 341; Burkill, p. 36; Dibelius, pp. 44, 224; Horstmann, p. 119; Kertelge, pp. 31–2; Kuhn, p. 217; Neirynck, pp. 82, 85; Pesch, n. 72, p. 58; Schreiber, pp. 95, 102; Schweizer, p. 50; Taylor, pp. 180–2.

1^{35} Bultmann, p. 155; Neirynck, pp. 47, 77, 94; Schreiber, p. 100; Sundwall, p. 10; Taylor, p. 183.

1^{37}; 1^{38-9} Best, p. 69; Bultmann, p. 155; Burkill, p. 37; Kuhn, p. 217; Marxsen, p. 61; Neirynck, pp. 50, 77, 82; Pesch, p. 57; Reploh, p. 14; Schreiber, n. 54, p. 101; Schweizer, p. 54; Sundwall, p. 10; Taylor, p. 184.

1^{40a} Best, p. 116; Burkill, p. 37; Kertelge, p. 62; Kuhn, p. 219; Neirynck, pp. 82, 123; Taylor, p. 186.

1^{41a}; 1^{43}; 1^{44a} Best, p. 40; Bultmann, p. 212; Burkill, pp. 39, 126; Neirynck, pp. 84–7, 123; Pesch, p. 57; Schreiber, p. 183; Schweizer, p. 57; Sundwall, pp. 10–11.

1^{45} Best, p. 69; Bultmann, p. 341; Burkill, pp. 39–40, 140; Dibelius, p. 74; Horstmann, pp. 121, 123; Kertelge, p. 63; Kuhn, p. 138; Neirynck, pp. 51, 75, 76, 77, 87, 94, 101, 131; Pesch, p. 57; Schreiber, pp. 163, 168, 214; Schweizer, p. 57; Sundwall, pp. 11ff.; Taylor, p. 190.

2^{1-2} Best, p. 70; Bultmann, p. 14; Burkill, p. 125; Dibelius, pp. 45, 219; Kertelge, p. 76; Kuhn, p. 89; Marxsen, n. 31, p. 62; Neirynck, pp. 52, 75, 96, 112, 131; Pesch, p. 57; Schmidt, pp. 78ff.; Sundwall, p. 13; Taylor, pp. 192–3.

2^{5a} Bultmann, p. 15; Neirynck, pp. 77, 114; Schreiber, pp. 110, 242; Sundwall, p. 13; Taylor, p. 192.

2^6 Bultmann, p. 52; Neirynck, p. 82; Schreiber, pp. 182ff.; Schweizer, p. 64; Taylor, p. 195.

2^{8-9} Bultmann, p. 331; Burkill, p. 131; Schreiber, p. 242; Neirynck, pp. 116, 125.

2^{10c} Bultmann, p. 131, pp. 149ff.; Burkill, p. 127; Neirynck, p. 77; Schweizer, p. 64; Taylor, p. 198.

2^{12-14} Best, p. 71; Bultmann, pp. 63, 341; Burkill, p. 123; Horstmann, p. 123; Kertelge, p. 130, n. 527; Kuhn, pp. 82, 86, 89, 200; Neirynck, pp. 65, 77, 119, 123; Schreiber, pp. 172, 209; Schweizer, p. 63; Sundwall, pp. 13ff.; Taylor, p. 201.

2^{14} Kuhn, p. 89; Neirynck, p. 77; Schweizer, p. 64; Sundwall, p. 15; Trocmé, p. 158.

2^{15ac} Bultmann, pp. 48, 66; Burkill, p. 123; Kuhn, n. 16, p. 87; Schreiber, n. 28, p. 164; Sundwall, p. 15; Taylor, p. 205.

2^{16a} Bultmann, pp. 18, 331; Burkill, p. 123; Kuhn, p. 88; Neirynck, pp. 114, 127; Trocmé, pp. 92, 128.

2^{17a} Bultmann, pp. 41, 81, 92, 155, 163; Sundwall, p. 15; Taylor, p. 207; Trocmé, p. 92; Neirynck, pp. 82, 90, 127.

2^{18a} Bultmann, n. 3, 52, but note also line 8, p. 19; Kuhn, p. 88; Neirynck, pp. 85, 108; Schreiber, pp. 85, 108; Taylor, p. 208; Trocmé, p. 71.

2^{23b} Bultmann, pp. 16, 47, 49; Neirynck, p. 114; Taylor, pp. 215–17; Trocmé, n. 72, p. 114.

2^{26b} Kuhn, p. 89; Sundwall, p. 18.

2^{27a} Bultmann, p. 16; Kuhn, p. 84; Schweizer, p. 71; Sundwall, p. 18; Taylor, p. 218.

2^{28}; 3^{1a} Bultmann, p. 12 restricts the R to πάλιν; Kertelge, p. 83; Neirynck, p. 75; Sundwall, p. 19; Taylor, p. 221.

3^{5a}; 3^{6} Bultmann, pp. 52, 63; Burkill, p. 132; Dibelius, pp. 45, 219, 223; Kertelge, p. 83; Kuhn, n. 15, p. 87; Neirynck, p. 108, 113, 131; Pesch, p. 57; Schweizer, p. 74; Sundwall, p. 20; Taylor, p. 224; Trocmé, pp. 29, 71.

3^{7-12} ($3^{7,9}$R,^{12})* Best, p. 73; Bultmann, p. 341; Burkill, pp. 55, 140; Dibelius, pp. 224ff., 223, 227; Horstmann, pp. 119, 126; Kertelge, pp. 34–5; Kuhn, p. 82; Marxsen, p. 62; Neirynck, pp. 96, 97–102, 116; Pesch, p. 58; Reploh, p. 14; Schreiber, pp. 174ff., Schweizer, pp. 78–81; Sundwall, pp. 20ff.; Taylor, p. 225; Trocmé, p. 37, n. 72, 128.

3^{13-19} (3^{13}R^{-16})* Best, p. 74; Bultmann, pp. 341ff.; Dibelius, p. 48, 224; Horstmann, p. 84; Neirynck, pp. 86, 97, 106, 119, 135; Pesch, p. 58; Reploh, pp. 35–50; Schreiber, n. 43, 166; Sundwall, p. 21; Taylor, pp. 229–34; Trocmé, p. 101, 139.

3^{20-1} Best, p. 74; Bultmann, pp. 29ff.; Burkill, pp. 121, 140; Dibelius, p. 47; Neirynck, pp. 77, 87, 98, 113; Pesch, p. 58; Schreiber, pp. 87, 163; Schweizer, p. 83; Sundwall, p. 21; Taylor, pp. 235–7; Trocmé, pp. 90, 105–6, 128, 182.

3^{22a} Best, p. 74; Bultmann, p. 330; Kuhn, p. 201; Schreiber, pp. 212, 234; Schweizer, p. 83; Sundwall, p. 21; Taylor, p. 238; Trocmé, pp. 79, 90, 108.

3^{23a} Best, p. 117; Dibelius, p. 237; Kertelge, n. 505, p. 126; Schreiber, p. 16; Schweizer, pp. 83; Sundwall, p. 23; Taylor, p. 239.

3^{28a} Best, p. 14; Bultmann, n. 1, p. 131; Schreiber, n. 24, p. 94; Schweizer, p. 83; Trocmé, p. 108.

3^{30-33a} Best, pp. 11, 74; Bultmann, pp. 29, 62, 332; Burkill, p. 121; Kuhn, p. 201; Neirynck, pp. 86, 102, 127, 131; Schreiber, n. 195, p. 197; Schweizer, p. 83; Sundwall, pp. 22–3; Taylor, pp. 244–6; Trocmé, pp. 90, 105.

3^{34a} Bultmann, p. 29; Neirynck, pp. 86, 90, 94, 113; Trocmé, pp. 104, 106.

3^{35b} Bultmann, p. 143; Burkill, p. 121; Schreiber, p. 231; Schweizer, p. 84; Trocmé, pp. 105–6, 144.

4^{1-2} Best, p. 71; Bultmann, p. 341; Burkill, p. 97; Dibelius, pp. 47, 112; Jeremias, *Parables of Jesus*, pp. 13ff.; Kuhn, pp. 131, 138; Marxsen, p. 67; Neirynck, pp. 70, 77, 86, 98, 103, 123, 131; Reploh, p. 59; Schreiber, pp. 169ff., 209; Schweizer, p. 89; Sundwall, p. 24; Taylor, p. 251; Trocmé, p. 127.

4^{3a} Bultmann, pp. 175, 326; Horstmann, p. 89; Neirynck, p. 131; Schreiber, p. 209; Schweizer, p. 90; Trocmé, n. 131, p. 35.

4^9 Bultmann, p. 326; Neirynck, p. 131; Pesch, p. 61; Schreiber, p. 209.

4^{10-12} Best, pp. 65, 74; Bultmann, pp. 199, n. 1, p. 325; Burkill, p. 98; Dibelius, p. 227; Horstmann, pp. 90, 115ff.; Neirynck, pp. 53, 108, 127, 133; Reploh, p. 60; Schreiber, p. 86; n. 224, p. 239; Schweizer, p. 93; Sundwall, p. 26; Taylor, pp. 254ff., 501; Trocmé, pp. 35, 127, n. 106, p. 139.

4^{13} Best, p. 72; Bultmann, p. 187; Horstmann, p. 117; Neirynck, pp. 57, 127; Schreiber, p. 127; Schweizer, p. 97; Trocmé, n. 131, p. 35.

4^{21a} Best, p. 74; Bultmann, pp. 87, 98; Dibelius, pp. 228; Kuhn, p. 131; Neirynck, p. 61; Reploh, p. 67; Schweizer, p. 99; Sundwall, p. 27; Taylor, p. 262; Trocmé, p. 25.

4^{22a}; 4^{23} Best, n. 2, p. 65; Bultmann, p. 325; Dibelius, p. 247; Horstmann, p. 89; Pesch, p. 61; Schweizer, p. 100; Taylor, p. 264.

4^{24a} Best, p. 74; Bultmann, pp. 91, 325; Kuhn, p. 131; Neirynck, p. 133; Reploh, p. 67; Schweizer, p. 100; Sundwall, p. 27; Taylor, p. 264.

4^{25a}; 4^{26a} Best, p. 74; Bultmann, p. 173; Dibelius, p. 228; Schreiber, n. 242, p. 209; Trocmé, p. 35.

4^{29a}; 4^{30a} Best, p. 74; Bultmann, p. 173; Neirynck, p. 57; Schreiber, p. 209; Trocmé, p. 35.

4^{31b} Taylor, p. 270.

4^{33-4} Best, p. 74, n. 2, p. 65; Bultmann, p. 341; Horstmann, p. 89; Kuhn, p. 134 (v. 34 only); Neirynck, p. 131; Schreiber, p. 12, n. 96, p. 111; Schweizer, p. 106; Sundwall, p. 24; Taylor, p. 271; Trocmé, p. 24, n. 71, p. 127.

4^{35-36a} Best, p. 105; Bultmann, p. 215; Dibelius, p. 227; Kertelge, p. 91; Marxsen, p. 67; Neirynck, pp. 48, 94; Pesch, pp. 58–9; Schreiber, pp. 12, 120–2; Sundwall, p. 30; Trocmé, n. 72, p. 128.

4^{37-8}; 4^{41} Best, p. 73; Bultmann, p. 216; Horstmann, p. 83; Neirynck, p. 116; Pesch, p. 59; Schreiber, n. 29, p. 96.

5^{1-2a} Best, p. 74; Bultmann, p. 344; Horstmann, p. 121; Kertelge, p. 112; Neirynck, p. 51; Marxsen, p. 67; Schreiber, p. 21; Schweizer, p. 112.

5^5; 5^8 Best, p. 168; Bultmann, p. 210; Burkill, p. 90; Kertelge, p. 202; Schweizer, p. 112; Taylor, p. 281.

5^{9c}; 5^{11}; 5^{15}; 5^{17}; 5^{18-20} Lightfoot, pp. 88ff.; Schweizer, p. 113; Trocmé, n. 15, p. 41 (against Burkill, p. 91); 5^{19}: Bultmann, p. 33; Dibelius, p. 70; Neirynck, p. 60; Schreiber, n. 42, p. 166; Taylor, p. 284; 5^{20}: Best, pp. 64, 72; Dibelius, p. 74; Marxsen, p. 67; Neirynck, p. 119; Pesch, pp. 59–60; Schweizer, p. 113; Sundwall, p. 31.

5^{21} Best, p. 74; Bultmann, p. 214 not R; Burkill, p. 121; Kertelge, p. 112; Neirynck, p. 76; Pesch, p. 59; Schreiber, pp. 158, 172; Schweizer, p. 15; Sundwall, p. 33; Trocmé, p. 182.

5^{23a}; 5^{24} Burkill, p. 121, Neirynck, pp. 114, 121; Rawlinson, pp. 42ff., 67; Schweizer, p. 116; Sundwall, p. 32; Taylor, p. 289; Trocmé, p. 158.

5^{25-6}; 5^{28} Best, n. 2, p. 118; Kertelge, p. 112; Neirynck, p. 116; Taylor, p. 290.

5^{30-1} Best, n. 2, p. 118; Neirynck, pp. 75, 78, 114; Schweizer, pp. 116–17; Taylor, p. 292; Trocmé, p. 128.

5^{33}; 5^{35a} Best, p. 173; Burkill, p. 121; Schreiber, p. 240; Schweizer, p. 116; Sundwall, p. 35; Trocmé, p. 182.

5^{41b} Neirynck, pp. 106, 111; Schreiber, n. 22, p. 28; Schweizer, p. 119; Taylor, p. 296.

5^{42} Horstmann, p. 122; Neirynck, pp. 76, 119; Schreiber, p. 240.

5^{43a} Best, p. 40; Bultmann, p. 214; Burkill, p. 80 (5^{43b}); Dibelius, p. 223; Horstmann, p. 122; Pesch, p. 59; Schreiber, p. 240; Schweizer, p. 116; Sundwall, p. 32; Taylor, p. 297; Trocmé, pp. 42, 182.

6^{1-2a} Best, p. 75; Bultmann, pp. 56, 60; Kertelge, n. 488, p. 122, n. 527, p. 130; Neirynck, pp. 52, 76, 78, 94; Pesch, p. 59; Schreiber, pp. 87, 205; Schweizer, p. 123; Sundwall, p. 36; Trocmé, pp. 128, 158.

6^{4a}; 6^{6a} Best, p. 71; Kertelge, n. 527, p. 130; Neirynck, p. 95; Schreiber, p. 205; Schweizer, p. 126; Sundwall, p. 36; Trocmé, p. 105.

6^{6b-13}(R: $6^{6b-7,10a,12-13}$; S: 6^{8-11}) Best, p. 72; Burkill, p. 55; Dibelius, p. 224; Neirynck, p. 133; Pesch, pp. 58–9; Reploh, pp. 50–8; Schreiber, p. 204; Schweizer, pp. 126ff.; Taylor, pp. 302ff.

6^{14-16} Best, p. 75; Bultmann, pp. 302, 332; Burkill, pp. 128, 131; Kertelge, p. 121; Kuhn, p. 201; Neirynck, p. 135; Schreiber, p. 214; Schweizer, p. 132; Sundwall, p. 37; Taylor, p. 307.

6^{17a}; 6^{18}; 6^{20ac}; 6^{21-2} Lohmeyer, p. 118; Pesch, p. 84; Schreiber, pp. 181ff.; Taylor, p. 311.

6²⁹ Best, p. 76; Bultmann, p. 301; Burkill, p. 121; Neirynck, p. 135; Pesch, p. 59; Schreiber, p. 181; Trocmé, p. 182.

6³⁰⁻³⁵ᵃ Best, pp. 5, 26, 72; Bultmann, pp. 66, 244, 340; Burkill, pp. 121, 140; Dibelius, p. 224; Kertelge, p. 129; Kuhn, p. 138; Neirynck, p. 113; Pesch, p. 60; Reploh, pp. 50ff.; Schmidt, p. 188; Schreiber, pp. 169, 204; Schweizer, pp. 135, 140; Sundwall, p. 39 (vi, 31–2), p. 127; Taylor, pp. 318ff.; Trocmé, n. 75, pp. 128, 142, 163.

6⁴¹; 6⁴⁵ Best, p. 73; Bultmann, pp. 216, 230; Dibelius, p. 219; Kertelge, p. 145; Neirynck, pp. 51, 95, 103; Schreiber, p. 96; Sundwall, p. 41; Trocmé, p. 155.

6⁴⁷⁻⁸ Best, pp. 73, 78, 183; Bultmann, p. 216; Dibelius, pp. 71–6, 277ff.; Neirynck, pp. 78, 113; Schreiber, pp. 97ff., 209; Schweizer, pp. 141ff.

6⁵⁰ᵃ Best, p. 78; Bultmann, p. 216; Horstmann, p. 126; Kertelge, p. 146; Kuhn, n. 1, p. 203; Pesch, p. 60; Reploh, p. 78; Schreiber, p. 98; Schweizer, pp. 137, 142; Sundwall, p. 41; Taylor, p. 330; Trocmé, p. 155.

6⁵²⁻⁶ Best, p. 79; Bultmann, p. 341; Burkill, p. 64; Dibelius, p. 224; Kertelge, pp. 35–9; Kuhn, pp. 217–18; Marxsen, n. 52, p. 69; Neirynck, pp. 75, 78, 122; Pesch, n. 73, p. 58; Schreiber, p. 102; Schweizer, p. 143; Sundwall, p. 41; Taylor, p. 331.

7¹ Best, p. 79; Bultmann, pp. 48, 324; Neirynck, pp. 107, 109; Pesch, p. 60; Schreiber, p. 182; Sundwall, p. 41; Trocmé, pp. 72, 79.

7²ᵇ Bultmann, p. 52; Neirynck, p. 91; Sundwall, p. 42; Taylor, p. 335; Trocmé, n. 75, p. 91.

7³⁻⁴ Best, p. 79; Burkill, p. 117; Neirynck, pp. 89, 96, 98, 109; Schreiber, p. 111; Schweizer, p. 145; Sundwall, p. 42; Taylor, p. 335.

7⁵ᵃ Best, p.120; against, Bultmann, p. 66; Neirynck, p. 91; Schweizer, p. 145; Sundwall, pp. 43ff.; Taylor, p. 336; Trocmé, p. 72.

7⁸ Bultmann, pp. 136, 146; Neirynck, pp. 83, 91, 124; Schreiber, n. 99, p. 111; S according to Sundwall, p. 43; Trocmé, 92.

7⁹ᵃ Best, p. 79; Bultmann, pp. 49, 329; Neirynck, pp. 91, 134; Schweizer, p. 145; Sundwall, p. 43; Taylor, p. 339; Trocmé, p. 82.

7¹⁰ᵃ; 7¹¹ᶜ Neirynck, p. 106; Schreiber, n. 22, p. 28; Taylor, p. 340.

7¹³ᶜ Bultmann, pp. 49, 329; Neirynck, pp. 76, 86, 91; Pesch, p. 60; Schreiber, p. 110; Schweizer, p. 146; Taylor, p. 341.

7¹⁴ Best, p. 79; Bultmann, p. 329; Horstmann, p. 90; Neirynck, p. 53; Pesch, p. 61; Sundwall, p. 44; Taylor, p. 343; Trocmé, p. 31.

7^{16-17} Best, p. 79; Bultmann, p. 92; Kuhn, p. 113; Neirynck, p. 53; Pesch, p. 61; Reploh, pp. 60, 79; Schreiber, p. 163; Schweizer, p. 146; Sundwall, p. 44; Taylor, p. 344.

7^{18a} Bultmann, p. 92; Horstmann, pp. 126–7; Neirynck, p. 57; Reploh, p. 79; Schreiber, p. 200; Schweizer, p. 146; Taylor, p. 344, cf. 6^{52}, 8^{17}.

7^{19-20a} Bultmann, pp. 92ff.; Neirynck, pp. 75, 78, 86; Sundwall, p. 45; Taylor, p. 345.

7^{21a}; 7^{23} Bultmann, pp. 48, 166; Neirynck, p. 53; Reploh, p. 229; Taylor, p. 501.

7^{24} Best, p. 79; Bultmann, pp. 38, 64; Horstmann, p. 124; Kertelge, p. 154; Neirynck, p. 52; Pesch, p. 61; Schreiber, p. 168; Schweizer, p. 151; Sundwall, p. 45.

7^{25}; 7^{26a}; 7^{27a} Taylor, p. 349.

7^{31} Best, p. 79; Bultmann, pp. 38, 213; Horstmann, p. 121; Kertelge, p. 157; Neirynck, pp. 75, 79; Pesch, pp. 59–61; Reploh, p. 14; Schreiber, p. 170; Schweizer, p. 154; Sundwall, p. 45; Taylor, p. 352.

7^{32a}; 7^{34c} Best, pp. 120–1; Neirynck, p. 106; Schreiber, n. 22, p. 28; Taylor, p. 355.

7^{35-7} Best, p. 72; Burkill, pp. 81, 140; Dibelius, pp. 74, 223; Horstmann, p. 129; Kertelge, p. 157; Neirynck, pp. 79, 92, 121, 123; Pesch, p. 61; Schreiber, p. 223; Schweizer, p. 154; Sundwall, p. 47; Taylor, p. 356.

8^1 Best, p. 104; Bultmann, p. 217 says 'almost no editorial additions'; Neirynck, pp. 115, 117; Pesch, p. 61; Schreiber, pp. 120, 122–3; Schweizer, p. 156; Taylor, p. 357.

8^{9b-10} Kertelge, p. 139; Neirynck, pp. 79, 117; Pesch, p. 61; Sundwall, pp. 50–1; Taylor, p. 360.

8^{11a} Best, n. 1, p. 106; Bultmann, pp. 52, 331; see, however, Dibelius, p. 159; van Jersel, 'Der Sohn in den synoptischen Jesusworten', $N.T.$ suppls. (1964), 167; Kertelge, pp. 23ff.; Neirynck, p. 79; Pesch, p. 61; Sundwall, p. 51; Taylor, p. 361.

8^{13} Bultmann, p. 331; Neirynck, pp. 83, 98; Pesch, p. 61; Schreiber, p. 204; Schweizer, pp. 159–60; Sundwall, p. 52.

8^{14-21}(S = $8^{17,18}$) Best, pp. 73, 78; Bultmann, vv. 16–21, p. 330; Dibelius, v. 19, pp. 228–9; Horstmann, pp. 90, 126; Kertelge, p. 131; Neirynck, p. 57, Pesch, p. 61; Reploh, p. 78; Schreiber, pp. 98, 118, 182, 217, 232; Schweizer, p. 160; Sundwall, p. 52 (v. 15); Taylor, p. 363; Trocmé, pp. 74–5, n. 111, p. 142.

8^{22a} Best, p. 79; Bultmann, pp. 64–5; Kertelge, pp. 161ff.; Pesch, p. 60; Schreiber, pp. 176, 207; Schweizer, p. 163; Sundwall, p. 53; Trocmé, p. 43.

8^{26} Best, p. 107; Burkill, p. 80; Dibelius, p. 223; Horstmann, p. 123;

Kertelge, p. 161; Neirynck, pp. 79, 92; Pesch, p. 60; Schreiber, p. 163; Sundwall, p. 53; Taylor, p. 373.

8^{27-33} Best, pp. 72ff.; Bultmann, pp. 258–9; Dibelius, pp. 115, 225–6; Horstmann, pp. 26–31, 118; Kuhn, p. 218; Neirynck, p. 70; Pesch, p. 62; Reploh, pp. 89ff., 100ff.; Schreiber, pp. 191, 197; Schweizer, p. 166; Sundwall, pp. 54ff.; Trocmé, pp. 94, 100, 103.

8^{34a} Best, p. 79; Bultmann, pp. 82, 330; Horstmann, pp. 34, 87; Pesch, p. 63; Reploh, pp. 104, 124; Schreiber, pp. 166, 238; Schweizer, p. 175; Sundwall, p. 56; Taylor, p. 380.

8^{35ac} Best, p. 109; Bultmann, pp. 75, 81, 93, 105, 111, 151; Reploh, p. 128; Sundwall, p. 56; Taylor, p. 382; Trocmé, p. 31.

8^{36a}; 8^{37a}; 8^{38ac} Horstmann, pp. 34, 136; Neirynck, p. 109; Pesch, p. 63; Reploh, pp. 135ff.; Schreiber, p. 110; Sundwall, p. 57; Taylor, p. 383; Trocmé, p. 135.

9^{1ac} Bultmann, pp. 121, 127; Horstmann, pp. 58, 65; Neirynck, p. 79; Pesch, p. 63; Reploh, pp. 112, 139ff.; Schreiber, p. 133; Schweizer, p. 178; Sundwall, p. 57; Taylor, p. 386; Trocmé, p. 157.

9^{2ab} Best, p. 81; Bultmann, pp. 259, 309; Dibelius, p. 213; Horstmann, pp. 59, 83ff.; Kuhn, p. 201; Neirynck, p. 95; Reploh, p. 112; Schreiber, p. 232: Trocmé, pp. 45, 100.

9^3; 9^{6-7a} Best (private communication of MS. to be published in *Studia Evangelica*); Horstmann, pp. 83, 88ff., 120; Neirynck, pp. 79, 87, 99; Reploh, p. 113; Schreiber, pp. 230ff.; Schweizer, p. 180.

9^{9-13}(R = $9^{9, 12, 13}$; S = $9^{10, 11}$) Best, pp. 76, 81, 123; Bultmann, pp. 26off.; Dibelius, p. 226; Horstmann, pp. 73, 128ff.; Neirynck, pp. 79, 89, 104; Pesch, p. 63; Reploh, pp. 113ff.; Schreiber, pp. 109–14; Schweizer v. 9, 10; Sundwall ($9^{9-10, 12-13}$), p. 57; Taylor, p. 501; Trocmé, p. 94.

9^{14-17a} Best, p. 81; Bultmann, pp. 52, 211; Horstmann, p. 107; Kertelge, p. 176; Neirynck, p. 53; Reploh, pp. 212ff.; Schreiber, p. 196; Schweizer, pp. 187ff.; Taylor, p. 395.

9^{20}; 9^{26}; 9^{28a} Bultmann, p. 211; Kertelge, p. 176; Kuhn, p. 167; Neirynck, p. 53; Reploh, pp. 60, 212ff.; Schreiber, p. 196; Schweizer, pp. 187ff.; Sundwall, pp. 58–9; Taylor, pp. 401, 501; Trocmé, pp. 90, 127.

9^{30-2} Best, pp. 72, 81; Bultmann, p. 331; Dibelius, p. 225; Kuhn, pp. 20, 138; Marxsen, p. 73; Neirynck, p. 70; Pesch, p. 62; Reploh, p. 14; Schreiber, pp. 196–7; Schweizer, p. 190; Sundwall, p. 60; Taylor, p. 402.

9^{33-7} Best, p. 73; Bultmann, p. 65 (v. 33), p. 149 (v. 37), v. 36 also p. 149; Horstmann, p. 128; Kuhn, p. 183; Neirynck, p. 52;

Pesch, p. 63; Reploh, p. 214; Schreiber, p. 163; Schweizer, pp. 191–2; Sundwall, p. 60; Taylor, p. 403.

9^{38a} Best, n. 1, p. 173; Bultmann, pp. 54, 149 'Mk. 9^{38-40} is an alien insertion', p. 142; Dibelius, p. 160; Kuhn, p. 200; Pesch, p. 63; Reploh, p. 230; Schreiber, p. 98; Schweizer, p. 197; Taylor, p. 403.

9^{39b}; 9^{40a}; 9^{41b} Best, p. 165; Bultmann, pp. 142–3; Reploh, p. 230; Neirynck, p. 104; Schweizer, pp. 15, 197; Sundwall, p. 61; Taylor, p. 408; Trocmé, p. 144.

9^{49a}; 9^{50c} Bultmann, pp. 87, 91, 98, 102; Dibelius, pp. 236, 247; Pesch, p. 63; Sundwall, p. 63; Taylor, p. 414.

10^1 Best, pp. 72, 82; Bultmann, p. 340; Kuhn, n. 63, p. 203; Marxsen, p. 74; Neirynck, p. 53; Pesch, p. 63; Schreiber, pp. 189–90; Schweizer, p. 202; Sundwall, p. 63.

10^{10-11a} Best, p. 82; Bultmann, p. 26; Kuhn, p. 188; Neirynck, p. 53; Reploh, pp. 60, 215; Schreiber, p. 163; Schweizer, p. 204; Sundwall, p. 64; Taylor, pp. 415, 419, 501.

10^{13} Best, p. 82; Bultmann, pp. 57, 60; Neirynck, pp. 115, 122; Pesch, p. 63; Schreiber, n. 41, p. 98; Sundwall, p. 65.

10^{15a} Best, p. 67; Bultmann, pp. 75, 81, 105; Neirynck, p. 99; Trocmé, p. 160.

10^{16-17a} Best, p. 82; Bultmann, p. 22; Pesch, p. 63; Schreiber, p. 230; Schweizer, p. 206; Sundwall, p. 65; Taylor, p. 425.

10^{22b} Bultmann, pp. 63, 329; Neirynck, p. 83; Schreiber, p. 230; Taylor, p. 430.

10^{23a} Best, p. 82; Bultmann, p. 329; Kuhn, p. 148; Neirynck, pp. 75, 79; Reploh, pp. 192, 197; Schreiber, p. 110; Schweizer, p. 213; Sundwall, p. 66; Taylor, p. 424.

10^{24ab} Best, p. 80; Bultmann, p. 22; Kuhn, p. 148; Neirynck, pp. 92, 97, 169; Schreiber, p. 110; Schweizer, p. 209; Sundwall, p. 66.

10^{26} Best, p. 109; Bultmann, p. 22; Schweizer, p. 209; Sundwall, p. 66.

10^{27ac} Neirynck, pp. 79, 128; Pesch, p. 63; Reploh, p. 197; Schreiber, p. 110; Schweizer, p. 209; Sundwall, p. 66.

10^{28} Best, p. 82; Bultmann, pp. 22, 130, 330; Neirynck, pp. 120, 128; Reploh, p. 201; Schreiber, p. 91; Schweizer, p. 214; Taylor, pp. 424, 433.

10^{29} Best, p. 63; Bultmann, pp. 22, 110; Neirynck, pp. 89, 96, 99; Schreiber, pp. 111ff., 233ff.; Taylor, p. 434.

10^{31-35a} Best, pp. 73, 80; Bultmann, p. 111; Dibelius, p. 225; Horstmann, p. 131; Lambrecht, pp. 21–55, 60; Marxsen, n. 74, p. 74; Neirynck, pp. 79, 83, 135; Reploh, p. 106; Schreiber, pp. 190ff., 107–9; Schweizer, p. 215; Taylor, pp. 435, 438; Trocmé, pp. 24, 101.

10^{41-5} Best, pp. 73, 82; Bultmann, pp. 143ff., 146, 148; Lambrecht, pp. 27–30; Neirynck, pp. 80, 93, 104, 135; Pesch, p. 63; Schreiber, pp. 19ff.; Schweizer, p. 223; Sundwall, p. 69; Taylor, pp. 442ff.; Trocmé, p. 125.

10^{46-52} Best, pp. 82, 107–8; Bultmann, p. 213; Horstmann, p. 124; Kertelge, pp. 179ff.; Kuhn, n. 22, p. 220; Marxsen, p. 74; Neirynck, pp. 80, 99, 120, 123, 132; Reploh, p. 222; Schreiber, pp. 222, 226; Schweizer, p. 224; Sundwall, pp. 69–70; Trocmé, p. 158.

11^{1-2b} Best, p. 82; Bultmann, p. 261; Lambrecht, p. 31; Neirynck, p. 51; Pesch, p. 62; Schreiber, p. 187; Sundwall, p. 70.

11^{3c}; 11^{9-10} Best, p. 83; Bultmann, p. 305; Lambrecht, n. 1, p. 31; Neirynck, pp. 83, 104; Schreiber, p. 193; Schweizer, p. 228; Taylor, p. 457; Trocmé, p. 158.

11^{11-12} Best, p. 82; Bultmann, p. 218; Burkill, p. 121; Lambrecht, p. 31; Neirynck, p. 52; Pesch, p. 64; Schreiber, p. 99; Schweizer, p. 230; Taylor, pp. 458–9; Trocmé, pp. 83, 128.

11^{13c} Best, p. 83; Lambrecht, pp. 33–4; Neirynck, pp. 75, 100; Schreiber, n. 62, p. 103; Schweizer, p. 230; Taylor, p. 460.

11^{14}; 11^{15a} Best, p. 83; Bultmann, pp. 36, 218; Kuhn, pp. 200–1; Lambrecht, p. 32; Neirynck, pp. 75, 80, 87; Schreiber, p. 187; Schweizer, p. 116; Taylor, pp. 461–3; Trocmé, p. 128.

11^{17a} Best, p. 72; Bultmann, p. 36; Kuhn, p. 138; Neirynck, p. 70; Schreiber, p. 43; Schweizer, p. 233; Sundwall, p. 72; Taylor, p. 463; Trocmé, p. 83.

11^{18-23a} Best, pp. 71, 83; Bultmann, pp. 36, 231; Dibelius, pp. 45, 223; Kuhn, p. 201; Lambrecht, pp. 32, 36; Neirynck, pp. 100, 109, 113, 133; Schreiber, pp. 52, 87, 98ff., 134–40; Schweizer, p. 233; Sundwall, pp. 71ff.; Taylor, pp. 464ff.; Trocmé, pp. 85, 128; Burkill, p. 122.

11^{27} Best, pp. 83, 86; Bultmann, pp. 20, 36, 218; Dibelius, n. 1, p. 45; Kuhn, p. 201; Lambrecht, pp. 32, 37; Neirynck, p. 52; Pesch, p. 64; Schreiber, pp. 185–8; Schweizer, p. 237; Sundwall, p. 72; Trocmé, pp. 79, 128.

11^{31-2} Best, p. 85; Bultmann, p. 20; Lambrecht, p. 38; Schreiber, p. 111.

12^{1a} Best, p. 86; Bultmann, p. 205; Burkill, p. 122; Dibelius, p. 237; Lambrecht, p. 38; Neirynck, p. 132; Schweizer, p. 239; Sundwall, p. 73.

12^{12} Best, p. 86; Lambrecht, p. 44; Neirynck, p. 132; Pesch, p. 64; Schreiber, p. 111; Schweizer, p. 239; Sundwall, p. 73.

12^{13} Best, p. 86; Bultmann, p. 26; Burkill, p. 203; Lambrecht, p. 46; Pesch, p. 64; Schreiber, p. 182; Sundwall, p. 73.

12^{17c} Best, p. 86; Bultmann, p. 63; Lambrecht, p. 46; Pesch, p. 64.

12[18a] Best, p. 86; Bultmann, p. 26; Burkill, p. 203; Neirynck, p. 115; Pesch, p. 64; Schreiber, p. 188.

12[28ab] Best, p. 86; Bultmann, pp. 34ff.; Burkill, pp. 123, 204; Lambrecht, p. 46; Neirynck, p. 115; Pesch, p. 64; Schreiber, p. 112; Schweizer, p. 250; Sundwall, p. 74.

12[34c] Bultmann, pp. 63, 341; Kuhn, p. 41; Burkill, pp. 123, 203; Kuhn, p. 41; Lambrecht, p. 47; Neirynck, p. 88; Pesch, p. 64; Schreiber, p. 183; Sundwall, p. 174; Taylor, p. 490.

12[35a] Best, p. 72; Bultmann, p. 136; Kuhn, p. 42; Lambrecht, p. 47; Schreiber, pp. 186ff.; Schweizer, p. 254; Sundwall, p. 75.

12[37b] Best, p. 88; Bultmann, p. 341; Kuhn, p. 41; Lambrecht, p. 47; Neirynck, p. 132; Schreiber, p. 184; Schweizer, p. 258; Sundwall, p. 75; Taylor, p. 493.

12[38a] Best, p. 71; Bultmann, p. 113; Burkill, p. 205; Dibelius, p. 236; Kuhn, p. 42; Lambrecht, p. 52; Schweizer, p. 254; Sundwall, p. 75; Taylor, p. 494; Trocmé, p. 24.

12[40a] Lambrecht, p. 52; Pesch, p. 64; Sundwall, p. 75.

12[41-2] Best, n. 1, p. 88; Bultmann, p. 56; Dibelius, p. 261; Lambrecht, pp. 80–1, 91; Neirynck, p. 106; Pesch, pp. 72ff.; Schweizer, p. 254.

12[43a] Lambrecht, n. 1, p. 54; Schweizer, p. 259; Taylor, p. 497; Trocmé, p. 128.

12[44ac] Bultmann, p. 60; Marxsen, p. 162.

13[1] Bultmann, pp. 36, 56; Lambrecht, p. 69; Neirynck, pp. 75, 83, 105; Pesch, p. 228; Schreiber, pp. 127ff.; Schweizer, p. 262; Sundwall, p. 76; Taylor, p. 500; Trocmé, p. 83.

13[2-3] Best, n. 1, p. 88; Bultmann, pp. 120, 125, 128, 324; Lambrecht, pp. 72–85; Marxsen, pp. 162, 167; Neirynck, p. 51; Pesch, p. 226; Schreiber, pp. 76, 187; Schweizer, p. 262; Sundwall, p. 76; Taylor, pp. 501–2.

13[4] Lambrecht, p. 88; Marxsen, pp. 162, 166; Neirynck, p. 54; Pesch, p. 228; Reploh, p. 33; Schreiber, pp. 128ff.; Schweizer, p. 266; Sundwall, p. 77; Taylor, p. 502.

13[5a] Bultmann, pp. 122, 125; Kuhn, p. 43; Lambrecht, pp. 92–3; Marxsen, pp. 162, 166; Neirynck, pp. 120, 132; Pesch, p. 225; Schreiber, p. 142; Schweizer, p. 266; Sundwall, p. 77; Taylor, p. 639.

13[6b] Kuhn, p. 43; Lambrecht, pp. 105–6; Marxsen, p. 162; Pesch, p. 225; Schreiber, p. 142; Taylor, p. 639.

13[7c] Kuhn, p. 43; Lambrecht, pp. 108, 113; Marxsen, pp. 166, 176; Neirynck, p. 93; Pesch, p. 225.

13[8c] Kuhn, p. 43; Lambrecht, p. 113; Marxsen, n. 41, p. 41, p. 166; Neirynck, p. 93; Pesch, p. 225; Schreiber, p. 155; Sundwall, p. 78; Trocmé, pp. 164–5.

13^{9a} Best, p. 63; Bultmann, p. 122; Lambrecht, p. 121; Marxsen, pp. 162, 166; Neirynck, p. 80; Pesch, p. 227; Schweizer, p. 269; Sundwall, p. 77; Taylor, pp. 640–3; Trocmé, p. 165.

13^{10} Best, pp. 63, 72; Lambrecht, p. 126; Marxsen, pp. 122, 166, 175; Neirynck, p. 105; Pesch, p. 227; Schreiber, p. 265; Sundwall, p. 78; Taylor, pp. 506–7, 640.

13^{11b}; 13^{13} Best, p. 109; Kuhn, p. 43; Lambrecht, pp. 141ff.; Marxsen, pp. 162, 173–6; Neirynck, p. 87; Pesch, p. 225; Schreiber, p. 238; Sundwall, p. 78.

13^{14b} Best, p. 183; Kuhn, p. 43; Lambrecht, p. 154; Pesch, p. 226; Schreiber, pp. 142–4; Sundwall, p. 78; Trocmé, p. 84.

13^{19a}; 13^{23} Bultmann, pp. 122, 130; Kertelge, p. 28; Kuhn, p. 43; Lambrecht, p. 172; Marxsen, pp. 162, 186; Pesch, p. 226; Rawlinson, p. 189; Schweizer, p. 263; Sundwall, p. 78; Taylor, pp. 517, 641; Trocmé, p. 166.

13^{24b} Best, n. 3, p. 98; Lambrecht, pp. 174, 192; Marxsen, pp. 162, 166; Neirynck, p. 48; Pesch, p. 226; Schreiber, pp. 132–4, 139–41; Schweizer, p. 275; Sundwall, p. 78; Taylor, pp. 517, 639; Trocmé, p. 167.

13^{28a} Bultmann, p. 123; Lambrecht, p. 201; Marxsen, p. 162; Schreiber, p. 139; Schweizer, p. 278; Sundwall, p. 78; Taylor, p. 520; Trocmé, p. 31.

13^{29-30a} Bultmann, p. 123; Lambrecht, p. 201; Marxsen, p. 162; Neirynck, pp. 80, 95, 130; Pesch, p. 227; Schreiber, p. 139; Schweizer, p. 279; Sundwall, p. 78; Taylor, pp. 520, 643.

13^{33} Bultmann, pp. 130, 174; Lambrecht, p. 241; Marxsen, pp. 162–6; Neirynck, p. 70; Schreiber, pp. 91–4; Schweizer, p. 279; Sundwall, p. 78; Taylor, p. 523.

13^{34a}; 13^{35a}; 13^{37} Best, p. 88; Bultmann, p. 130; Lambrecht, p. 253; Marxsen, p. 162; Neirynck, p. 81; Pesch, p. 226; Schreiber, pp. 129–31; Schweizer, pp. 280ff.; Sundwall, p. 78; Taylor, p. 524; Trocmé, p. 100.

14^{1a} Best, p. 90; Bultmann, pp. 262ff., 277–9; Lambrecht, p. 61; Neirynck, pp. 85, 100; Pesch, p. 66; Schreiber, pp. 89ff., 148; Schweizer, p. 287; Sundwall, p. 79; Taylor, p. 527.

14^{2a}; 14^{3a} Bultmann, pp. 277–9; Burkill, p. 121; Dibelius, p. 181; Neirynck, p. 52; Pesch, p. 66; Schweizer, p. 290; Taylor, pp. 529ff., 653, 658ff.

14^{4a}; 14^{5a}; 14^{7a}; 14$^{8-9}$ Best, p. 90; Bultmann, pp. 263, 277; Burkill, p. 121; Dibelius, p. 264; Horstmann, p. 98; Neirynck, pp. 80, 94, 132; Pesch, p. 66; Schreiber, p. 185; Schweizer, pp. 29–31; Taylor, pp. 529, 534, 653.

14$^{9-10}$ Best, p. 91; Bultmann, pp. 262, 277; Burkill, p. 121;

Lambrecht, pp. 58, 61; Neirynck, p. 133; Schreiber, pp. 89, 173; Taylor, p. 534.

14^{11}; 14^{12a} Best, p. 90; Bultmann, pp. 262, 264, 277–8; Burkill, p. 232; Dibelius, p. 181; Lambrecht, p. 59; Neirynck, p. 48; Pesch, pp. 66, 69; Schweizer, p. 294; Taylor, pp. 536ff.

14^{17-21} Best, p. 91; Bultmann, pp. 264–5; Dibelius, pp. 187, 206; Neirynck, pp. 87, 100, 109, 118; Pesch, p. 69; Schreiber, p. 103; Schweizer, p. 298; Taylor, pp. 539ff.; Trocmé, p. 50.

14^{22a} Best, p. 91; Bultmann, pp. 265, 277–8; Neirynck, pp. 80, 100; Schreiber, p. 241; Schweizer, p. 300; Taylor, p. 543.

14^{25-31} Best, p. 92; Bultmann, pp. 266–7, 285; Burkill, p. 222; Dibelius, pp. 181, 183, 214; Horstmann, p. 129; Neirynck, pp. 87, 88, 93, 130, 135; Pesch, p. 66; Reploh, p. 14; Schreiber, p. 185; Schweizer, pp. 307–8; Sundwall, p. 80; Taylor, pp. 548, 654.

14^{32a} Best, pp. 92–3; Bultmann, pp. 267–9; Burkill, p. 232; Schreiber, p. 185; Schweizer, p. 310; Taylor, pp. 551, 653.

14^{33} Best, p. 93; Schreiber, p. 241; Schweizer, p. 310; Trocmé, p. 101.

14^{38} Best, p. 93; Bultmann, p. 268; Neirynck, p. 80; Schreiber, pp. 100, 122–7; Sundwall, p. 81; Taylor, p. 554.

14^{39}; 14^{40} Neirynck, p. 81; Schreiber, p. 241; Taylor, p. 555.

14^{41} Best, p. 93; Bultmann, p. 268; Neirynck, pp. 81, 85, 94, 130; Schreiber, pp. 101–3; Schweizer, p. 310; Sundwall, p. 81.

14^{42} Burkill, p. 232; Neirynck, pp. 81, 85, 94; Pesch, p. 66; Schreiber, p. 101; Sundwall, p. 81.

14^{43a} Best, p. 94; Bultmann, pp. 267–8; Burkill, p. 236; Neirynck, p. 95; Pesch, p. 66; Schreiber, p. 84; Sundwall, p. 80.

14^{47-52} Bultmann, pp. 268–9, 282; Dibelius, pp. 184, 296; Neirynck, pp. 81, 95, 97, 100; Pesch, p. 66; Schweizer, p. 316; Taylor, pp. 557, 564, 654.

14^{53a} Best, p. 94; Bultmann, pp. 269, 278–9; Burkill, p. 237; Neirynck, p. 81; Pesch, p. 66; Schreiber, p. 182; Schweizer, p. 321; Sundwall, pp. 81, 536.

14^{57-9} Bultmann, pp. 269–70; Burkill, p. 217; Dibelius, pp. 192, 198; Neirynck, p. 100; Schreiber, p. 41; Schweizer, p. 329; Taylor, pp. 563, 566, 653; Trocmé, n. 55, p. 85.

14^{61}; 14^{65-66a} Bultmann, pp. 269, 278; Burkill, p. 237; Neirynck, p. 51; Pesch, p. 66; Schreiber, p. 233; Taylor, pp. 572, 653.

14^{67}; 14^{69-70a}; 14^{71a}; 14^{72}; 15^{1a} Bultmann, p. 272; Burkill, p. 243; Dibelius, p. 182; Pesch, p. 66; Taylor, p. 577; Trocmé, pp. 50, 79.

15^{2} Best, p. 95; Bultmann, pp. 272, 284; Neirynck, pp. 87, 131; Schreiber, p. 238.

15^{7-8};15^{10} Schreiber, p. 173; Schweizer, p. 337.

15^{12-13a};15^{14b};15^{15c} Best, p. 113; Neirynck, pp. 81, 100; Schreiber, p. 173.

15^{16b} Best, p. 96; Bultmann, pp. 272, 277; Neirynck, p. 107; Pesch, p. 66; Schreiber, p. 58; Schweizer, p. 341; Taylor, pp. 585, 653.

15^{18};15^{20c} Best, p. 97; Bultmann, pp. 272–3; Burkill, p. 243; Neirynck, p. 100; Schreiber, pp. 62–6, 32ff.; Schweizer, p. 341; Taylor, p. 586.

15^{22b} Taylor, p. 588.

15^{25-7} Best, p. 97; Bultmann, pp. 272–4, 284; Burkill, p. 244; Dibelius, p. 213; Neirynck, pp. 77, 81, 101; Schreiber, pp. 69ff.; Schweizer, p. 342; Taylor, pp. 587, 654.

15^{29-32} Best, p. 96; Bultmann, p. 273; Burkill, p. 244; Dibelius, p. 193; Schreiber, p. 41; Trocmé, p. 85, n. 55.

15^{29-32} Best, p. 97; Bultmann, p. 273; Burkill, p. 243; Dibelius, p. 187; Neirynck, pp. 81, 83, 85; Schreiber, p. 43; Schweizer, p. 350; Taylor, pp. 591–2.

15^{33} Best, p. 97; Bultmann, p. 274; Burkill, p. 243; Neirynck, p. 81; Schreiber, p. 39; Taylor, pp. 587, 593, 654.

15^{34b} Best, p. 97; Bultmann, pp. 273–4; Burkill, pp. 222, n. 50, p. 246; Dibelius, p. 186; Neirynck, p. 107; Schreiber, pp. 26, 50; Taylor, p. 593.

15^{36a};15^{39} Best, p. 97; Bultmann, p. 274; Horstmann, p. 120; Neirynck, p. 113; Pesch, p. 59; Schreiber, p. 26; Schweizer, p. 352; Taylor, pp. 598, 654.

15^{40a};15^{42} Best, p. 102; Bultmann, p. 274; Burkill, p. 243; Neirynck, p. 48; Pesch, p. 67; Schreiber, pp. 87–9.

15^{43b} Best, p. 65; Schreiber, p. 181; Taylor, p. 600.

15^{46} Bultmann, p. 274; Burkill, p. 243; Neirynck, pp. 81, 84; Schreiber, pp. 18off.; Taylor, p. 654.

16^{2a} Neirynck, p. 48; Schreiber, pp. 101ff.; Taylor, p. 605.

16^{4b} Taylor, p. 606.

16^7 Best, n. 3, p. 102; Bultmann, p. 285; Burkill, p. 251; Dibelius, p. 190; Horstmann, pp. 83, 129; Marxsen, pp. 8off.; Neirynck, pp. 85, 94; Reploh, p. 14; Schreiber, pp. 87ff.; Sundwall, p. 84; Trocmé, n. 42, p. 186.

16^{8c} Burkill, p. 157; Horstmann, pp. 83, 129; Neirynck, pp. 88, 101; Pesch, p. 66; Schreiber, p. 113; Taylor, pp. 609ff.

Redactional verses are classified under the following headings: Chronology; Command to silence; Editorial; Explanatory comment; M.L.C.; Saying link; S.S.P.; Topography and chronology; Topography

Chronology. 1^{9a}, $8^{1,13}$, $13^{7c,8c,24}$, $14^{1a,12,17,39}$, 15^{25}, 16^{2a}.

Command to silence. 1^{44a}, 3^{12}, 5^{23a}, 5^{43a}, 7^{36}, $8^{26,30}$, $9^{9,30}$.

Editorial. $1^{6,8a,11a,14-15,16ac,18,20a,26,31,40a,41}$, $2^{8-9,14,16a,17a}$, $2^{18a,28}$, $3^{34a,35b}$, $4^{9,23,29,41b}$, $5^{5,9c,11,15,17,25-6,30-1,42,43a}$, 6^{6a}, $6^{17a,20,22,29,41,48b}$, $7^{5a,8,13c,14,16-17,18a,19-20a,25,27c}$, $8^{9b,11a}$, $8^{35c,38c}$, $9^{3,6-7a,20,26,38a,50c}$, $10^{13,16-17a,24ab,26,28,31-5a}$, 11^{9-10}, $11^{13c,14}$, $12^{17c,18a,28ab,37b}$, $13^{4,5a,7a,9a,13b,14b,24b,28a,33,34a}$, $14^{28,33,38a,42,43a,57-9,61,65,66a,67-70a,71a,72}$, $15^{15c,20c,22b,26,29,(39)}$, $15^{43b,(46)}$, 16^{7}.

Explanatory comment. $1^{16ac,30,43}$, $2^{6,15ac,26b}$, $3^{5a,7-12,30-1,33a}$, 4^{22a}, $4^{25a,31b}$, $5^{8,28,33,41b}$, $6^{14-16,18,50a,52}$, $7^{2b,3-4,10a,11c,19-20a,21a}$, $7^{23,26a,31a,34c,36-7}$, $8^{36a,37a}$, $9^{39b,40a,41b,49a}$, 10^{22b}, $11^{1-2b,3c}$, $11^{18-23a,31-2}$, $12^{1a,12,18a,34c,40a,42,44c}$, $13^{6b,8c,10,11b,19a,23,37}$, $14^{2a,4a,8-9,40-1}$, $15^{2,10,14b,16b,31-2,34b}$, $16^{4b,8c}$.

M.L.C. $1^{1-4,10,35-8(?)}$, $3^{7-12,13-19,20-1}$, $4^{10-12,33-4}$, $6^{6b-13,14-16}$, $6^{30-4,53-6}$, $8^{14-21,27-33}$, $9^{9-13,30-2,33-7}$, $10^{31-5a,41-5,46-52}$, $14^{10-11,17-21,26-31}$, $15^{7-8,12-13a,18,36a,40a}$.

Saying link. $2^{5a,10c,27a}$, $3^{23a,28a}$, $4^{3a,10-12,13,21a,24a,(26a),(30a)}$, $6^{4a,10a,35a}$, 7^{9a}, 8^{34a}, $9^{1ac,17a}$, $10^{15a,23a,27a,29ac}$, 11^{17a}, $12^{38a,43a}$, $13^{5a,29-30a}$, 14^{27a}.

S.S.P. $1^{21-2,27-8,32-4,38-9,45}$, 2^{1-2}, $3^{6,7-12,20-1}$, 4^{1-2}, $5^{20,24}$, $6^{1-2a,6b-13,30-4,53-6}$, 9^{14-17a}.

Topography and chronology. $1^{12,23a,35}$, 4^{35-6a}, $6^{35a,47-8}$, 9^{2ab}, $11^{11-12,19,20}$, 13^{29-30a}, $15^{33,42}$.

Topography. $1^{21,29a}$, $2^{1-2,12-13,15ac,23b}$, $3^{1a,22a}$, 4^{38}, $5^{1-2a,21,35a}$, 6^{45}, $7^{1,31a,24,31}$, $8^{10,22a}$, $9^{28a,33}$, $10^{1,10,11a,32,46}$, $11^{1-2b,15a,27}$, $12^{12-13,35a,41}$, $13^{1,2-3}$, $14^{3a,22a,26,32a,53a}$, 15^{1a}.

B. LINGUISTIC CRITERIA
FOR REDACTION

I MARCAN LINGUISTIC STUDIES
SINCE HAWKINS AND TURNER

The aim of the book is to discover a method which may integrate both linguistics and literary studies as independent ways of distinguishing editorial and source material in the Gospel so as to lead on to a detection of the theology of the evangelist as redactor. While certain verses of the Gospel have been marked as editorial by literary, form-critical and linguistic judgements, the present chapter attempts to discover whether linguistic criteria for redaction may alone be deduced from an examination of the author's syntax and vocabulary.

Turner and Kilpatrick,[1] among others, refer from time to time to 'Marcan usage'. Taylor,[2] in his commentary on the Gospel, lists a fair number of unusual traits in the author's syntax and vocabulary, a well-known example being the frequent use of the historic present. Best refers not infrequently in his chapter on the 'Markan seams' to literary and linguistic features of Mark, and from these argues the redactional nature of the writing, e.g. ἄρχομαι + διδάσκειν and 'intercalation'. 'Marcan usage' may not have exactly the same sense in Taylor's and Turner's work as in that of Best,[3] for form-critical studies naturally lead on to an investigation of the evangelist's role as a redactor. So far, however, those characteristics classified as redactional have not been thoroughly tested as to whether they are to be traced to the sources rather than to the hand of the evangelist.

One presupposition for the search for either linguistic or literary criteria must be the possibility of the division of the

---

[1] See Bibliography, p. 181; see British and Foreign Bible Society ed. of Greek N.T., p. xxiii, footnote, where Kilpatrick commends Turner's papers on Marcan usage in *J.T.S.* 25–9 (1924–8). [2] Pp. 44–54.

[3] Pp. 83, 118, n. 2 on 'intercalation' and the variations in Greek style vv. 25–34 and vv. 21–4, 35–43 (cf. the participles of 25–7). For ἤρξατο διδάσκειν, 'a Markan phrase...incorporating his favourite use of ἄρχομαι', see p. 75.

Gospel into form-critical pericopae.[1] There is, however, no agreement among scholars whether Mark was handling continuous written sources, though we should not deny the possibility. But even if he did so, these written sources were evidently made up of what the form-critics mean by pericopae. The question which would then arise would be who was responsible for the 'seams' which link the sources. Are they always the work of the editor, or did he in some cases find these connectives already made for him in the written source which he was employing? These linguistic investigations may have contributions to make in solving the enigma of the material which the evangelist used, whether for example he deployed continuous written sources, or oral pericopae, or both. The evangelist would seem to have been a pioneer in the construction of the Gospel as a whole,[2] so his hand would be most likely detected linguistically in the first place in those passages which act as a cement between either pericopae or written sources.

The architects of Marcan studies of syntax and vocabulary, to whom we have to return again and again, were Turner[3] and Hawkins. They analysed in great detail the curious features of syntax and vocabulary, which Matthew and Luke changed, rejected and modified. Only comparatively recently in England, following the German school, and under the leadership of R. H. Lightfoot,[4] redactional studies in the Gospels have found qualified acceptance, but if the literary arguments for redaction are sound, they should have at least some support from linguistic study of syntax and vocabulary. If there is no correlation or meeting point of the two disciplines, then either one or both methods need further investigation and revision.

The term 'Marcan usage' can itself be considered ambiguous. Is it intended to refer to features of the whole Gospel as it stands? This would appear to be how Turner and others have used it. Should it not be used if we are speaking solely of those features and characteristics of the evangelist's own style, as distinct from the style of his sources, whether oral or written?

---

[1] Taylor, in his commentary; United Bible Societies Greek N.T.; also N.E.B.

[2] So Bultmann, p. 369: 'It is in Mark that the *Gospel type* is first to be met.'

[3] For Turner's articles see Bibliography, pp. 185–6.

[4] *History and Interpretation in the Gospels* (London, 1935); *Locality and Doctrine in the Gospels* (London, 1938).

Jeremias makes such a distinction, while Taylor is moving in that direction, but never carried his judgements to their logical conclusions.

A distinction has been made between source and redaction on literary-critical and linguistic grounds, the listed passages at the beginning of this chapter being the result of that investigation. In this research these same passages are investigated by means of syntactical and vocabulary tests. The method is to reverse the order, begin with linguistics, and then to combine the latter with the literary method to see if the two approaches find common ground. We take certain linguistic features which stand out in such a way that Turner and others regarded them as 'Marcan usage', and then investigate what percentage of such features belongs to the passages marked R, and what proportion is to be apportioned to what has been regarded as S, in the light of literary judgements. (A statistical[1] summary of the findings is appended to this chapter.) Some eighteen linguistic features of 'Marcan usage' have been examined in some detail with the intention of discovering, if possible, whether the style of the evangelist is homogeneous throughout his Gospel, or whether statistical evidence suggests that the syntax is more characteristic of redactional passages. We may cite as examples three of these tests, which illustrate the width of the spectrum. Out of the twenty-nine passages which include parentheses, all with one exception are redactional. In the case of πάλιν the figure is 60% R, and 40% S, there being seventeen examples of πάλιν in redactional passages, and eleven in source. In the case of ὥστε + inf. the redactional figure is lower, 53% in R and 47% in S, i.e. seven in editorial passages and six in source material. As for the historic present,[2] well known as a particular illustration of Marcan usage, the figures (64R, 87S, approximate ratio 2S to 1R) are inconclusive for our study, and might be held to argue the homogeneity of the style of the Gospel.

There is, however, one important factor which is independent

---

[1] (a) parenthesis; (b) genitive absolute; (c) part. used as m.v.; (d) πολλά accusative; (e) λέγω ὅτι; (f) ἄρχομαι + inf.; (g) εὐθύς and καὶ εὐθύς; (h) πάλιν; (i) 'redundant' part.; (j) periphrastic tenses; (k) 'impersonals'; (l) ὥστε + inf.; (m) two or more parts. before or after m.v.; (n) explanatory γάρ.

[2] Hawkins, pp. 113–19. A similar inconclusive result was found in examining: (a) the position of the verb in the sentence; (b) asyndeta; (c) the use of δέ and καί.

of literary-critical and syntactical investigations, and that is the vocabulary of the Gospel. A vocabulary analysis of the Gospel, which is analysed from the highest frequency in descending order of numerical use, shows the author to master a much wider and more extensive vocabulary than is sometimes realised. There are, for example, 618 words used only once, 227 only twice, 99 three times, 68 four times. Words used five or more times are listed in descending order of frequency, so that they may furnish evidence pointing to the evangelist's own predilections, and thus we may ask whether some of the words of high frequency are to be found in passages which on literary or linguistic grounds we have come to regard as redactional. Thus, for example, the word 'Galilee' is used twelve times in the Gospel, nine of which at least there are good grounds for regarding as editorial. Again, the word 'Gospel' is used seven times, all of which are probably redactional. 'To proclaim'[1] is used twelve times, eleven of which are most probably redactional.

A complete list in alphabetical order was taken of what is judged to be redactional vocabulary on the basis of literary, syntactical, and vocabulary tests. In the vocabulary list those words which are judged to be the vocabulary of the tradition are bracketed and not counted in the main statistics, in spite of the fact that they are to be found in verses marked R. When a word is used often in redaction and seldom in source it is considered as an indication of the evangelist's own special interests and theology, the reasoning being that these words are more frequent in his own seams than in the source he is using. We must not lose sight of the other end of the scale and must realise that infrequency may be as powerful an indicator of the evangelist's own vocabulary as frequency. So attention must also be paid to words which occur less than five times, and particularly those words which are used only once in the whole of the New Testament[2] (e.g. μογιλάλος, ἐξουδενεῖσθαι). Such words are tentatively placed in the redactional vocabulary[3] even when they are

---

[1] P. 137.

[2] Swete, p. xliv: 'Words in St. Mark (excepting proper names) which occur in no other N.T. writing'. For example, μογιλάλος 7³² may or may not be R. Probably the traditional pericope begins at 7³² καὶ φέρουσιν. Possibly originally the evangelist may have read κωφόν and added μογιλάλος. N.B. 7³⁷ κωφούς...ἀλάλους (see 9¹⁷).

[3] They are marked †.

not in redactional verses, because they are pointers to the author's theology, and probably indications of literary sophistication, though it still remains an open question whether he took this theology, and the accompanying vocabulary which expressed it, from the oral tradition. The vocabulary test could therefore corroborate the syntactical and literary criteria, and in those cases where statistics in relation to syntax themselves are inconclusive, they can be of value in either sustaining or rejecting tendencies which seem only half proven.

The reasons why the syntactical tests produce such varied results are not hard to find, and need to be stated if only to illustrate exactly what kind of writer or author Mark probably was. He is neither what we would call an author nor is he purely an editor.[1] He tends to be the latter rather than the former, but the fact that he was a personality with a style of his own, and a vocabulary of his own, should not be forgotten. Severely restrained and subordinate to the tradition he almost certainly was, but he was still a writer with a considerable degree of inspiration and creativity.

Secondly, probably not being a good Greek scholar, and Greek almost certainly being his second language, he reveals himself as limited in his powers of literary expression.[2] This would not be surprising if the sources he handled were oral rather than written, and so we may assume that his style is that of the speaker rather than that of the writer, e.g. he cannot sustain indirect speech for very long, and slips into direct, yet paradoxically he can use two or more participles,[3] he can employ the genitive absolute correctly as well as imperfectly,[4] occasionally he employs μέν,[5] although more often in his sources

---

[1] F. W. Beare's review of E. Haenchen, *Der Weg Jesu: eine Erklärung des Markus-Evangeliums und der kanonischen Parallelen* (Berlin, 1966).
'More significant is the fact that he applies in his synoptic treatment the distinctive new emphasis on the evangelists as theologians in their own right, and as authors rather than compilers; he regards this approach as a second stage of form criticism, and sees it especially in the work of Marxsen on Mark, Stendahl on Matthew, and Conzelmann on Luke.' In place of Marxsen's term 'Redaktionsgeschichte', he suggests 'Kompositionsgeschichte' (*J.B.L.* 85 (December 1966), 507–8).
[2] Trocmé, p. 57: 'The author of Mark was a rustic who merits not the least mention in the literary histories.'
[3] See pp. 119–26.   [4] 13 times correctly, 16 times incorrectly.
[5] Two out of five times μέν is combined with δέ; once is redactional.

than in his redaction. Probably it would be a reasonable conjecture that his literary ability however minimal – and it has been sometimes underestimated – was learnt as a participant in the oral and written traditions of the Church in its various forms of ecclesiastical catechesis, preachings, and liturgy.

Such a writer would have to borrow heavily from the sources he is employing. Sundwall has demonstrated the plausibility of Mark's learning and using catchword linking from his sources. But when we find εὐθύς,[1] πάλιν,[2] the impersonals,[3] to mention the clearest examples, used in both R and S, we are able to see why the editor has adapted his redaction in some ways as an imitation of his sources, for that at least makes a more harmonious and smoother flow in his overall plan for linking up the separate pericopae.

Some of the sources may have already been joined together by catchwords,[4] such as καὶ εὐθύς; πάλιν, and other devices. Mark extended the usage and refined it, but this is what makes it difficult to be always dogmatic or absolutely sure about delineating redactional and source material. The catchwords he uses in the 'seams' are more literary and self-conscious than those long retained in the oral tradition. When καὶ εὐθύς introduces a pericope it is possible that the author is preserving something already there in the source, but when the verses themselves are background, and include redactional vocabulary of high frequency there is a strong likelihood that such links are those of the narrator, and when repeated fairly frequently as e.g. καὶ ἔλεγεν αὐτοῖς, they are editorial passages.

Literary analysis, based on form criticism, enables us to detect approximately 106 pericopae,[5] or 'paragraphs' in the Gospel, which are held together by the redaction of the author, and built into seven major sections,[6] or what we would term today 'chapters'. Naturally it is at the beginnings and endings of pericopae (the so-called 'seams')[7] where redaction is mainly to

---

[1] Pp. 87ff.   [2] Pp. 96ff.   [3] Pp. 107ff.

[4] Sundwall, pp. 5–6; Taylor, pp. 409–10: 'Together with 37 and 38–41, they [9, 41–50] appear to have been compiled under a catechetical impulse by the aid of catchwords intended to assist the memory' (p. 408).

[5] Taylor, pp. 107–11; see pp. 10–24.

[6] I = 1^{1-13}; II = $1^{14}-3^6$; III = 3^7-6^{13}; IV = $6^{14}-8^{26}$; V = $8^{27}-10^{52}$; VI = 11^1-13^{37}; VII = $14-16^8$ [16^9-16^{20}].

[7] Best, 63–102.

be found. Nevertheless, unless his work was simply the assembling of sources already in Greek, his own hand may also be present in his sources, in so far as he was himself responsible for the translation or paraphrase of already existing Aramaic oral or written tradition. Further, his own redaction may not have been uninfluenced by linguistic usages already belonging to the tradition. One would expect to find in such a writing as a 'Gospel' sometimes redaction in the source, and traditional sayings or expressions preserved, or repeated and used in editorial links. If this is the correct estimate of Mark's situation as a writer, any neat and tidy solution to the problem of redaction and linguistics in Mark must be ruled out of court.

II SYNTACTICAL FEATURES
CONSIDERED AS POSSIBLE GUIDELINES
TO THE AUTHOR'S STYLE

(a) PARENTHETICAL CLAUSES

Matthew's and Luke's avoidance of Mark's parentheses is clear from the analysis below. Only three are retained by Matthew, and one by Luke. Leaving out the passages with ὅ ἐστιν there are twenty-one parenthetical passages for consideration. Thirteen of the twenty-one are clear redactional passages, while three of the twenty-one are editorial, but may be at the same time traditional or community sayings. Three of the passages are partly redactional, and partly traditional or from source material, while five of the total are redactional but only in a portion of the total verse. A proportion of at least eighteen out of twenty-one shows that use of parenthesis is a stylistic feature bringing us close to the author's hand, and is characteristic of the evangelist's Greek. Of the eight short passages with ὅ ἐστιν, only one is source, which would suggest that the Latinism is not in the oral or source material, nor is it the work of a later redactor, as suggested by Trocmé,[1] but is to be regarded as a Marcan redactional or editorial mannerism.

C. H. Turner[2] established parenthesis as a definite feature of Marcan usage. Here we shall analyse the phenomenon in Mark from two aspects: the reasons which induced the evangelist to use parenthesis so often in his syntax, and its proportion in the Gospel.

The reasons

The evangelists had no footnotes or brackets. Everything, including quotations, had to go into the main text. If the editor wished to explain a word or a custom, or to quote from the Old Testament or from the classics, there were no punctuation

---

[1] P. 191, n. 57.
[2] *J.T.S.* 26 (January 1925), 145–46.

Mark	Matthew	Luke	Marcan Editor	Non-R
(i) $\big\{$ 1^{1-4}	g.c. (3^{1-3})	g.c. (3^{2-6})	R	
7^{6-8}	g.c. (15^{6b-9})	NP	7^8PR(?)	7^{6-7}
(ii) 2^{15b}	omitted (9^{10})	omitted (5^{29})	PR 2^{15bc}	2^{15a}
6^{14b-16}	g.c. (14^1)	g.c. (9^{7-8})	PR $14a+$ $16a$	$14b$–15
16^{4b}	omitted (28^2)	omitted (24^2)	R(?)	$16b$
(iii) 3^{21b}	omitted (12^{22-4})	omitted (11^{14-16})	R (M.L.C.)	
3^{30}	omitted ('Q', 12^{32})	omitted ('Q', 12^{10})	R	
11^{31-2}	g.c. (21^{25-6})	g.c. (20^{5-6})	R	
16^{8c}	g.c. (28^8)	omitted (24^9)	R(?)	
4^{31b}	g.c. (13^{32})	omitted ((Q) 13^{19})	R	
12^{12b}	m.a. (21^{45})	same (20^{19})	R(?)	
2^{10c}	9^6	g.c. (5^{24})	R	
(iv) 7^{2b}	omitted (15^{1-20})	NP	PR	
7^{3-4}	omitted (15^{1-20})	NP	R	
7^{6-7}	15^{7-9}	NP	7^8R	7^{6b-7} (S)
7^{19c}	omitted (15^{17})	NP	R(?)	
7^{26a}	g.c. (15^{22})	NP	R	

Mark	Matthew	Luke	Marcan Editor	Non-R
(v) $\{$ 13^{10}	m.a. (10^{18})	omitted (21^{13})	R	
8^{15}	m.a. (16^{6})	m.a. (12^{1})	R(?)	
14^{49b}	g.c. (25^{56})	22 omitted	R(?)	
13^{14b}	24^{15}	omitted (21^{20})	R	
(vi) $\{$ 3^{17c}	omitted	omitted	R	
5^{9c}	omitted	g.c. (8^{30})		
5^{41b}	omitted (13^{25})	omitted (8^{54})	R	
7^{11c}	omitted (15^{1-20})	omitted	R	
7^{34c}	omitted (15^{29-31})	NP	R	
12^{42}	NP	omitted (21^{2})	12^{42b}R	
15^{16}	omitted (27^{27})	NP	R	
15^{34}	(27^{46})	NP	15^{34a}R	(?)
29	3 retd.	1 retd.	28/29	13
	11 g.c.	7 g.c.		
	15 omitted	21 omitted		

NP = No Parallel; PR = Part Redactional; m.a. = meaning altered; g.c. = grammar changed; retd. = retained

34

marks to distinguish the author's work from his quotations. Also, it is well known that ancient authors, in common with the lazy student, borrowed large extracts from sources, without any acknowledgement whatsoever.

The following are some of the possible reasons for parenthesis in his syntactical usage: (i) the insertion of quotations; (ii) loose sentence construction; (iii) explanatory clauses related to Christ's life, to the parables, and to the Church's ministry of forgiveness; (iv) problems of the admission of Gentile converts and of their eating with Jewish Christians; (v) catechetical, liturgical, and Biblical usage; (vi) translations, mainly from the Aramaic.

(i) *The insertion of quotations*

We may analyse in detail two examples[1] of parenthesis which are quotations inserted into the middle of the sentence.

¶ 1^{1-4}(R). The first example, the opening of the gospel, 1^{1-4}, has provoked considerable discussion because of the ambiguity of its syntax, and the difficulty of translating it. What a sobering reflection on the style of the author that both the beginning and the ending of his work are still matters of debate, leaving much to be desired from a literary point of view!

One commentator outlines ten possible ways of arranging the syntax:[2] The opening phrase of the gospel ἀρχὴ τοῦ εὐαγγελίου Ἰησοῦ Χριστοῦ [υἱοῦ θεοῦ] may be the title of the book, but as εὐαγγέλιον is 'the announcement of the good news by/of Jesus Christ', and the word εὐαγγέλιον is never used of a book in the gospel,[3] such an interpretation is unlikely. The words ἀρχὴ... θεοῦ could perhaps be an introduction of 'the good news' which is concentrated in 1^{2-8} or 1^{2-13}, and which consists of the pre-

---

[1] 1^{2-3}, 7^{6-8}.

[2] Cranfield, p. 34; see also Trocmé, pp. 120, 121, n. 53.

[3] 'It is remarkable that Mark always uses the noun εὐαγγέλιον in the absolute sense...Thus εὐαγγέλιον in 1. 1 must be understood from the standpoint of Mark's own time and so the term "title" does not completely meet the case...' (Marxsen, p. 84). In commenting on ἀρχή Marxsen says that its meaning is the crux of the matter; that it is not the 'point of departure of an event to be described, but the point back to which this event is to be traced' and that there is not a 'beginning' because God is the author of the event (*ibid.*, p. 87).

paratory work of the Baptist. Such a view is highly acceptable
to many critics. But the evangelist does not introduce any other
section in his work in this manner, and certain problems are
still outstanding with such an interpretation. The first is that
the other two synoptic evangelists do not appear to have read
Mark 1[2b] ἰδού... ἀποστέλλω τὸν ἄγγελόν μου πρὸ προσώπου
σου, ὃς κατασκευάσει τὴν ὁδόν σου, but both commence at
φωνὴ βοῶντος ἐν τῇ ἐρήμῳ. This may not be a difficulty, however, since Matthew and Luke may have omitted this passage
because it is not to be found in Isaiah, the prophet, as the
original reading in Mark asserts; their reasons for omission
would then be explained, and we do not necessarily have to
argue a later insertion by a redactor. An alternative explanation
would be that they used it elsewhere, in the 'Q' passage, Mt.
11[10]/Lk. 7[27].

Secondly, ἐγένετο in verse 4 probably looks back to ἀρχή...
as its subject. The evangelist has a varied use with γίνεσθαι, the
main uses being: as an auxiliary + participle periphrastically
used, with a participle as the predicate; the LXX usage of
καὶ ἐγένετο + temporal use of ἐν + inf.; and the linking of subject
and predicate. Thus in ἔκφοβοι γὰρ ἐγένοντο· καὶ ἐγένετο
νεφέλη ἐπισκιάζουσα αὐτοῖς, καὶ ἐγένετο φωνὴ ἐκ τῆς νεφέλης...[1]
ἔκφοβοι is used as an adjective, with καὶ ἐγένετο plus the participle ἐπισκιάζουσα used as a predicate periphrastically. The
third usage, 'impersonally with a subject, designating a thing
or an event' is very common in Mark.

1[9]R καὶ ἐγένετο ἐν ἐκείναις ταῖς ἡμέραις ἦλθεν is explained as
a Hebraism 'and it came to pass...that Jesus came', i.e.
καὶ ἐγένετο + main verb. 4[4] καὶ ἐγένετο ἐν τῷ σπείρειν may be
traced to the influence of the Septuagint with ἐν + infinitive
used in a temporal sense ('while'). 15[33], sometimes regarded
as a redactional verse, comes nearest to ἐγένετο in 1[4]. καὶ
γενομένης ὥρας ἕκτης σκότος ἐγένετο ἐφ' ὅλην τὴν γῆν ἕως ὥρας
ἐνάτης. γενομένης...ἕκτης is a genitive absolute; σκότος is the
subject and ἐγένετο the main verb. Thus ἀρχὴ τοῦ εὐαγγελίου
Ἰησοῦ Χριστοῦ [υἱοῦ θεοῦ] is linked by ἐγένετο to Ἰωάννης ὁ
Βαπτίζων ἐν τῇ ἐρήμῳ κηρύσσων βάπτισμα μετανοίας εἰς ἄφεσιν
ἁμαρτιῶν. καθὼς γέγραπται...τὰς τρίβους αὐτοῦ is in parenthesis. If ἰδοὺ ἀποστέλλω τὸν ἄγγελόν μου πρὸ προσώπου σου

_____
[1] 9[7].

ὃς κατασκευάσει τὴν ὁδόν σου is an interpolation, the length οι the parenthesis is reduced, but there is no textual evidence to support this.

Thirdly, an examination of the way the evangelist uses quotations elsewhere in the gospel might indicate his practice, and serve as a guide to the interpretation of 1¹⁻⁴. Out of thirteen[1] quotations of one or two verses' length, in four the evangelist suspends the quotation in the middle of the sentence. The other three besides 1¹⁻⁴ are 7⁶⁻⁸R, 10⁵⁻⁸, and 14²⁷⁻⁸R.

(1) καλῶς ἐπροφήτευσεν 'Ησαίας περὶ ὑμῶν τῶν ὑποκριτῶν, – ὡς γέγραπται ὅτι
οὗτος ὁ λαὸς τοῖς χείλεσίν με τιμᾷ,
ἡ δὲ καρδία αὐτῶν πόρρω ἀπέχει ἀπ' ἐμοῦ·
μάτην δὲ σέβονταί με,
διδάσκοντες διδασκαλίας ἐντάλματα ἀνθρώπων –
ἀφέντες τὴν ἐντολὴν τοῦ θεοῦ κρατεῖτε τὴν παράδοσιν τῶν ἀνθρώπων (7⁶⁻⁸).
(2) ὁ δὲ 'Ιησοῦς εἶπεν αὐτοῖς, Πρὸς τὴν σκληροκαρδίαν ὑμῶν ἔγραψεν ὑμῖν τὴν ἐντολὴν ταύτην. ἀπὸ δὲ ἀρχῆς κτίσεως ἄρσεν καὶ θῆλυ ἐποίησεν αὐτούς. ἕνεκεν τούτου καταλείψει ἄνθρωπος τὸν πατέρα αὐτοῦ καὶ τὴν μητέρα . . . καὶ ἔσονται οἱ δύο εἰς σάρκα μίαν· ὥστε οὐκέτι εἰσὶν δύο ἀλλὰ μία σάρξ. ὃ οὖν ὁ θεὸς συνέζευξεν, ἄνθρωπος μὴ χωριζέτω (10⁵⁻⁸).
(3) καὶ λέγει αὐτοῖς ὁ 'Ιησοῦς ὅτι Πάντες σκανδαλισθήσεσθε, ὅτι γέγραπται,
Πατάξω τὸν ποιμένα,
καὶ τὰ πρόβατα διασκορπισθήσονται·
ἀλλὰ μετὰ τὸ ἐγερθῆναί με προάξω ὑμᾶς εἰς τὴν Γαλιλαίαν (14²⁷⁻⁸).

1¹ and 1⁴ in vocabulary[2] would seem Marcan and redactional, with one striking exception. 'Ιησοῦς Χριστός is used in 1¹ as a personal name, whereas Mark always has the full title ὁ Χριστός, with the article. υἱοῦ θεοῦ, although omitted in some very good MSS, could have dropped out very easily and is used elsewhere in the gospel. ὁ Βαπτίζων in 1⁴ is a title, while κηρύσσω[3] is used twelve times.

The other possible syntactical arrangement is to regard 1¹ as

---

[1] 1¹⁻⁴; 4¹¹⁻¹³; 4²⁹,³²; 7⁶⁻⁸; 10⁵⁻⁸; 11¹⁷; 12¹⁰⁻¹¹; 12¹⁹,²⁹⁻³¹,³²⁻³; 12³⁶⁻⁷; 14²⁷⁻⁸.
[2] ἀρχή (2/4 times); εὐαγγέλιον (7/7 times); 'Ιησοῦ Χριστοῦ (once); υἱοῦ θεοῦ (3/5 times) = 1¹, 3¹¹, 15³⁹.
[3] κηρύσσων may be used here periphrastically.

the heading to 1²⁻⁸ or 1²⁻¹³, commencing the second sentence at καθὼς γέγραπται with either a full stop or comma at the end of the citation. ἐγένετο is then regarded as an auxiliary to the participle κηρύσσων which is periphrastically used. But the habit of the evangelist being to use parenthesis especially in quotations, the positioning of ἐγένετο at the beginning of the clause, but chiefly the meaning and the probable reference of ἀρχὴ τοῦ εὐαγγελίου to the ministry of the Baptist, make the Baptist's preaching the logical connecting link, and argue against such a syntax. The quotation referring to the messenger who prepares the way, and to the voice crying in the wilderness, opens up the eschatological vista of the forgiveness of sins, and forges 1¹ and 1⁴ inseparably together. In spite of the fact that the sentence seems long and somewhat clumsy, the most satisfactory solution is to take ἐγένετο as copula. The Baptist's mission is the heralding of the impending work of Jesus Christ, the preacher and central figure of the coming eschatological age. The Greek runs:

ἀρχὴ τοῦ εὐαγγελίου 'Ιησοῦ Χριστοῦ υἱοῦ θεοῦ – καθὼς γέγραπται ἐν τῷ 'Ησαΐᾳ τῷ προφήτῃ·
ἰδοὺ ἀποστέλλω τὸν ἄγγελόν μου πρὸ προσώπου σου,
   ὃς κατασκευάσει τὴν ὁδόν σου·
φωνὴ βοῶντος ἐν τῇ ἐρήμῳ·
   'Ετοιμάσατε τὴν ὁδὸν κυρίου,
   εὐθείας ποιεῖτε τὰς τρίβους αὐτοῦ –
ἐγένετο 'Ιωάννης ὁ βαπτίζων ἐν τῇ ἐρήμῳ κηρύσσων βάπτισμα μετανοίας εἰς ἄφεσιν ἁμαρτιῶν.

This would yield as a translation:

The beginning of the good news about Jesus Christ (as it is written in Isaiah, the prophet, 'Behold I send my messenger before you, to prepare your way. A voice crying in the desert, Prepare the Way of the Lord, and make his paths straight') was John, the Baptizer, proclaiming a baptism with a view to remission of sins.

¶ 7⁶⁻⁸. The second example, 7⁶⁻⁸, from the pericope on the question of the washing of hands, has three parenthentical clauses,[1] one of which is similar in character to the quotation in the opening of the gospel.

---

[1] (a) 7² = τοῦτ' ἔστιν ἀνίπτοις, (b) 7³⁻⁴ = οἱ γὰρ Φ.... χαλκίων, (c) 7⁶ = ὡς γέγραπται... ἀνθρώπων.

ὁ δὲ εἶπεν αὐτοῖς· καλῶς ἐπροφήτευσεν Ἠσαΐας περὶ ὑμῶν τῶν
ὑποκριτῶν, – ὡς γέγραπται ὅτι
οὗτος ὁ λαὸς τοῖς χείλεσίν με τιμᾷ,
  ἡ δὲ καρδία αὐτῶν πόρρω ἀπέχει ἀπ᾽ ἐμοῦ·
μάτην δὲ σέβονταί με,
  διδάσκοντες διδασκαλίας ἐντάλματα ἀνθρώπων –
ἀφέντες τὴν ἐντολὴν τοῦ θεοῦ κρατεῖτε τὴν παράδοσιν τῶν ἀνθρώπων
(7⁶⁻⁸).

As with the previous example, the quotation well illustrates
the sentence. In 1¹⁻⁴ the Baptist heralds the good news, preparing the way of the Lord: in 7⁶⁻⁸, in 'teaching the com-
mandments of men', the scribes and Jewish leaders 'disregard
the command of God, and follow the traditions of men'. Because
the Greek Bible is quoted here, Rawlinson[1] regards the quotation as probably coming from the evangelist or his sources
rather than as the actual words of Christ. Swete[2] suggests that
8 is a doublet of 9, which reads:– καὶ ἔλεγεν αὐτοῖς· καλῶς ἀθετεῖτε
τὴν ἐντολὴν τοῦ θεοῦ, ἵνα τὴν παράδοσιν ὑμῶν στήσητε (7⁹).
10⁵⁻⁸ is not a quotation suspended in the middle of a statement,
but a quotation skilfully interwoven into the deductions which
the speaker makes from it. When the editor uses a quotation it
is not always clear whether he is using his own words or if his
argument is assisted by Biblical injunctions. ἀπὸ δὲ ἀρχῆς
κτίσεως is probably a reference to Genesis Creation stories but
it also implies perhaps a principle of creation, something which
belongs to the natural order. ἄρσεν... μίαν is a combination of
Genesis 1²⁷ᵇ and 2²⁴, but ἕνεκεν τούτου refers not to 1²⁷ᵇ but to
2²³, i.e. woman originating from man's rib. The consequence of
the two statements is expressed in Mark's ὥστε + indicative,
followed by the injunction (μή + imperatives) not to
separate.

14²⁷⁻⁸ is similar to 1¹⁻⁴ and the previous passage in its use of
quotations as part of the general argument, yet the quotation
still seems to stand as an entity in itself. Jesus opens the statement with a warning that they are going to be affronted by His
death, which He does with a paraphrase of Zechariah. In the
LXX we read: πατάξατε τοὺς ποιμένας καί ἐκσπάσατε τὰ

[1] Rawlinson, p. 94.
[2] P. 147 reads: ἀφέντες τὴν ἐντολὴν τοῦ θεοῦ κρατεῖτε τὴν παράδοσιν
τῶν ἀνθρώπων.

πρόβατα... (Zech. 13⁷).[1] Mark reads πατάξω τὸν ποιμένα καὶ τὰ πρόβατα διασκορπισθήσονται.

The meaning here seems quite different from the original, having been changed to apply to the death of Jesus and the dispersal of the disciples. ἀλλὰ μετὰ τὸ ἐγερθῆναί με προάξω ὑμᾶς εἰς τὴν Γαλιλαίαν is a redactional[2] preparation for 16⁷, so the promise to appear (either a Resurrection or Parousia intimation) is a reversal of the death and scattering of the flock by a resurrection and regathering of them in Galilee. ὅτι γέγραπται gives a providential design to the death of Jesus, especially with the first person singular being used of God Himself. So, in fact, πατάξω and προάξω are not the same subject; one is God, the other is Christ.

(ii) Loose sentence construction

The second type of parenthesis is caused by the loosely constructed sentence, which appends a phrase as an afterthought to clarify a previously obscure statement. As sometimes with Paul a secondary argument leads the author astray, disturbing the logic and syntax of the preceding clause. The writer either leaves a verb or phrase in suspense, or picks it up again later in the sentence. A good example of such a broken construction is 2¹⁵.

¶2¹⁵ᵇR. This runs: καὶ γίνεται κατακεῖσθαι αὐτὸν ἐν τῇ οἰκίᾳ αὐτοῦ, καὶ πολλοὶ τελῶναι καὶ ἁμαρτωλοὶ συνανέκειντο τῷ Ἰησοῦ καὶ τοῖς μαθηταῖς αὐτοῦ · –ἦσαν γὰρ πολλοί, καὶ ἠκολούθουν αὐτῷ – . Taylor's comment on the parenthetical clause (ἦσαν γὰρ πολλοί, καὶ ἠκολούθουν αὐτῷ) is interesting: 'It reveals the Evangelist's consciousness that he has not mentioned the large company of disciples earlier, and that he must do so now.'[3] The explanatory phrase[4] follows an ambiguous opening, καὶ γίνεται κατακεῖσθαι αὐτὸν ἐν τῇ οἰκίᾳ αὐτοῦ, where it is very uncertain who is entertaining whom, and in whose house. Probably the opening of 2¹⁵ is partly redactional, added to a vague

[1] Q.Z.D. reads the same text as the LXX and Hebrew.
[2] Taylor, p. 549.
[3] Ibid., p. 205.
[4] Ibid., p. 308, notes how often γάρ is the second word of the explanatory phrase: 1²², 2¹⁵, 3¹⁰,²¹, 5⁸,²⁸, 6¹⁷,²⁰, 7³, 11¹³, 16⁸. See pp. 126ff.

reference to house and person from an early pericope. After the next phrase, καὶ πολλοὶ τελῶναι καὶ ἁμαρτωλοὶ συνανέκειντο, Mark adds καὶ τοῖς μαθηταῖς αὐτοῦ, for he wishes to bring them into the narrative for the first time. In his explanatory phrase he cannot resist the comment that they were numerous, and devout in their following of Christ, but whether 'they' are disciples or taxgatherers is far from obvious. ἠκολούθουν[1] together with the difficult phrase, 'the scribes of the Pharisees' may reflect the underlying motive of the story itself, that of the question of table-fellowship at the Palestinian-Gentile community table. Perhaps the evangelist is unconsciously contrasting Christ's willingness to eat with the excommunicated 'publicans and sinners' and the attitude of the Jewish-Christian 'scribes' of Pharisaical outlook[2] who hestitated to eat with the uncircumcised in the days of primitive Christianity. καλεῖν can also be used of invitations to meals as well as calls to repentance, so there is a possibility that Jesus was in fact the host, and that He said: 'I did not *invite* the "pious" but the sinners (to the meal).'

¶6[14-16](R). This, a Marcan literary construction,[3] also illustrates the evangelist's struggle to write clearly, and how he sometimes uses the parenthesis to repair the obscurity of his syntax. The section on 'Herod's Fears about Jesus' opens so badly that Goguel suggests that the suspension of the subject and verb without a complement or object was caused by the evangelist consciously softening down the details contained in the original complement which he has omitted. But what Herod heard is revealed in the explanatory parenthesis in 14b–15; the verb ἤκουσεν left suspended is picked up again by ἀκούσας δέ in v. 16 at the end of the parenthesis; then Herod's reaction to the various rumours circulating about Jesus and their connection with John the Baptist is stated. Thus the pericope opens with καὶ ἤκουσεν ὁ βασιλεὺς Ἡρῴδης followed by the paren-

[1] ἀκολουθεῖν may mean more than a physical following. Out of the eighteen (1[18], 2[14 (2), 15], 5[24], 6[1], 8[34 (2)], 9[38(2)], 10[21, 28, 32, 52], 11[9], 14[13, 54], 15[41] (11/18R)) times it is used in the gospel, six (5[24]R, 6[1]R, 10[52]R, 11[9]R, 14[13, 54]) imply a physical following, two (8[34], 9[38]) a mental allegiance; in seven (1[18]R, 2[14, 15] R, 10[21, 28]R, [32]R, 15[41]) instances it means both. οἱ δὲ ἀκολουθοῦντες in 10[32]R could mean the adherents or disciples, those who deny themselves, take up their cross and follow Christ in His spiritual pilgrimage.

[2] Trocmé, p. 143.   [3] See also Taylor, pp. 82–5.

thesis which consists of: φανερὸν γὰρ ἐγένετο τὸ ὄνομα αὐτοῦ, καὶ ἔλεγον ὅτι Ἰωάννης ὁ βαπτίζων ἐγήγερται ἐκ νεκρῶν, καὶ διὰ τοῦτο ἐνεργοῦσιν αἱ δυνάμεις ἐν αὐτῷ. ἄλλοι δὲ ἔλεγον ὅτι Ἠλίας ἐστίν· ἄλλοι δὲ ἔλεγον ὅτι προφήτης ὡς εἷς τῶν προφητῶν (6¹⁴⁻¹⁵).

¶16⁴ᵇ. Sometimes the delay in the parenthesis is so protracted that the commentators follow the scribal emendations of the text to make a more logical and polished sequence. In the final pericope on the Empty Tomb, after the question of the women about the removal of the stone, in 16³, the size of the stone is referred to rather late in the day in 16⁴. Some Western MSS place the explanatory comment after the question, but as it would be in accordance with Marcan usage to delay the explanation, Taylor prefers the phrase after v. 4. But equally well it could be argued that the phrase in its present position serves to enhance the miracle, and when one reflects that k and the Gospel of Peter contain further miraculous details, and that the Marcan tendency is to provide an explanation sometimes immediately after the previous statement, one concludes that the Western MSS may not in fact be correct in this instance.

(iiia) *Explanatory: of Christ's Life*

¶3³⁰(R), 3²¹ᵇ(R). The next two examples are similar in kind: a charge of possession by evil spirits, 3³⁰R, instead of 'madness' or 'spiritual ecstasy', 3²¹ᵇR. Both comments come at the end of editorial sections. They are ἔλεγον γὰρ ὅτι ἐξέστη (3²¹) and ἔλεγον, Πνεῦμα ἀκάθαρτον ἔχει (3³⁰).[1] The two[2] sections are related, suggests Trocmé, in several ways: spirit possession and madness were connected in the minds of the ancients; the family of Jesus (the James party in Jerusalem) and the scribes are identified and condemned by the author; thus Mark shows a strong animus against the brother of the Lord and his Jerusalem episcopate, with its Jewish-Christian tendencies:

[1] See 'Impersonals', pp. 107ff.

[2] 3¹⁹ᵇ⁻²¹ᵇ = fears of the family of Jesus, which naturally leads on to 3³¹⁻⁵ 'the true kindred of Jesus'. 3²²⁻³⁰, in two sections, has a unifying theme in the scribes' accusation of Christ's being in league with evil spirits, and the slander of πνεῦμα ἀκάθαρτον ἔχει which brings the passage on the Binding of the Strong Man to an end. Trocmé, pp. 108–9.

'One should consequently consider the author of Mark person-
ally responsible for the strange redactional work which we have
just been considering, as a declared enemy of James, brother
of the Lord, and unique head of the Jerusalem Church, during
the long years before his martyrdom in the year 62.'[1]

¶ 11³¹⁻²(R). The pericope on the Question of Authority (11²⁷⁻³³),
containing a parenthesis in 11³¹⁻²R, is an explanatory dialogue,
analysing the reasons for the death of Christ, and relating one
of its primary causes to the cleansing of the Temple. The section
should also be viewed as a justification and defence of the
Church's authority being ascribed to Christ Himself. From
either approach, the opening verse is a good example of the
combination of primary and secondary source material.[2] The
historic present is found in a short verse καὶ ἔρχονται πάλιν εἰς
Ἱεροσόλυμα. Sometimes it is a feature of redactional verses to
have a very short sentence followed by a reasonably long one.
Preceding the second ἔρχονται (πρὸς αὐτόν) is a genitive
absolute badly constructed according to classical rules: καὶ ἐν τῷ
ἱερῷ περιπατοῦντος αὐτοῦ ἔρχονται πρὸς αὐτόν.

The section 11³¹⁻² runs as follows: 31 καὶ διελογίζοντο πρὸς
ἑαυτοὺς λέγοντες· τί εἴπωμεν; ἐὰν εἴπωμεν· ἐξ οὐρανοῦ, ἐρεῖ
Διὰ τί οὖν οὐκ ἐπιστεύσατε αὐτῷ; ἀλλὰ εἴπωμεν· ἐξ ἀνθρώπων;
– 32 ἐφοβοῦντο τὸν ὄχλον. ἅπαντες γὰρ εἶχον τὸν Ἰωάννην
ὄντως ὅτι προφήτης ἦν. These verses are off-stage thinking
aloud for the benefit of the understanding of the reader or
listener. The real parenthesis is 11³². Fear is the main statement,
followed by the explanatory clause: first ἐφοβοῦντο τὸν ὄχλον·
followed by the explanation of this fear of the people: ἅπαντες
γὰρ εἶχον τὸν Ἰωάννην ὄντως ὅτι προφήτης ἦν. Mark makes
two grammatical errors here. He breaks off the second condi-
tional sentence (ἀλλὰ εἴπωμεν· ἐξ ἀνθρώπων;) without supply-
ing the apodosis, and replaces it with the explanatory clause
ἐφοβοῦντο... Even here instead of writing εἶχον τὸν Ἰωάννην
ὄντως ὡς προφήτην, he uses a ὅτι clause: ὄντως προφήτης ἦν.
The religious authorities' fear of the people on account of the
popularity of Jesus or John is a familiar motif, but here while

---

[1] *Ibid.*

[2] Bultmann, p. 344; Taylor, p. 469, thinks that the three parties (only
here in the gospel) may be an expansion of the original.

John's ministry is regarded by all as genuine, that of Jesus is uncertain. The text, however, does not say what was felt about the ministry of John but about his baptism, and the explanation produces some indifferent syntax.

¶ 16⁸ᶜ(R). Another fascinating example of parenthesis explaining the narrative is the famous ending of the Gospel in 16⁸. καὶ ἐξελθοῦσαι ἔφυγον ἀπὸ τοῦ μνημείου, εἶχεν γὰρ αὐτὰς τρόμος καὶ ἔκστασις. καὶ οὐδενὶ οὐδὲν εἶπαν. [ἐφοβοῦντο γάρ.] Does Marcan usage, particularly in parenthetical clauses, throw any light on this vexed and controversial question? φοβεῖσθαι is used twelve times in the Gospel, eight of these being in redactional verses. The most significant are 11¹⁸R and 12¹²R with the addition of γάρ, and 10³² and 11³² without it.

11¹⁸ runs: καὶ ἤκουσαν οἱ ἀρχιερεῖς καὶ οἱ γραμματεῖς, καὶ ἐζήτουν πῶς αὐτὸν ἀπολέσωσιν. ἐφοβοῦντο γὰρ αὐτόν, πᾶς γὰρ ὁ ὄχλος ἐξεπλήσσετο ἐπὶ τῇ διδαχῇ αὐτοῦ. In this redactional verse, the antipathy of the scribes and chief priests, and the impression made by the teaching of Jesus on the crowd, are repeated editorial motifs. The intention of the Jewish leaders to seize Christ is explained in the next sentence by the inference that His influence on the crowd was deplored by the authorities. Four other φοβεῖσθαι redactional passages with and without γάρ will now be examined.

10³² runs: ἦσαν δὲ ἐν τῇ ὁδῷ ἀναβαίνοντες εἰς Ἱεροσόλυμα, καὶ ἦν προάγων αὐτοὺς ὁ Ἰησοῦς, καὶ ἐθαμβοῦντο, οἱ δὲ ἀκολουθοῦντες ἐφοβοῦντο. Textual complications in this verse have arisen because of the ambiguity in ἐθαμβοῦντο and ἐφοβοῦντο, as 'they' may be one group of the disciples (οἱ δὲ ἀκολουθοῦντες) or two separate groups. Mark's fondness for amazement, and wonder (θαυμάζω, θαμβοῦμαι), fear (φοβοῦμαι) is also striking.

The next examples, 11³² and 12¹², are also part of parenthetical passages referred to elsewhere in this chapter.[1]

16⁸ now follows as the last of the redactional passages being examined: καὶ ἐξελθοῦσαι ἔφυγον ἀπὸ τοῦ μνημείου, εἶχεν γὰρ αὐτὰς τρόμος καὶ ἔκστασις. καὶ οὐδενὶ οὐδὲν εἶπαν · ἐφοβοῦντο γάρ. In this sentence two main statements are made: (1) καὶ ἐξελθοῦσαι ἔφυγον ἀπὸ τοῦ μνημείου; (2) καὶ οὐδενὶ οὐδὲν εἶπαν.

---

[1] Pp. 43, 47.

The women fled from the tomb and said nothing to anyone. Double negatives are familiar Marcan style, especially at the end of the pericopae, e.g. in the commands to silence.[1] Both these main clauses are explained by subsidiary γάρ clauses: (a) εἶχεν γὰρ αὐτὰς τρόμος καὶ ἔκστασις; (b) ἐφοβοῦντο γάρ. Once again the words for fear, and astonishment, with silent awe as the result, dominate the sentence (τρόμος, ἔκστασις, φοβεῖσθαι). An analysis of the twelve sentences with φοβεῖσθαι reveals that half[2] of them simply state the fear of the parties concerned, which are the people,[3] the disciples,[4] or the women at the tomb.[5] The other six are more precise, referring to Herod's fear of John,[6] the disciples' inability to answer,[7] the scribes' and the chief priests' fear of Jesus,[8] the scribes', the chief priests' and the elders' fear of the people.[9] With so many grammatical and stylistic errors in a Gospel which also abounds in parenthesis, asyndeton, and anacolouthon, and in the case of an author who is no literary genius, arguments based on style can be very precarious. Considering, however, that in 9[6], 11[18], 12[12] γάρ is found, the usage seems well in keeping with the redactional style and theology of the author. The positioning of the explanatory γάρ clause after the main statements does not support Taylor's plea that 'the natural sequel to ἐφοβοῦντο γάρ would be a μή clause'.[10] It might be so if the author were a better writer, or other than Mark. Such a sequence is well supported by the redactional syntax, and theology, elsewhere in the Gospel. Coupled with this, we should recall the ambiguity and difficulty of interpretation in the opening of the Gospel. Marcan usage then would support 16[8] as the genuine ending of the Gospel, and in keeping with style and literary ability.

[1] 1[44], 5[43], 7[36], 8[26,30], 9[9].   [2] 4[41], 5[15,33] R, [36]R, 10[32]R, 16[8]R.

[3] 5[15].   [4] 4[41], 10[32]R.   [5] 16[8]R.

[6] 6[20]R.   [7] 9[32]R.   [8] 11[18]R.

[9] 11[32]R, 12[12]R; 9[6], from the Transfiguration narrative, should be included with its ἔκφοβοι clause suggesting supernatural fear rather than fright. When Peter makes an obscure comment, the editorial explanation is οὐ γὰρ ᾔδει τί ἀποκριθῇ, ἔκφοβοι γὰρ ἐγένοντο, which is near in spirit and syntax to 16[8]. However, the unpardonable stylistic ending in γάρ is not committed here, the adjective being followed by ἐγένοντο.

[10] Pp. 609–10.

(iiib) *Explanatory: of parables*

The following two redactional parenthetical phrases are attempts to clarify the parables of the Seed Growing Quickly,[1] and of the Wicked Husbandmen.[2] The first is 4[31b]:

¶4[31b](R?). This runs: μικρότερον ὂν πάντων τῶν σπερμάτων τῶν ἐπὶ τῆς γῆς. Black[3] proposes that the original text or Aramaic source did not include the comment, on the grounds that the parallelism is destroyed by ὅταν σπαρῇ being repeated. The question, πῶς ὁμοιώσωμεν τὴν βασιλείαν τοῦ θεοῦ, ἢ ἐν τίνι αὐτὴν παραβολῇ θῶμεν; is Rabbinic in style. Remoulding the interpolation the emended Greek text runs:

> ὡς κόκκῳ σινάπεως,
> ὃς ὅταν σπαρῇ ἐπὶ τῆς γῆς μικρότερόν ἐστι
> πάντων τῶν σπερμάτων τῶν ἐπὶ τῆς γῆς,
> ὅταν αὐξηθῇ γίνεται μεῖζον
> πάντων τῶν λαχάνων,
> καὶ ποιεῖ κλάδους μεγάλους, ὥστε δύνασθαι
> ὑπὸ τὴν σκιὰν αὐτοῦ τὰ πετεινὰ τοῦ οὐρανοῦ κατασκηνοῦν.

Dodd commends the Lucan 'Q' version, which is short and has no reference to the smallness of the seed: ὁμοία ἐστὶν κόκκῳ σινάπεως, ὂν λαβὼν ἄνθρωπος ἔβαλεν εἰς κῆπον ἑαυτοῦ, καὶ ηὔξησεν καὶ ἐγένετο εἰς δένδρον, καὶ τὰ πετεινὰ τοῦ οὐρανοῦ κατεσκήνωσεν ἐν τοῖς κλάδοις αὐτοῦ (Luke 13[18-19]). His view is that

the emphasis on the smallness of the seed is in Mark alone, and is probably intrusive. The clause μικρότερον ὂν πάντων τῶν σπερμάτων τῶν ἐπὶ τῆς γῆς has disturbed the grammar of the sentence. Moreover, the mustard seed is not the smallest seed in common use. The evangelist seems to have interpolated a clause to indicate the sense in which he understood the parable: the Church is a small affair in its beginnings, but it is the germ of the universal Kingdom of God.[4]

However, the Lucan version seems to lack the parallelism of the Marcan and Matthaean versions, and may be an edition of

---

[1] 4[26-9].　　　　　　　　　　[2] 12[1-12].

[3] ἐπὶ τῆς γῆς is certainly a R phrase, cf. 4[1]R, 6[47]R.

[4] C. H. Dodd, *The Parables of the Kingdom*, rev. ed. (London, 1926), p. 190 and n. 1.

Mark's. Furthermore, Jeremias sees these parables as parables of contrast – in this instance between smallness and great height and protectiveness. 'Thus did Jesus' audience understand the parables of the Mustard Seed and the Leaven as parables of contrast. Their meaning is that out of the most insignificant beginnings, invisible to human eye, God creates his mighty kingdom, which embraces all the peoples of the world.'[1] With Black's suggestion of a change from the second σπαρῇ to αὐξηθῇ (read by Matthew[2] and Luke[3]), the repetition of σπαρῇ is avoided, but if Matthew had a double version of the parable clearly the Marcan version is more primitive in its paronomasia which in Black's view would be present in the Aramaic. The evangelist has mistranslated or misunderstood the second σπαρῇ and then developed an original authentic part of Christ's poetry into one of his parentheses. One possible explanation is that Mark may have been not only translating here, but also interpreting, and that he was trying to write Greek prose, not to render the original Aramaic into poetry.

¶ 12¹²ᵇ. The parenthesis in Mark 12¹² is part of a redactional verse, explaining the parable of the Wicked Husbandmen.[4] The vocabulary and syntax are Marcan;[5] the verse also contains the evangelist's second reference to the hostility of the Sanhedrin.[6] The parenthetical phrase ἔγνωσαν γὰρ ὅτι πρὸς αὐτοὺς τὴν παραβολὴν εἶπεν explains the previous ἐζήτουν αὐτὸν κρατῆσαι, whereas ἐφοβήθησαν τὸν ὄχλον anticipates καὶ ἀφέντες αὐτὸν ἀπῆλθον. The syntax is very simple: the sentences are all three made up of four words only, with no particles.

> καὶ ἐζήτουν αὐτὸν κρατῆσαι, . . .
> καὶ ἐφοβήθησαν τὸν ὄχλον, . . .
> – ἔγνωσαν γὰρ ὅτι πρὸς αὐτοὺς τὴν παραβολὴν εἶπεν –
> καὶ ἀφέντες αὐτὸν ἀπῆλθον.[7]

The scribes' fear of the populace because of Christ's popularity with them is a familiar redactional motif.

---

[1] J. Jeremias, *The Parables of Jesus*, trans. S. H. Hooke, rev. ed. (London, 1963).   [2] Matthew 13³².   [3] Luke 13¹⁹ ηὔξησεν.   [4] 12¹⁻¹².

[5] ζητέω (6/10 times), κρατῆσαι (9/15 times), φοβοῦμαι (8/12 times), γινώσκω (7/12 times), παραβολή (12/13 times), ἀφίημι (11/34 times).

[6] 11¹⁸.

[7] Matthew 22²² uses the same phrase in a different context; see p. 100.

(iiic) Explanatory: The Church's ministry of forgiveness

¶2¹ᵒᶜR. The next parenthesis, λέγει τῷ παραλυτικῷ, is a short but important one. The 'Paralytic and Forgiveness' is composite, for a fusion has been made of a primitive miracle story in 2¹⁻⁵ᵃ + 2¹ᵒᵇ⁻¹² with a linked dialogue on the Church's authority to forgive sins in the middle section (2⁵ᵇ⁻¹ᵒ). Does Marcan usage help us to decide whether the fusion has been made in the oral or written tradition?

λέγει τῷ παραλυτικῷ is repeated in 2¹ᵒᶜ, with the historic present, a Marcan characteristic, in both instances.

The redactional opening of 5a has a sequence of καί + part. + subj.: καὶ ἰδὼν ὁ Ἰησοῦς τὴν πίστιν αὐτῶν followed by the historic present, λέγει. If this is linked with σοὶ λέγω, ἔγειρε ἆρον...in 11b–12, the result is a primitive miracle story with the expression of astonishment at the end of the pericope.

2⁶ with the scribes 'reasoning in their hearts', plus the verb 'to be' with a participle periphrastically used,[1] has a strong redactional ring: ἦσαν δέ τινες τῶν γραμματέων ἐκεῖ καθήμενοι καὶ διαλογιζόμενοι ἐν ταῖς καρδίαις αὐτῶν. 2⁸ has a similar syntax and meaning – καί + part. + ὁ Ἰησοῦς + two historic presents: καὶ εὐθὺς ἐπιγνοὺς ὁ Ἰησοῦς τῷ πνεύματι αὐτοῦ ὅτι οὕτως διαλογίζονται ἐν ἑαυτοῖς, λέγει (repeated from 2⁶),[2] the ambiguous ἐν ἑαυτοῖς explained in ἐν ταῖς καρδίαις ὑμῶν.

With v. 5b ἀφίενταί σου αἱ ἁμαρτίαι may be compared v. 9a ἀφίενταί σοὐ αἱ ἁμαρτίαι and with v. 9b ἔγειρε καὶ ἆρον τὸν κράβαττόν σου καὶ περιπάτει may be compared v. 11b ἔγειρε ἆρον τὸν κράβαττόν σου καὶ ὕπαγε εἰς τὸν οἶκόν σου. It is difficult to resist the conclusion that doublets and editorial work are the reasons for the similarity in these phrases.

The vividness of the primitive section seen in the faith of the four, the astonishment at the miracle, not at the forgiveness of sins, is quite different in character from the middle section: Jesus arguing with the scribes, a difficult charge of blasphemy concerned with the right of the 'Son of Man' to forgive sins, the

---

[1] Pp. 103ff.
[2] 2⁶: καὶ διαλογιζόμενοι ἐν ταῖς καρδίαις αὐτῶν.
2⁸: διαλογίζονται ἐν ἑαυτοῖς...
τί ταῦτα διαλογίζεσθε ἐν ταῖς καρδίαις ὑμῶν;

idea that forgiveness of sins and a command to be healed are one and the same, and that the proof of the former is to be supported by the latter, the failure to develop the charge of blasphemy – all are signs of development and lateness. '11f. is more closely related to 1–5a than to 5b–10.'[1] Matthew[2] alters πάντας to οἱ ὄχλοι which is probably Mark's original meaning. Behind the middle section is the Church's relating sin and sickness, and its need to justify its own ministry of healing and forgiveness by the authority of Christ, based on some incident in His earthly life.

The redactional work, the vocabulary, the doublets, the historic presents make it very difficult to resist the conclusion that the final fusion has been made in the literary process, although it does not preclude the oral as well.

(iv) *Ministry of Jewish Christians to Gentile converts*

¶7,[2b](PR). In its practical evangelism the early Church had to translate Jewish ideas and language into the Greek language, and to adapt Hebraic food and ritual laws to foreign social customs. Sometimes Christians relaxed the Jewish food and ritual taboos; sometimes the Church had to explain the reasons for ritual and cleansing rules, even when it no longer insisted on Gentile converts rigidly obeying them. The pericope on the Question of the Washing of Hands has three parenthetical passages dealing with such matters.[3] Two of them explain Jewish ritual customs; the third is an example of a quotation in parenthesis.[4] The first is a kind of footnote, or definition of κοιναῖς χερσίν, τοῦτ' ἔστιν ἀνίπτοις (·7[2b]). Taylor rightly says: 'The explanatory phrase τοῦτ' ἔστιν ἀνίπτοις is added by Mark for the benefit of his Gentile readers.'[5]

¶7,[3–4]R. The next two and a half verses comprise the second and longer parenthetical explanation, in the same vein as the footnote to 'unclean hands'. – οἱ γὰρ Φαρισαῖοι καὶ πάντες οἱ

---

[1] Taylor, p. 199; Bultmann, pp. 14–15.   [2] Matthew 9[8].
[3] 7[2b]; 7[3–4]; 7[6–7].   [4] 7[6–7].
[5] P. 335: The phrase is part of the second sentence of the pericope which runs: καὶ ἰδόντες τινὰς τῶν μαθητῶν αὐτοῦ ὅτι κοιναῖς χερσίν, [τοῦτ' ἔστιν ἀνίπτοις,] ἐσθίουσιν τοὺς ἄρτους...τινὰς τῶν μαθητῶν becomes the subject of ἐσθίουσιν, creating a hyperbaton.

'Ιουδαῖοι ἐὰν μὴ πυγμῇ νίψωνται τὰς χεῖρας οὐκ ἐσθίουσιν, κρατοῦντες τὴν παράδοσιν τῶν πρεσβυτέρων, καὶ ἀπ' ἀγορᾶς ἐὰν μὴ ῥαντίσωνται οὐκ ἐσθίουσιν, καὶ ἄλλα πολλά ἐστιν ἃ παρέλαβον κρατεῖν, βαπτισμοὺς ποτηρίων καὶ ξεστῶν καὶ χαλκίων –. οἱ 'Ιουδαῖοι is a very curious phrase, found nowhere else in the Gospel. πυγμῇ is notoriously difficult to explain, so its virtue as an explanation seems questionable. Turner quotes a writing of Palladius where an old lady remonstrates with a young man for washing πυγμῇ ὕδατι ψυχροτάτῳ whereas she only washed ἐκτὸς τῶν ἄκρων τῶν χειρῶν i.e. πυγμῇ = a good length, perhaps fist to elbow. πυγμῇ can also be translated 'with the fist', but it probably signifies a longer wash than just to the wrist.[1] πάντες οἱ 'Ιουδαῖοι is reminiscent of the Fourth Gospel's 'the Jews'; Trocmé[2] suggests that James' party in Jerusalem, with its insistence on keeping the food, circumcision, and ritual laws is being indicted by the author. The sentence is a very long one (forty-one words), with very unusual vocabulary, the following words only being found here in Mark: νίπτεσθαι, πυγμῇ, ῥαντίζεσθαι,[3] ξέστης, χαλκίον, πάντες οἱ 'Ιουδαῖοι. ἀπ' ἀγορᾶς may be translated '(anything) from the market-place'.[4] The possible Semitisms and the inclusion of so many unusual words suggest special material, while the three parentheses of explanatory nature and the phrase πάντες οἱ 'Ιουδαῖοι betray the author's hand also.

¶ 7[19c](R?). The next phrase, καθαρίζων πάντα τὰ βρώματα, is a reflection on the whole passage vv. 14–23, which is a Marcan construction including dominical sayings to which are appended lists[5] of sins, similar in kind to passages in the Pauline epistles. When the passage is broken down the hand of the evangelist is to be seen in at least three out of ten verses (7[14, 16–17, 19]) of the passage in question.

7[14] καὶ προσκαλεσάμενος πάλιν τὸν ὄχλον ἔλεγεν αὐτοῖς· ἀκούσατέ μου πάντες καὶ σύνετε. [15]οὐδέν ἐστιν ἔξωθεν τοῦ ἀνθρώπου εἰσπορευόμενον εἰς αὐτὸν ὃ δύναται κοινῶσαι αὐτόν· ἀλλὰ τὰ ἐκ τοῦ ἀνθρώπου ἐκπορευόμενά ἐστιν τὰ κοινοῦντα τὸν ἄνθρωπον.

---

[1] Black, p. 9; Turner, J.T.S. 29 (April 1928), 278–9; Trocmé, p. 156.
[2] P. 108.
[3] ῥαντίζω = sprinkling for purification purposes; Taylor, p. 336.
[4] Black, p. 54.   [5] 7[21-2].

¹⁶(εἴ τις ἔχει ὦτα ἀκούειν ἀκουέτω.) ¹⁷καὶ ὅτε εἰσῆλθεν εἰς οἶκον ἀπὸ τοῦ ὄχλου, ἐπηρώτων αὐτὸν οἱ μαθηταὶ αὐτοῦ τὴν παραβολήν. ¹⁸καὶ λέγει αὐτοῖς, οὕτως καὶ ὑμεῖς ἀσύνετοί ἐστε; οὐ νοεῖτε ὅτι πᾶν τὸ ἔξωθεν εἰσπορευόμενον εἰς τὸν ἄνθρωπον οὐ δύναται αὐτὸν κοινῶσαι, ¹⁹ὅτι οὐκ εἰσπορεύεται αὐτοῦ εἰς τὴν καρδίαν ἀλλ' εἰς τὴν κοιλίαν, καὶ εἰς τὸν ἀφεδρῶνα ἐκπορεύεται; – καθαρίζων πάντα τὰ βρώματα. ²⁰ἔλεγεν δὲ ὅτι τὸ ἐκ τοῦ ἀνθρώπου ἐκπορευόμενον ἐκεῖνο κοινοῖ τὸν ἄνθρωπον. ²¹ἔσωθεν γὰρ ἐκ τῆς καρδίας τῶν ἀνθρώπων οἱ διαλογισμοὶ οἱ κακοὶ ἐκπορεύονται, πορνεῖαι, κλοπαί, φόνοι, ²²μοιχεῖαι, πλεονεξίαι, πονηρίαι, δόλος, ἀσέλγεια, ὀφθαλμὸς πονηρός, βλασφημία, ὑπερηφανία, ἀφροσύνη. ²³πάντα ταῦτα τὰ πονηρὰ ἔσωθεν ἐκπορεύεται καὶ κοινοῖ τὸν ἄνθρωπον.

Certain verses here are probably redactional: v. 14, introducing the Lord's saying in v. 15, and v. 16 which is similar in style and function to 4¹⁰. Taylor says of v. 14 'The introduction to the section in 14a consists of common Markan words and is almost certainly the Evangelist's free composition.'[1] ὄχλος is a well known Marcan word (thirty-eight times). προσκαλεῖσθαι is used nine times[2] by Mark, with eight[3] out of the nine in redactional verses. ἀκούσατέ μου πάντες καὶ σύνετε recalls the introduction to the parable of the Sower, which reads: καὶ ἔλεγεν αὐτοῖς ἐν τῇ διδαχῇ αὐτοῦ ἀκούετε. The principle is laid down by the Lord in 7¹⁵, and the linking phrase, also used twice in the parabolic material[4] in Ch. 4, is repeated here in a similar situation, when the disciples enter 'the house', and ask the Lord to explain the 'parable' (4¹⁰).[5] οὕτως καὶ ὑμεῖς ἀσύνετοί ἐστε; in 7¹⁸ picks up the opening πάντες καὶ σύνετε in 14c, which seems to be repeated and developed in the following adaptation of the Lord's saying in v. 18 οὕτως καὶ ὑμεῖς ἀσύνετοί ἐστε; while οὐδέν ἐστιν ἔξωθεν τοῦ ἀνθρώπου εἰσπορευόμενον εἰς αὐτὸν ὃ δύναται κοινῶσαι αὐτόν (7¹⁵ᵃ) is also found in πᾶν τὸ ἔξωθεν εἰσπορευόμενον εἰς τὸν ἄνθρωπον οὐ δύναται αὐτὸν κοινῶσαι (7¹⁸). The second part of 7¹⁵ is explanatory: ἀλλὰ τὰ ἐκ τοῦ ἀνθρώπου ἐκπορευόμενά ἐστιν τὰ κοινοῦντα τὸν ἄνθρωπον being further explained in vv. 19–20, τὸ ἐκ τοῦ ἀνθρώπου ἐκπορευόμενον ἐκεῖνο κοινοῖ τὸν ἄνθρωπον (7²⁰) ὅτι οὐκ εἰσπορεύεται αὐτοῦ εἰς τὴν καρδίαν ἀλλ' εἰς τὴν κοιλίαν, καὶ εἰς τὸν

---

[1] P. 343.   [2] 3¹³,²³, 67, 7¹⁴, 8¹,³⁴, 10⁴², 12⁴³, 15⁴⁴ (26/38R).
[3] 3¹³,²³, 67, 7¹⁴, 8¹,³⁴, 10⁴², 12⁴³.
[4] εἴ τις ἔχει ὦτα ἀκούειν ἀκουέτω.   [5] Black, pp. 211ff.

ἀφεδρῶνα ἐκπορεύεται; together with the evangelist's comment – καθαρίζων πάντα τὰ βρώματα. Black, however, does not regard καθαρίζων... as originally a parenthesis, but postulates an Aramaic mistranslation as the reason for the textual confusion, and rejects the parenthetical hypothesis. Both the list of vices and the development of the dominical saying reveal the influence of the catechist. They are reflections of the problems of Gentile Christians who need to have some relaxation of the Jewish food and ritual regulations. καθαρίζων π. τ. β. is probably the evangelist's heading for the pericope, and betrays his strong dislike of ritual cleansing.[1]

¶7[26a]. The next parenthesis, from the pericope[2] on the Syro-Phoenician Woman, reads: ἡ δὲ γυνὴ ἦν Ἑλληνίς, Συροφοινίκισσα τῷ γένει. The opening half of the first verse is probably redactional: ἐκεῖθεν δὲ ἀναστὰς ἀπῆλθεν εἰς τὰ ὅρια Τύρου.[3] The following verse also gives several signs of being from the author's hand; one indication is the parenthesis already quoted. The first phrase[4] is written with ἀλλά + εὐθύς + participle (ἀκούσασα) + subject (γυνή).[5] The next phrase is either a vulgarism or a Semitism, i.e. the relative followed by a resumptive pronoun, ἧς εἶχεν τὸ θυγάτριον αὐτῆς πνεῦμα ἀκάθαρτον. The last two words ἀκάθαρτος (eleven times) and πνεῦμα (twenty-three times) are familiar Marcan language. Of the two participles the second[6] is almost meaningless. The description of the woman is first by her religion (of Gentile origin) and secondly by nationality. The importance and relevance of such a description to a Gentile church in Rome would be obvious, especially if one includes the problems and hesitancy about accepting Gentiles into the Christian Church. The parenthesis has almost the feeling of a postscript in a letter, when the schoolboy asks for

[1] Such a comment has as its background the epistle to the Galatians, the dispute and deliberations of the council of Jerusalem when it enacted the necessity for Gentile Christians to follow the Jewish food regulations, and the vision of Peter when he was told by God not 'to call unclean what God had cleansed'. Cf. Acts 10[15] and Cadbury and Lake's suggestion that there may be an allusion to Mk. 7[14]ff. It is tempting to see an allusion here in 'cleansing all meats' to Peter's vision, i.e. Mark reflecting aloud.

[2] 7[24–30].   [3] 7[26a], see Kertelge, pp. 153ff.
[4] 7[24].   [5] 7[25] ἀλλ' εὐθὺς ἀκούσασα γυνὴ περὶ αὐτοῦ, ἧς εἶχεν...
[6] ἐλθοῦσα; see p. 120.

a loan, the request being the main reason for writing, but it has been consigned to the postscript as if it were an afterthought. The attitude of Jesus to the Gentile woman would be of great interest to a Gentile congregation in a missionary situation, and her status needs emphasis not soft-pedalling.

(v) Catechetical, liturgical and Biblical usage

¶13¹⁰(R). The next passage, 13¹⁰, from the Marcan apocalypse, is a Marcan redactional passage which the evangelist believes expresses the mind of Christ, although it may not be His exact words. The main reasons for regarding this verse as parenthetical and redactional are the vocabulary[1] and the fact that the poetry of the passage and its main theme are interrupted by the parenthetical phrase καὶ εἰς πάντα τὰ ἔθνη πρῶτον δεῖ κηρυχθῆναι τὸ εὐαγγέλιον. The vocabulary consists of ἔθνη, πρῶτον, δεῖ, κηρύσσω, εὐαγγέλιον. The poetic structure might have an Aramaic basis. The Greek stanzas could possibly be:

9 βλέπετε δὲ ὑμεῖς ἑαυτούς·
παραδώσουσιν ὑμᾶς εἰς συνέδρια
καὶ εἰς συναγωγὰς δαρήσεσθε
καὶ ἐπὶ ἡγεμόνων καὶ βασιλέων
σταθήσεσθε ἕνεκεν ἐμοῦ, εἰς μαρτύριον αὐτοῖς.

10 – καὶ εἰς πάντα τὰ ἔθνη πρῶτον δεῖ
κηρυχθῆναι τὸ εὐαγγέλιον –

11 καὶ ὅταν ἄγωσιν ὑμᾶς παραδιδόντες,
μὴ προμεριμνᾶτε τί λαλήσητε,
ἀλλ᾿ ὃ ἐὰν δοθῇ ὑμῖν ἐν ἐκείνῃ τῇ ὥρᾳ
τοῦτο λαλεῖτε,
οὐ γάρ ἐστε ὑμεῖς οἱ λαλοῦντες ἀλλὰ
τὸ πνεῦμα τὸ ἅγιον.

12 καὶ παραδώσει ἀδελφὸς ἀδελφὸν
εἰς θάνατον καὶ πατὴρ τέκνον.
καὶ ἐπαναστήσονται τέκνα ἐπὶ γονεῖς
καὶ θανατώσουσιν αὐτούς.
καὶ ἔσεσθε μισούμενοι ὑπὸ πάντων

[1] δεῖ: 8³¹R, (9¹¹), 137R¹⁰R¹⁴, 14³¹R 4/6; ἔθνος: 10³³R⁽⁴²⁾, 11¹⁷S, 13⁽⁸⁾·¹⁰R (2/6R); πρῶτον (3/6R): 3²⁷S, 4²⁸S, 7²⁷R, 9⁽¹¹⁾·¹²R, 13¹⁰R; κηρύσσω: 14R, 7S, 14R, 38R, 39R, 45R, 3¹⁴R, 5²⁰R, 6¹²R, 7³⁶R, 13¹⁰R, 14⁹R (11/12R); εὐαγγέλιον: 1¹R, 14R, 15R, 8³⁵R, 10²⁹R, 13¹⁰R, 14⁹R (7/7R). Lambrecht, pp. 127ff.

διὰ τὸ ὄνομά μου·
ὁ δὲ ὑπομείνας εἰς τέλος
οὗτος σωθήσεται.

V. 10 is sometimes deprived of its parenthetic character by a reconstruction of the sentence. Kilpatrick and others take the first half of v. 10 with v. 9, arguing from MS evidence and from the fact that the Marcan verb normally stands at the beginning of the sentence, and would read σταθήσεσθε ἕνεκεν ἐμοῦ εἰς μαρτύριον αὐτοῖς καὶ εἰς πάντα τὰ ἔθνη. πρῶτον δεῖ κηρυχθῆναι τὸ εὐαγγέλιον, καὶ...¹ There are three powerful arguments against this:

(a) The poetical structure of vv. 9 and 11 is destroyed by the prose of v. 10 as Lohmeyer rightly suggested. παραδώσουσιν... δαρήσεσθε...ἡγεμόνων...βασιλέων ... σταθήσεσθε... ἄγωσιν ...προμεριμνᾶτε...λαλήσητε...λαλεῖτε...παραδώσει etc.

(b) Mark does not always commence with a verb, but, as Turner points out, quite often follows a Latin order and ends with one.

(c) Parenthesis is part of Marcan usage to judge from the numerous examples of it. Here it is almost as if the evangelist were thinking aloud. In the previous verse he has warned the followers of Christ of impending persecutions by Jew and Gentile. In v. 11b² (perhaps also an interpolation) the Holy Spirit will assist the accused when arraigned before his accusers, but the thought is then present that it is the preaching of the Gospel throughout the world, which is an urgent matter before the impending return of the Lord in the Parousia, that will involve the Christian in accusation and imprisonment and so necessitate the guidance of the Holy Spirit.

¶8¹⁵. Mark 8¹⁵ is thought by Turner to be parenthetical: καὶ διεστέλλετο αὐτοῖς λέγων, ὁρᾶτε, βλέπετε ἀπὸ τῆς ζύμης τῶν Φαρισαίων καὶ τῆς ζύμης Ἡρῴδου. Probably the saying has been adapted by Mark in an esoteric sense and should be regarded as a footnote or secondary. The whole section is more like a

¹ G. D. Kilpatrick, 'The Gentile Mission in Mark and Mark xiii 9–11', in Nineham (ed.), *Studies in the Gospels*, pp. 145–58; Trocmé in favour, p. 166, Taylor, p. 507, Cranfield, pp. 398ff., against.

² Lambrecht, pp. 139ff.

passage from the Fourth Gospel, with hidden allusions such as the 'leaven of the Pharisees and of Herod',[1] the 'hardness' of the disciples' heart,[2] the use of the dialogue form. The recalling of the Miracles of the Five Thousand[3] and Four Thousand[4] stamp the section as redactional and editorial, linking the previous pericopae together, and leading on to the cure of the blind man (v. 18) and the revelation of Jesus' Messiahship[5] to the blind Peter. Two notable signs have been given and yet the Pharisees demand a further sign, and even the disciples do not trust the sufficiency of Christ to meet the demands of life.

The Miracles of the Five and Four Thousand are stressed in the dialogue leading to the climax of the poignant question, οὔπω συνίετε; Taylor admits that 'the story illustrates the beginnings of a type of Gospel narrative found often in the Fourth Gospel and which has persisted in Christian teaching down to the present day. Touch with history is not lost, but catechetical interests supervene.'[6] V. 14 is regarded by Bultmann as 'the introduction to the saying about leaven'.[7] The narrative is really meant to show the disciples as unbelieving as the Pharisees, still seeking a sign when they had received two already. The unexplained 'leaven' is twofold: demanding a sign of Messiahship, and 'hardness of heart' (lack of faith). The first half of v. 15[8] introduces the enigmatic saying, while the next verse[9] is redactional, followed by the artificial dialogue[10] leading to the Isaianic quotation[11] exemplifying persistent unbelief and blindness of perception. Many commentators regard vv. 19–21 as redactional.[12] The author is trying to link his previous sections together to form cycles of simple ideas which will teach his readers and catechumens the basic facts of the life and teaching of the Lord, but he reveals at the same time certain scars of his own experience, and that of the early Church, which force him to rethink, and sometimes to reinterpret, the traditional material

---

[1] 8[15].   [2] 8[17].   [3] 8[19]; 8[20].

[4] 8[29]; Schweizer, p. 160: 'Mark has revised this section extensively'.

[5] Taylor, p. 364.   [6] P. 364.

[7] P. 331. καὶ ἐπελάθοντο λαβεῖν ἄρτους, καὶ εἰ μὴ ἕνα ἄρτον οὐκ εἶχον μεθ' ἑαυτῶν ἐν τῷ πλοίῳ.

[8] καὶ διεστέλλετο αὐτοῖς λέγων· ὁρᾶτε, βλέπετε...

[9] καὶ διελογίζοντο πρὸς ἀλλήλους ὅτι ἄρτους οὐκ ἔχουσιν. καὶ γνοὺς λέγει αὐτοῖς, τί...

[10] 8[17].   [11] Is. 6[9]; see Mk. 8[18].   [12] See p. 16.

which he is handling. The attitude of Agrippa and the Herodian family to the early Christians, and their attempt to gain the favour of the Pharisees, has perhaps influenced the text in v. 15.[1] The Pauline idea of the hardening of the Jewish people's heart[2] and their blindness to the signs of the coming of the Messiah is illustrated by the attitude of Herodian Pharisee, and Christian disciples in varying degrees of unbelief.

¶ 14[49b]. Mark 14[49b], which Turner regards as parenthetical, is probably not to be considered as such. Coming in Ch. 14 in the account of the arrest of Christ, the Greek seems strange even for Mark,[3] and can only be translated by taking the ἵνα as imperatival. After καθ' ἡμέραν ἤμην πρὸς ὑμᾶς ἐν τῷ ἱερῷ διδάσκων, καὶ οὐκ ἐκρατήσατέ με we read ἀλλ᾽ ἵνα πληρωθῶσιν αἱ γραφαί.[4] The best way out of the impasse is to regard ἵνα as an imperatival wish: Let the scriptures be fulfilled! It is very difficult to regard ἵνα as a purpose clause. However, both the verb πληροῦσθαι (three times) and the noun γραφή (two times) are Marcan usage. (Taylor asserts that 'the phrase is not in Mark's manner'.)[5] Trocmé, interestingly enough, considers this phrase as evidence that Chs. 14–16 are not part of the original Mark.[6] It could also be a scribal note. 5[23] is a similar imperatival use of ἵνα. τὸ θυγάτριόν μου ἐσχάτως ἔχει, ἵνα ἐλθὼν ἐπιθῇς τὰς χεῖρας αὐτῇ ἵνα σωθῇ καὶ ζήσῃ.[7] However, if ἵνα is regarded as imperatival it is difficult to see why it can also be a parenthesis.

¶ 13[14b]. A true parenthesis is the well-known ὁ ἀναγινώσκων νοείτω from the section on the 'Abomination of Desolation' in Mark 13[14]. Interpreters often regard this phrase as a 'warning taken from the apocalyptic fly-sheet which Mark is using', or a clear reference back to the Daniel apocalypse.[8] Perhaps the Dead Sea Scrolls may throw some light here, for in the pesher commentaries when the text is quoted or a paraphrase of it, there follow the words 'the meaning or interpretation is'.[9] τότε οἱ ἐν...[10] in that case might be an application or interpretation of

---

[1] Trocmé, pp. 73–5.   [2] Romans 9–11.
[3] According to Schweizer, p. 316, 49a is R but 49b 'does not conform to his style'. See also Lambrecht, p. 34, n. 3, p. 47, n. 2, p. 51.
[4] 14[49].   [5] P. 561.   [6] Pp. 176–94, 184.
[7] 5[23].   [8] Daniel 9[27], 11[31], 12[11]. Taylor, p. 511.
[9] IQp Hab. I, 8, 13; II, 1, 12 – passim.   [10] 13[14].

the quotation from Daniel. The reader is instructed to follow the advice given, if he sees the profanation of the Temple or the appearance of Anti-Christ in the Holy Place. Although ἀναγινώσκειν (four times) and νοεῖν (three times) are not used a great deal in Mark, it may prove constructive to investigate the context where the evangelist has used them.

In the dispute about the plucking of corn on the Sabbath Jesus replies to the Pharisees: Οὐδέποτε ἀνέγνωτε τί ἐποίησεν Δαυίδ, ὅτε χρείαν ἔσχεν καὶ ἐπείνασεν αὐτὸς καὶ οἱ μετ' αὐτοῦ;[1] Secondly, at the end of the parable of the 'Wicked Husbandmen' the allegory is supported by Scriptural quotation which is preceded by the question οὐδὲ τὴν γραφὴν ταύτην ἀνέγνωτε[2] (quotation of Psalm 117²²ᶠ· LXX). Taylor says: 'It may be that Mark has appended 10f., but there are no decisive arguments in favour of this view.'[3] The third example is from the Sadducaic argument about the Resurrection, to which Jesus replies by quoting Scripture, and saying: περὶ δὲ τῶν νεκρῶν ὅτι ἐγείρονται, οὐκ ἀνέγνωτε ἐν τῇ βίβλῳ Μωϋσέως ἐπὶ τοῦ βάτου πῶς εἶπεν αὐτῷ ὁ θεὸς λέγων...[4]

7¹⁸, the first of the three[5] examples of νοεῖν, is from a section on 'Cleansing', which gives many indications of being a Marcan construction. The dialogue, a favourite Marcan form of developing catechetical instruction, depicts the inner circle asking for elucidation of a dominical saying. Jesus replies to them in almost Johannine wonder at their failure to perceive the inner truth: οὕτως καὶ ὑμεῖς ἀσύνετοί ἐστε; οὐ νοεῖτε ὅτι πᾶν τὸ ἔξωθεν... This repetition of the saying of the Lord in 7¹⁵ has been developed and explained in 7¹⁸⁻¹⁹ with the Marcan parenthesis καθαρίζων πάντα τὰ βρώματα at the end.[6]

The second example, 8¹⁷, is also from a Marcan construction, the 'Mystery of the Loaves'. Again we find the dialogue method in an almost cryptic style, with literary recapitulations of previous points in the story. After an esoteric phrase καὶ διελογίζοντο πρὸς ἀλλήλους ὅτι ἄρτους οὐκ ἔχουσιν[7] Christ again remonstrates with the unbelievers (this time the disciples) saying τί διαλογίζεσθε ὅτι ἄρτους οὐκ ἔχετε; οὔπω νοεῖτε οὐδὲ συνίετε; πεπωρωμένην ἔχετε τὴν καρδίαν ὑμῶν; A direct citation is then quoted from LXX Isaiah 6⁹ᶠᶠ·, which is also found in a Marcan

---

[1] 2²⁵. [2] 12¹⁰. [3] P. 477. [4] 12²⁶.
[5] 7¹⁸, 8¹⁷, 13¹⁴. [6] 7¹⁹. [7] 8¹⁶.

bridge passage from 4¹⁰⁻¹² about parables. In the Targum LXX form of Isaiah 6¹²ᶠᶠ· συνίημι and ἀκούω are linked, while οὔπω συνίετε;[1] is the climax of the Marcan construction. In the previous passage 7¹⁴⁻²³ ἀσύνετοί ἐστε and οὐ νοεῖτε are in close proximity.[2] Thus all the uses of ἀναγινώσκειν including 13¹⁴³ are concerned with Old Testament texts and disputes about interpretations of the Scripture or the Law. Two[4] out of the three sayings with νοεῖν are clarifying or interpreting doubtful and misunderstood sayings of Christ Himself. Finally, out of the six[5] texts (knowing that parenthesis is a marked feature of Marcan style, we should add 13¹⁴ to the list) three[6] are certainly, and four[7] are possibly, redactional passages.

Returning to the passage in question, 13¹⁴, if we presume that ὁ ἀναγινώσκων νοείτω is a Marcan parenthesis, the previous passages[8] would suggest that the manner of the evangelist is to use ἀναγινώσκειν of reading the scriptural text, and νοεῖν as a synonym for συνίημι of the comprehension of the work of Christ. The context of misunderstanding and lack of perception is the lot of the unbeliever, and of the believer in the first stages of understanding. When the disciple approaches the Lord for elucidation of the parable, or the 'leaven of the Pharisees, or of the Herodians', or of the 'mystery of the loaves', he may then proceed to a state of real knowledge. One obvious interpretation of ὁ. ἀ. ν. in the light of the previous usage is a prayer or wish: 'May the reader (or Biblical student) be enlightened.' The phrase is a devout opening to scriptural study, or like the prayer of the Qumran or Christian expositor that both writer and reader, both preacher and congregation, may grasp the inner meaning of the esoteric or hidden reference of the text or saying.

[1] 8²¹.

[2] 7¹⁸.

[3] 2²⁵, 12¹⁰·²⁶, 13¹⁴.

[4] 7¹⁸, 8¹⁷.

[5] 2²⁵, 12¹⁰·²⁶, 13¹⁴, 7¹⁸, 8¹⁷.

[6] 7¹⁸, 8¹⁷, 13¹⁴.

[7] 12¹⁰R?, 7¹⁸R, 8¹⁷R, 13¹⁴.

[8] 7¹⁸, 8¹⁷. See also Lambrecht, p. 153, and an apt comment from Lagrange quoted by him: 'Enfin c'est le texte de Marc que nous expliquons. Dans sa pensée le v. 14 répond précisément à la question posée au v. 4, sur le signe qui doit précéder la ruine du Temple' (13¹⁴).

(vi) Translations, mainly from the Aramaic

The Aramaic and other foreign words, with their translations, are a well-known feature of the Marcan gospel. When laid out they exhibit a common pattern or stylistic feature.

Βοανηργές, ὅ ἐστιν υἱοὶ βροντῆς (3¹⁷ᶜR).

καὶ λέγει αὐτῷ, Λεγιὼν ὄνομά μοι, ὅτι πολλοί ἐσμεν (5⁹ᶜ).

λέγει αὐτῇ Ταλιθα κουμ, ὅ ἐστιν μεθερμηνευόμενον, Τὸ κοράσιον, σοὶ λέγω, ἔγειρε (5⁴¹ᵇR).

Κορβᾶν, ὅ ἐστιν Δῶρον, ὃ ἐὰν ἐξ ἐμοῦ ὠφεληθῇς, οὐκέτι ἀφίετε αὐτὸν οὐδὲν ποιῆσαι τῷ πατρὶ ἢ τῇ μητρί (7¹¹⁻¹²R).

καὶ λέγει αὐτῷ, Εφφαθα, ὅ ἐστιν Διανοίχθητι (7³⁴R).

ἔβαλεν λεπτὰ δύο, ὅ ἐστιν κοδράντης (12⁴²ᵇR).

οἱ δὲ στρατιῶται ἀπήγαγον αὐτὸν ἔσω τῆς αὐλῆς, ὅ ἐστιν πραιτώριον (15¹⁶ᵇR).

καὶ τῇ ἐνάτῃ ὥρᾳ ἐβόησεν ὁ Ἰησοῦς φωνῇ μεγάλη **Ελωι ελωι λεμα σαβαχθανι** ὅ ἐστιν μεθερμηνευόμενον **ὁ θεός μου ὁ θεός μου εἰς τί ἐγκατέλιπές με;** (15³⁴R).

Of these eight passages six use the same phrase ὅ ἐστιν while two use the extension of the latter to ὅ ἐστιν μεθερμηνευόμενον. It is also interesting to note that the latter phrase is used both in the early chapters and in the Passion narrative in a verse[1] which Bultmann regards as secondary material, principally because the time sequence is noted by the evangelist. Trocmé regards these verses amongst others as the work of a redactor who has added Chs. 14–16 to the primitive edition of Mark, Chs. 1–13. ὅ ἐστιν he regards as a Latinism derived from the expression *hoc est* or *id est*. The presence of Latin words and expressions is explained by Trocmé[2] as part of the spoken language of the day, the author not being a purist in style, and quite content to reproduce the vernacular. Hawkins[3] refers to ὅ ἐστιν as 'characteristic of Marcan style', while the only other examples of the phrase in the New Testament are Col. 1²⁴, Hebrews 7² and Rev. 21¹⁷.[4] Of the eight passages, five are trans-

---

[1] 15³⁵.   [2] P. 191.

[3] P. 28. Out of the eight, seven are redactional; five translate Aramaic into Greek.

[4] ὑπὲρ τοῦ σώματος αὐτοῦ, ὅ ἐστιν ἡ ἐκκλησία (Col. 1²⁴); βασιλεὺς Σαλήμ, ὅ ἐστιν βασιλεὺς εἰρήνης (Heb. 7²); μέτρον ἀνθρώπου, ὅ ἐστιν ἀγγέλου (Rev. 21¹⁷).

lations of Aramaic words or phrases, one is a translation of a Latin word, while two are translations of Greek or oriental background into Latinisms. Thus the complexity of the Gospel comes into view: Aramaisms are translated into Greek but also orientalisms into Latin words. If 5⁹ was intended for Roman readers, it seems a little otiose to explain 'legion' to a Roman audience.

¶ 14³⁶. The Aramaism in 14³⁶ is not to be classified as an explanatory comment along with the previous examples, although at first it appears in this light: καὶ ἔλεγεν ἀββά, ὁ πατήρ, πάντα δυνατά σοι. The expression in Romans 8¹⁵ reads: ἐν ᾧ κράζομεν ἀββά ὁ πατήρ... Galatians 4⁶ reads: κρᾶζον ἀββά ὁ πατήρ. Its origin is liturgical, and it is obviously an explanatory comment reflecting a bilingual situation, but that ὁ πατήρ is retained in Mark, Galatians, and Romans shows that it has attained some kind of permanence. A modern parallel might be when the Anglican liturgy was changed from Latin to English at the Reformation, and in the psalms and canticles of Morning and Evening Prayer, the first word of the canticle becomes almost a title, and is retained in its original language. The priest announces the canticle with its Latin words: 'Te Deum', 'Magnificat', he invariably says and then the congregation sings or says, 'We praise Thee', or 'My soul doth magnify'. Turner says that 'ἀββά differs from his other parentheses in being provided for him, so to say, ready made... It was in familar use – possibly in connexion with the Lord's Prayer – in the church of the apostolic age.[1] Both Matthew[2] and Luke[3] use πάτερ, the vocative, but the three instances of the expression in early documents are strong proof of its originality.[4]

Conclusions

An attempt has been made to analyse some of the reasons for the parenthetical clauses in Mark, and they may be summarised as follows:

(1) To provide quotations or bracketed Biblical texts which

[1] *J.T.S.* 26 (January 1925), 154–5. [2] 26³⁹. [3] 22⁴².
[4] W. Sanday and A. C. Headlam, *The Epistle to the Romans*, 5th ed. (Edinburgh, 1902), p. 203; Moulton, vol. 1, p. 10, n. 1.

support a statement, but are subsidiary to it. Mark 1^{1-4}, 7^{6-8}.

(2) A loose sentence-construction, when the author wishes to clarify a previous statement, or to emphasise a point, but the final result is sometimes greater obscurity or ambiguity. E.g. 2^{15}, 6^{14-16}, 16^4.

(3) To provide explanatory clauses, used in catechetical or liturgical situations concerned with the elucidation of the traditions of the life and teaching of Christ. E.g. 3^{21b}, 3^{30}, 11^{31-2}, 16^8, 4^{31b}, 12^{12b}.

(4) Some parenthetical clauses reflect the Church's concern with ritualistic and other problems, and its desire to trace its authority for action and precedent to the earthly ministry of the Risen Lord. Thus 2^{11b} is an editorial or form-critical linking parenthesis concerned with the Church's right to forgive sins related to its mission of healing and exorcism. Ch. 7 has as its subject matter the problems which arise when the Jewish Christians minister to Gentile converts. Three of the parentheses are from one pericope, and are explanatory comments of Jewish ritual customs (7^{2b}, $7^{3-4, \, 6-7}$). In the same category comes 7^{20a}, while 7^{26a} is a parenthesis which is like some footnotes in scholarly works, more interesting and important than the main text itself. 13^{10} is a paraphrase of the Lord's words, or the Church's interpretation of its mission, which disturbs the flow of the previous argument. In the same spirit is the enigmatic 8^{15}. 13^{14} is concerned with the Church's exegetical and inspirational ministry.

(5) Aramaisms or Latinisms which are prefixed by a Greek form of a Latinism, *id est* = ὅ ἐστιν. Most of these are translations of Aramaic for the benefit of Greek readers or listeners (3^{17}R, 5^{41}R, 7^{11}R, 7^{34}R, 15^{34}R), but the others reflect the dual influence of Aramaic and Latin and also a trilingual situation, Greek, Latin, and Aramaic. 5^9 is a translation of a Latinism; 12^{42} a Latinism paraphrasing an oriental coinage, while 15^{16} is obscure but looks like a Latinism to explain a Greek word.

(6) Of these parenthetical clauses twenty-four are fairly certainly redactional, while four are almost certainly so, one probably not. Such a high percentage would suggest that Turner blazed a way for understanding not so much Marcan source style, but rather editorial style.

(b) GENITIVE ABSOLUTE

R: 1^{32}, 4^{35}, $5^{2, 21, 35}$, $6^{2, 54}$, 8^{1}, $9^{9, 28}$, $10^{17, 46}$, $11^{11, 12, 27}$, $13^{1, 3}$, $14^{3, 17, 18, 22, 43, 66}$, 15^{42} = 24 times
S: $5^{15}(?)$, $6^{21(?), 22(?), 35(?), 47(?)}$ = 5 times

Out of 29 uses of the genitive absolute, 24R out of a possible total of 29 is very high – sufficiently so to command respect as a guide to the redactor's hand. Twenty[1] out of twenty-four examples occur in the first or second verse of the pericope. Fourteen[2] are to be found in topographical and chronological framework while the remainder[3] are part of literary constructions, or summary statements of progress.

The fact that most of these genitive absolutes are to be found opening the pericope, and that their subject matter is chronological or topographical or comments on the 'progress of the gospel', as well as the literary nature of the genitive absolute,[4] suggest that the editor is opening his pericope with a linking phrase, and thus developing material which was originally without time or place references, so as to make of it a continuous narrative.

A few examples will illustrate the function of the construction. 4^{45}, commencing a new section, reads: 'That day, when evening came...'; 5^{2}: 'When He came out of the boat...'; 5^{21}: 'When Jesus had crossed over in the boat...'; 5^{35}: 'While He was still speaking, they came...'; 6^{2}: 'And when the sabbath came He began to teach...'; 6^{54}: 'And when they disembarked from the boat...'; 8^{1}: 'In those days the multitude again being great, and having nothing to eat,...'; 9^{9}: 'On their way down the mountain,...'; 10^{17}: 'And as He was going forth for His journey...'; 10^{46}: 'And as He was going forth to Jericho, and His disciples and much people...'; 11^{12}: 'And on the morrow

---

[1] 4^{35}, $5^{2, 21, 35}$, $6^{2, 54}$, 8^{1}, 9^{9}, $10^{17, 46}$, $11^{11, 12, 27}$, $13^{1, 3}$, $14^{3, 22, 43, 66}$, 15^{42} (11^{11} is the last verse) = 20 times.

[2] Topography = $5^{2, 21, 35}$, 9^{28}, 10^{46}, 11^{27}, $13^{1, 3}$, $14^{3, 22}$. Topography and Chronology: 4^{35}, 11^{11-12}, 15^{42}. Chronology: 8^{1}.

[3] 1^{32}, $6^{2, 54}$, 9^{9}, $10^{17, 46}$, $14^{17, 18, 43, 66}$.

[4] Blass–Debrunner, p. 218, point out that the g.a. is in Mark 'only temporal, and, except for 4: 35, 16: 2, it is always in postposition'. Both Zerwick and the latter emphasise the freer use in the N.T., but at the same time cite classical authors as well as the LXX and N.T. in this respect.

when they came out from Bethany...'; 11^{27}: 'And in the
temple as He was walking about, there...'; 13^1: 'And as He
was going out of the temple...'; 13^3: 'And as He was sitting on
the Mount of Olives over against the temple...'; 14^3: 'And
when He was in Bethany in the house of Simon the leper, as He
lay at table...'; 14^{17}: 'And when it was evening...'; 14^{22}:
'And as they were eating...'; 14^{43}: 'And forthwith, as He was
still speaking...'; 14^{66}: 'And whilst Peter is below...'; 15^{42}:
'And when it was already evening, since it was the preparation...' All these short clauses, constructed in the participial
genitive absolute, link the previous pericope to the new section
which originally existed independently of them, their presence
being superfluous to the story, and their only *raison d'être* being to
move on the 'Gospel' narration with a semblance of time and
place.

Strictly speaking, the genitive absolute must not be constructed with its participle(s) agreeing with the subject or
object of the sentence. No doubt even in classical Greek this
was sometimes ignored, but even more often in the Koine. Out
of thirteen correct uses in the Gospel ten are editorial. In three[1]
instances, the evangelist uses the genitive absolute twice in the
same sentence, one example of which, 14^3, is grammatically
disastrous.[2] Its place in the Passion narrative is significantly at
a break in the literary construction of the earliest Passion
narrative in which according to Taylor 14^{10} followed on from
14^{1-2}, the natural flow from 14^2 to 14^{10} being interrupted by the
incident of the anointing, so that 14^{3-9} with its well-known 14^9[3]
is a Marcan insertion, 14^3 being the opening of the new pericope. The only explanation of the anacolouthon in 14^3 can be
that Mark has added another genitive absolute to one which
was already there in his source. 'As He sat at table...' was what
Mark found in his source, and so he supplied the topographical
link 'Jesus was at Bethany, in the house of Simon the leper.'[4]

[1] 6^{21-2}, 8^1, 14^3.

[2] καὶ ὄντος αὐτοῦ ἐν Βηθανίᾳ ἐν τῇ οἰκίᾳ Σίμωνος τοῦ λεπροῦ,/κατακειμένου
αὐτοῦ ἦλθεν γυνὴ...

[3] See Marxsen, p. 86; J. Jeremias, 'The Gentile world in the Thought of
Jesus', *S.N.T.S.* 3 (1952), 21f.

[4] Taylor, p. 530 'and the suggestion of Lohmeyer, 292, that Mark inserted the first into a narrative which originally began (καὶ) κατακειμένου
αὐτοῦ is attractive'.

The Johannine tradition places this story in another context, while the highly redactional vocabulary of the conclusion of the story, 14⁸⁻⁹, suggests that the evangelist has adapted the whole incident to the 'anointing of the Messiah', and the woman's part in the original story to her place in His proclaiming of the *kerygma* in the Church's mission.[1]

Returning to the question of methodology, the twenty-four examples of the genitive absolute which have been marked R are to be found at the beginnings of pericopae, and belong to passages which have been marked redactional on literary and higher-critical grounds. There remain, however, at least five passages containing a genitive absolute, which do not seem to mark the beginning of a story, and which would not naturally be regarded as redactional on critical grounds. Here, as later, we shall, therefore, in the light of our previous examination of the redactional use of the genitive absolute, look again at these residual passages, to see whether there might be grounds for putting them under redactional rather than source usage. There is something of a parallel, here, to the vocabulary test. If, for example, one discovers a word is 5/8 R then the remaining three verses are usually examined to see if on other grounds they have been omitted in the search for redactional material. Of the five, all five[2] seem possible R verses, but particularly 5¹⁸ and 6³⁵.

¶5¹⁸. Taylor[3] states: 'The vocabulary and style are clearly Markan.' He comments on the genitive absolute, and notes the parallel of ὁ δαιμονισθείς with τὸν ἐσχηκότα τὸν λεγιῶνα in v. 15. Again, comparing v. 10, he notes the repetition in this verse of παρεκάλει + ἵνα + subjunctive. Also, the phrase ἵνα μετ' αὐτοῦ ᾖ is very near to ἵνα ὦσιν μετ' αὐτοῦ in the literary construction, 'The Appointment of the Twelve' (3¹⁴R). As far as the vocabulary is concerned, πλοῖον is marked in the high-frequency test 12/17, ἐμβαίνειν is used 5/5R, and δαιμονίζεσθαι in 1³² is redactional.

---

[1] Marxsen, p. 86: 'But that God remembers the fame of this woman (as Lohmeyer continues) is not there. Rather we find here (and only here in Mark *expressis verbis*) the theme of the memorial, which must be understood in the sense of a "repraesentatio", a realisation of the action.'

[2] 5¹⁸, 6²¹,²²,³⁵,⁴⁷.   [3] P. 284.

As far as vocabulary is concerned ἀπέρχεσθαι, ἐμβαίνειν in 5[18f.] are high-frequency words. Both R. H. Lightfoot and Burkill give additional notes to 5[18-20], the former inclining to the view that they are R. The latter, after considering Dibelius'[1] and Wrede's opinion that the verses describe Jesus' command to silence being disregarded, considers them as S. Taylor and Trocmé comment on the strange theology of passages like 5[7-20], and Matthew and Luke's abridgement of them. Schweizer remarks: 'Certainly vs. 18a can be traced to the one who has added this story to 4: 36 (which see, and cf. 3: 7–12; 4: 1–9). He has added vss. 18f. as a primary point.'[2] He goes on to state that 5[20] with its affinity with 1[45], and change from 'God' to 'Lord' (see Luke 8[39]) denotes it as R. So we may conclude that commentators of repute seem to regard 5[18-20] as R, and the language used would seem to support them.

6[35] from the 'Feeding of the Five Thousand' is regarded by Taylor as unlikely to be the original beginning of the pericope.[3] The whole question of this pericope is complicated by the doublet or other account of the feeding. Best[4] observes that the reference to 'teaching' in 6[34], which is regarded by the present writer as Marcan introduction to the miracle, could suggest that the 'Five Thousand Feeding' is the Marcan model and that of the Four Thousand is the secondary account. However it seems equally possible that Mark created the Five Thousand from the Four Thousand as the primary account. To be noted in the introductory section are the familiar vocabulary,[5] and particularly the way the vocabulary in 6[35-6] is anticipated in the preceding section. Repetition is continued even in the feeding itself and in this verse under discussion ἤδη ὥρας πολλῆς γενομένης is repeated in the second half of the verse, ἤδη ὥρα πολλή. Taylor is emphatic that originally the pericope 'cannot

---

[1] Burkill, pp. 86–95; cf. Lightfoot, pp. 88–90.

[2] Schweizer, p. 113.

[3] 'It is better to conclude either that the story began with 31 or that Mark has interwoven its beginning with 30–4', p. 322.

[4] 'vi[53-6] appears to be a Markan summary based on tradition which he has received...; Mark however continually in his own seams introduces Jesus as teacher. In that he would seem to be correcting the tradition he has received', p. 79.

[5] 6[34]: πολὺν ὄχλον, ἤρξατο διδάσκειν, πολλά. 6[35] πολλῆς γενομένης...οἱ μαθηταὶ αὐτοῦ, λέγω ὅτι. N.B. ἔρημός ἐστιν ὁ τόπος: see ibid., p. 26.

have begun so abruptly.' Therefore, if we are to regard the pericope as having begun in the source with ἤδη ὥρα πολλή it may be that these words prompted the evangelist's own genitive absolute, καὶ ἤδη ὥρας πολλῆς γενομένης with the favourite οἱ μαθηταὶ αὐτοῦ and ἔρημός ἐστιν ὁ τόπος being a free paraphrase, or already in the text. Normally speaking the evangelist uses γενομένης when he is opening with a comment on the 'early hour'; cf. 1³², 4³⁵, 6⁴⁷, 14¹⁷, 15⁴², 1³² ὀψίας δὲ γενομένης (Taylor says ὥρα is understood). Sundwall[1] is of the opinion that 6³⁴ is redactional, and that the story originally had no reference to time and place, Mark having supplied the connections by 6³⁰⁻⁴ and with one passage also at the beginning of the pericope.

6⁴⁷ is from the 'Storm on the Lake', and we are reminded by Best that there are two[2] accounts of this incident just as there are two feedings. 6⁵²R links up the storm and the feeding. Best[3] thinks that redactional work may be found in vv. 47 and 48, but he is also open to the possibility that the feeding and the miracle on the water have been linked by Mark, the references to eating, leaven, loaves, etc. being symbolic allusions to Jesus' teaching. The vocabulary[4] in 6⁴⁷ is highly redactional, while 6⁴⁸ has already been marked as partly redactional on account of the evangelist's use of the participle as a main verb and parenthesis.[5] Bultmann and Dibelius[6] point out the development within the narrative and the possible influence of the storm motif from 4³⁷⁻⁴¹.

The remaining two texts from Ch. 6 are 6²¹,²², both these texts being found in 'The Death of the Baptist', 6¹⁴⁻²⁹. The latter, says Taylor, contains many unusual words, which may be 'accounted for by the subject-matter, and signs of the Markan style are not wanting'. Evidence to support this opinion would

---

[1] P. 38: 'The beginning of the story of the feeding has disappeared in the redaction (Bultmann, p. 259), and v. 34 would be for the most part the word of the redactor (Klostermann, p. 72).'

[2] Pp. 73, 183.

[3] *Ibid.*, p. 78: 'Verses 47, 48 show Mark's hand and perhaps he has made the link at this point between the feeding narrative and the walking on the water.'

[4] πλοῖον, θάλασσα, μόνος, ὀψίας, ἐπὶ τῆς γῆς.

[5] See p. 70, where 6⁴⁸ is made R on linguistic grounds and one of my tentative changes from S to R.

[6] Bultmann, p. 216; Dibelius, pp. 71, 76, 277ff.

be the parenthesis in 6[14-16], two γάρ clauses in 6[18], and 6[20], λέγω ὅτι in 6[18], καὶ εὐθύς in 6[27] and an unusual diminutive which is regarded by Hawkins as part of distinctive Marcan vocabulary, κοράσιον. In 6[21,22] we find three high-frequency examples of Marcan vocabulary: Γαλιλαία, Ἡρῴδης, κοράσιον; and worthy of note is συνανακειμένοις, which is only used twice, here and in 2[15] (which is R). The evangelist is of course much interested in John the Baptist and his relationship to Jesus. Lohmeyer comments on the 'cultivated style through which an Aramaic basis can be traced'. So Taylor says 'it may be inferred, if this description [i.e. Lohmeyer's] is warranted, that Mark is using a source'.[1] Marcan interest in Herod, and the 'Herodians', is marked (cf. 3[6]).

6[21,22] are now marked R. These five texts have been discussed in some detail partly to show that the linguistic method can be useful in confirming or rejecting as redactional texts which are perhaps still a little doubtful from a literary or higher-critical point of view. The final statistics, 29/29, are very high indeed, and comparable to 'parenthesis'.

(c) PARTICIPLE AS A MAIN VERB

R: 1[39], 2[1], 6[6], 7[2,19]; add 6[48](?).

There are at least five examples of the participle replacing the finite verb.

1[39] reads καὶ ἦν[2] κηρύσσων εἰς τὰς συναγωγὰς αὐτῶν εἰς ὅλην τὴν Γαλιλαίαν καὶ τὰ δαιμόνια ἐκβάλλων. Is καὶ τὰ δαιμόνια ἐκβάλλων to be linked with the periphrastic ἦν?[3] If so, it is a long way from its auxiliary. The participle, if regarded strictly as a participle, should be linked to the main verb, which is in this case 'proclaiming' (a highly redactional word), and also the evangelist elsewhere links exorcism and/or healing with preaching or proclaiming.

Zerwick has drawn our attention to the possibilities of a literary

---

[1] E. Lohmeyer, *Das Evangelium des Markus* (Göttingen, 1937), p. 118; Pesch, p. 84; Schreiber, pp. 181ff.

[2] W.H. with ABθ 892 Cop. sa. bo. Aeth. read ἦλθεν instead of ἦν AC DWΓΔΘΠΣΦ etc. Probably as Taylor suggests (p. 184) ἦν is the harder reading, εἰς after κηρύσσων seeming harsh to the scribe.

[3] See p. 104.

chiastic placing in certain[1] of the verses, of which 1 [39] is one. The juxtaposition of similar or contrasting words is combined with what he calls a 'rhythmic thought-process' of chiasmus.[2] If this is correct it may be of considerable importance in a study which attempts to separate R and S, if it be granted that chiasmus is predominantly a literary rather than an oral feature of style. As Zerwick states, the chiasmus 'is to be found in the narrative part also (as distinct from "sayings"), and in fact predominantly in passages where we think we can recognise the evangelist himself (in contrast to the inherited tradition)'.

καὶ ἦν[3] κηρύσσων εἰς τὰς συναγωγὰς αὐτῶν...
καὶ τὰ δαιμόνια ἐκβάλλων.

Presumably we are to see κηρύσσων contrasted with ἐκβάλλων, and δαιμόνια with συναγωγάς.[4] A further complication is that 1 [39] is the end of a section, and 1 [40] produces three more participles which may link up with the first two in 1 [39]: κηρύσσων ἐκβάλλων (1 [39]), παρακαλῶν...γονυπετῶν λέγων (1 [40]).[5]

Both Taylor and Best, in spite of considerable complexity of textual variation here, and in 1 [39] also, reject the idea that the clause is interpolated by a redactor (not the author). Mark is probably looking ahead to 1 [43] when he writes 1 [39], anticipating the reference to the expulsion of evil spirits in the synagogue. And so ἐκβάλλων in 1 [39] gets ready for 1 [43] καὶ ἐμβριμησάμενος αὐτῷ εὐθὺς ἐξέβαλεν αὐτόν.

Like 1 [39], 2 [1] καὶ εἰσελθὼν πάλιν εἰς Καφαρναοὺμ δι' ἡμερῶν ἠκούσθη ὅτι ἐν οἴκῳ ἐστίν also is a 'seam', and links on to the ending verse of 1 [39–45], which is the adjoining verse. Elsewhere in this thesis the possibility of conscious catchwords manipulated by the evangelist has been discussed,[6] but here 2 [1] εἰσελθὼν πάλιν[7] presents an anacolouthon (so Taylor and Best).

[1] M. Zerwick, *Untersuchungen zum Markus-Stil, Ein Beitrag zur Durcharbeitung des Neuen Testamentes* (Rome, 1937), pp. 125–6.
[2] *Ibid.*, p. 125.   [3] See p. 67, n. 2.
[4] Probably we are meant to contrast δαιμόνια and συναγωγάς.
[5] P. 121.   [6] See p. 4.
[7] Taylor, p. 192; Best, p. 69: 'ii, 1, 2 certainly bear some signs of Markan editorial work. The anacolouthic εἰσελθὼν and Mark's favourite πάλιν are an indication of this.'

The main verb, the impersonal ἠκούσθη, is ambiguously[1] related to δι' ἡμερῶν. In addition to the 'anacolouthic εἰσελθών, and Mark's favourite πάλιν,' mentioned by Best,[2] we may add the impersonal, ἠκούσθη, and catchwords related to the previous closing verse, plus the enigmatic reference to a house where Jesus was wont to stay.[3] These various considerations might well argue that the passage is to be considered as R.

6⁶ is regarded by Taylor as 'an editorial summary based on tradition', but it is theologically related to our first text, 1³⁹, and grammatically to at least another Marcan text, 2²³, where it is not clear whether the main verb or the participle is the dominant thought of the sentence. περιῆγεν is ostensibly the main verb, but κύκλῳ διδάσκων, the participle, may really express the evangelist's primary emphasis. Did Jesus go around teaching, or did He teach as He went around? According to Best[4] it is 'teaching' which dominates to the exclusion of all else and is to be contrasted with the following verse which shows Jesus delegating authority to deal with unclean spirits, on the grounds that He has already demonstrated His own charismatic power in that field. The natural translation of κύκλῳ διδάσκων would be 'teaching in a circle', but in view of 6³⁶, κύκλῳ may be still related to 'going round' – a kind of circular teaching tour. Matthew accepts the m.v. περιῆγεν but uses three participles, διδάσκων, κηρύσσων, and θεραπεύων to link up the itinerary movement with the threefold activities of mission, thus ignoring and changing the main Marcan emphasis on Jesus as teacher in this particular text.

7² and 7¹⁹ are both part of parentheses and dealt with more fully elsewhere,[5] but they both demonstrate the redactor–editor demanding of a participle an extension of usage which even in koine Greek it should not be asked to bear. The N.E.B. translates ἰδόντες by 'noticed' and makes a whole sentence of the

---

[1] 'Probably this note of time should be taken with εἰσελθών rather than with ἠκούσθη (cf. Swete, 32; Klostermann, 25; Lohmeyer, 50)' (Taylor, p. 192).   [2] P. 69.

[3] Allen, p. 25: 'Noticeable also is the frequent reference to a house as the scene of Christ's activity.' 1²⁹(?), 2¹R, ¹⁵R, 3²⁰R, 7¹⁷R, ²⁴R, 9²⁸R, ³³R, 10¹⁰R.

[4] P. 75: 'Thus Jesus is seen by Mark primarily as a teacher, but also as one who can delegate authority over demons because he already possesses that authority.'   [5] Pp. 49–51.

concluding clause of 7¹⁹, καθαρίζων πάντα τὰ βρώματα: 'Thus he declared all foods clean.' Probably the small parenthesis in 7² τοῦτ' ἔστιν ἀνίπτοις plus the main parenthesis in 7³⁻⁴ have disturbed the grammatical thought of the writer. In any case he has gone astray with a mixture of constructions in his ἰδόντες τινάς...ἐσθίοντας and ἰδόντες ὅτι ἐσθίουσιν τὸν ἄρτον.¹ More probably he read in his source 7⁵ ἀλλὰ κοιναῖς χερσὶν ἐσθίουσιν τὸν ἄρτον, which he reproduces in 7²ᵇ by interpolating the comment τοῦτ' ἔστιν ἀνίπτοις in between his own introduction, καὶ ἰδόντες τινὰς τῶν μαθητῶν αὐτοῦ (7²ᵃ), and the same phrase altered only by changing the singular ἄρτον to the plural τοὺς ἄρτους.²

In the case of 7¹⁹ Zerwick reminds us of the possibility of chiastic construction in the first part of the sentence,³ while D. Daube has demonstrated in the Hebrew language the influence of the participle as a substitute for the imperative, or the present or future.⁴

6⁴⁸⁵ is an interesting example where both parenthesis and a broken construction suggest that the evangelist is once again using ἰδών as a main verb. 6⁴⁷ was tentatively changed from S to R on linguistic grounds from the last section (genitive absolute).⁶ Further confirmation of 6⁴⁸ as R comes from this broken construction with the participle used as a main verb. Note also the use of γάρ explanatory in typical redactional style; the employment of the historic present, the phrase ἐπὶ τῆς γῆς (6⁴⁷), and a possible hidden parenthesis in ἦν γὰρ ὁ ἄνεμος ἐναντίος αὐτοῖς.

(d) πολλά ACCUSATIVE

R: 1³⁴, 4², 6¹³, 7⁴, ¹³, 8³¹, 9¹², 10²² = 8 times
S: 12⁴¹R(?), 15³S = 2 times

---

¹ So Taylor, p. 334.
² καὶ ἰδόντες...χερσίν, τοῦτ' ἔστιν ἀνίπτοις, ἐσθίουσιν τοὺς ἄρτους – οἱ γάρ... ³ *Unters. zum Markus-Stil*, p. 125.
⁴ D. Daube, 'Participle and Imperative in 1 Peter' in E. G. Selwyn, *The First Epistle of St. Peter* (London, 1946), pp. 467–88: The English 'he cries', 'should cry', and imperative ('cry!') would all be rendered by the Hebrew participle, 'crying'.
⁵ ἰδὼν αὐτοὺς βασανιζομένους ἐν τῷ ἐλαύνειν... – ἦν γὰρ ὁ ἄνεμος ἐναντίος αὐτοῖς, – περὶ...ἔρχεται... ἰδών seems to be the m.v., ἦν...αὐτοῖς is in parenthesis.
⁶ P. 66.

The verbs employed with πολλά accusative are as follows: ἐκβάλλειν (1³⁴, 6¹³) and διδάσκειν (4²), παραλαμβάνειν (7⁴), πάσχειν (8³¹, 9¹²), ποιεῖν (7¹³), and periphrastic ἔχειν (10²²).

Seven of these eight redactional uses of πολλά can be classified theologically as follows: (i) setting the scene for teaching, healing or exorcism: 1³⁴, 4², 6¹³; (ii) teaching that the Son of Man must suffer: 8³¹, 9¹²; (iii) explanations of Jewish customs and 'defilement': 7⁴, ¹³.

(i) 1³⁴ᵇ and 6¹³ᵃ are almost identical. 1³⁴ reads καὶ δαιμόνια πολλὰ ἐξέβαλεν (6¹³ ἐξέβαλλον). Best[1] writes of Mark possibly adopting the word ἐκβάλλειν in welding together the Baptism and Temptation accounts. 6¹³ is the conclusion of the M.L.C., 'the Commissioning of the Twelve'. In both 1³⁴ and 6¹³, in contrast to 4², the verb comes at the end of the clause, as it does in most of the eight examples. 6¹³ might well be partly redactional or partly traditional, while 1³⁴ with its command to silence, and significantly its more literary πολλοὺς κακῶς ἔχοντας, can be safely regarded as editorial. 4² is composed also of the redactional διδάσκειν, followed by καὶ ἔλεγεν αὐτοῖς, widely accepted as redactional.[2]

(ii) 8³¹, ³ and 9¹², ⁴ are both from Marcan Literary Constructions, 8³¹ being the first of the three prophecies of the Passion, and 9¹² the sequel to the Transfiguration. Both are explicit expressions of the Marcan theology of predestined suffering for the 'Son of Man', expressed by δεῖ...πολλὰ παθεῖν in 8³¹, and a rhetorical question in 9¹² καὶ πῶς γέγραπται ἵνα πολλὰ πάθῃ καὶ ἐξουδενηθῇ – so δεῖ is employed in 8³¹, and γέγραπται in 9¹², to convey the belief that in the Old Testament scriptures, as well as in the mind of God, the enigma of the Passion is to be resolved. I have noted elsewhere[5] that certain rare occurrences in vocabulary may indicate the redactor's hand, and this could apply to ἐξουδενηθῇ.† The employment of ἵνα + subjunctive in 9¹² is a grammatical usage comparable to δεῖ + inf. in the other text, 8³¹, where added redactional pointers are ἄρχομαι + a high

---

[1] P. 4. 'To describe the action of the Spirit in initiating the Temptation Mark adopts the word ἐκβάλλειν.'

[2] See Kuhn, p. 84; Reploh, p. 61.

[3] καὶ ἤρξατο...πολλὰ παθεῖν.

[4] καὶ πῶς γέγραπται ἐπὶ τὸν υἱὸν τοῦ ἀνθρώπου, ἵνα πολλὰ πάθῃ, καὶ ἐξουδενηθῇ;

[5] See pp. 28ff.

frequency (διδάσκειν). πολλά (παθεῖν) in 8³¹ is similarly placed to its position in the purpose clause, πολλά πάθῃ, in 9¹².

(iii) 7⁴ᵇ¹ and 7¹³² are from the teaching section on 'Defilement', 7¹⁻²³. 7⁴ᵇ is a small clause found in the long parenthesis which explains the ritual and cleansing practices of the 'Pharisees and the Jews' to Gentile readers (7³⁻⁴). It is fully dealt with under 'parenthesis'.[3] Here it is relevant to note that πολλά in 7⁴ᵇ comes early in the clause, while the verb is at the end of the clause, for unlike 7¹³, it is in the middle of the long sentence, whereas the latter is an 'editorial summary' (so Taylor).[4] The evangelist has produced a good alliteration in καὶ παρόμοια τοιαῦτα πολλά ποιεῖτε (7¹³).

10²², like 4², places πολλά as the last word in the sentence. To be also noted as indications of redactional usage are the periphrastic ἔχων, the enclitic γάρ,[5] and the literary catchword by response:

ἦν γὰρ ἔχων (10²²) κτήματα πολλά.
οἱ τὰ χρήματα (10²³) ἔχοντες

Probably there is also chiastic placing of ἔχων and ἔχοντες with χρήματα and κτήματα.[6] The story has a nicely delayed climax at the end which could almost pass for the skill of the preacher, were it not for the typically Marcan habit of saying something ('he went away sorrowing'), and then explaining the statement in the next clause (ἦν γάρ....).

The remaining two examples of πολλά acc. are 12⁴¹ and 15³. The latter, with its V.S.O. and πολλά at the end, as it comes from the most primitive part of the Passion narrative would probably be S, but the former, 12⁴¹, with its familar alliteration,[7] and placed just at the end of one major section and leading into the famous Ch. 13, would be more likely to be editorial. Ropes comments on 'the perfect literary art', and Lambrecht's denoting κατέναντι, a redactional trait,[8] with the parenthesis in the next verse, would encourage us to transfer 12⁴¹ to R.

---

[1] οἱ γὰρ Φαρισαῖοι..., καὶ ἄλλα πολλά ἐστιν ἃ παρέλαβον κρατεῖν,... χαλκίων (7³⁻⁴). [2] καὶ παρόμοια τοιαῦτα πολλά ποιεῖτε (7¹³).

[3] Pp. 49ff. [4] P. 341.

[5] P. 47. [6] See p. 7.

[7] καὶ πολλοὶ πλούσιοι ἔβαλλον πολλά.

[8] Note the repeating of γαζοφυλάκιον and βάλλω, and also ὄχλος, πῶς, πολλά, R vocabulary of high frequency.

(e) λέγω ὅτι

R: $1^{15,40}$, $2^{12,17}$, $3^{11,21,22,28}$, 4^{21}, $5^{28,35}$, $6^{14-16}(3)$, 7^{20}, 8^{28}, $9^{1,11(?),13,31,41}$, 10^{32}, 11^{23}, 12^{43}, $13^{6,30}$, $14^{18,27(2),57.58(2)} =$
32 times

S: 1^{37}, 5^{23}, $6^{4,18(?),35(?)}$, $12^{6(?)}$, $14^{25(?),71(?),69(?)} = 9$ times

Possible conversion of S to R: 1^{37}, $6^{18,35}$, $14^{25,69,71} = 6$ times

To remain S: 5^{23}, 6^4, $12^{6(?)} = 3$ times

Turner,[1] Sundwall,[2] and Zerwick[3] have drawn our attention to Mark's avoidance of indirect speech, and his preference for direct speech. Zerwick points out that Mark quite often uses the rhetorical question,[4] and direct speech where there is no necessity for it at all.[5] He also quotes Larfeld's researches which show the evangelist as 'one who reproduces in direct speech (viz.) unexpressed thoughts (5.28, 9.10), and the words uttered by several persons or at various times (1.37; 3.11; 6.14, 16...)'. Zerwick, in an important passage, outlines the significance of indirect speech in determining sources.[6]

Thus, having seen that the most prolific use of direct speech is essentially a characteristic of popular writers, and that it stands out particularly clearly in the gospels, with Mark in the lead over others, we must pay all the more careful attention to the little in the way of indirect speech that we find in him, especially since the presence of this indirect speech has, understandably enough, occasionally been employed as a criterion of style, at least by way of confirmation, for the purpose of determining the limits of the sources (Wendling in various places).'

The most striking feature of Mark's few attempts to sustain

[1] *J.T.S.* 28 (October 1926), 9-15.

[2] P. 8.

[3] *Unters. zum Markus-Stil*, pp. 4ff., 45.

[4] Zerwick, *Unters. zum Markus-Stil*, pp. 24-5. He cites 1^{27}R, 2^7, 3^{33}R, 4^{13}R, 2^1R, 4^0R, 5^{35}R$^{(?)}$,39, $8^{12,36}$R, 9^{19}, 11^{17}R, 12^{14}, 14^{37}R,^{63}. Duplication of the question is to be found in: 1^{27}R, $2^{7,9}$R, 6^2R,^{3}, 7^{18}R, 8^{17}S, 1^8S, 9^{19}, 11^{28}, 14^{37}. See also Neirynck, pp. 114ff., 63ff.

[5] Zerwick, *ibid.*, cites 1^{37}R, 4^{39}S, 5^8R, 8^{19}R, 2^0R, 9^{25}S, 10^{49}R, 13^1R, 16^3S.

[6] *Ibid.*, p. 25. See also Neirynck, pp. 71-2: 'use of oratio recta and oratio obliqua has shown that the progressive double-step expression is a more general Markan characteristic'.

indirect speech for any length is that they soon collapse, and he resorts to direct speech.[1] The nearest he comes to anything approaching the finesse of literary Greek is 1⁴, referring to the Baptist's mission as κηρύσσων βάπτισμα μετανοίας εἰς ἄφεσιν ἁμαρτιῶν. When he is summarising the content of Jesus' preaching in a celebrated bridge passage 1¹⁴⁻¹⁵, he soon resorts to λέγω ὅτι, which is probably to be regarded as something like our colon, according to Zerwick.[2]

Summarising the main reasons for this phenomenon, which is in the main a feature of redactional rather than source style and therefore can, as Sundwall suggested, be a guide to the redactor's hand,[3] we suggest the following: (i) summaries of what has been said over and over again: 1¹⁵, 3¹¹ (2 times); (ii) direct speech overcoming indirect: 1⁴⁰, 2¹², 3²², 10³², 13⁶, 14⁵⁸⁽²⁾ (7 times); (iii) impersonals (sometimes in parentheses: 3²¹, 5³⁵, 6¹⁴⁻¹⁶⁽³⁾, 8²⁸⁽²⁾ (7 times); (iv) explanatory parentheses: 3²¹, 5²⁸, 6¹⁴⁻¹⁶⁽³⁾ (5 times); (v) introduction to sayings, classified as follows: emphatic (ἀμὴν λέγω (ὑμῖν) ὅτι): 3²⁸, 9¹,¹³,⁴¹, 11²³, 12⁴³, 13³⁰, 14¹⁸ (8 times); unemphatic (καὶ ἔλεγεν αὐτοῖς): 4²¹, 9¹,³¹ (3 times); and miscellaneous: 2¹⁷, 7²⁰, 14²⁷ (3 times) = 14 times.

These may be taken in turn.

(i) *Summaries*

3¹¹ ⁴ reads καὶ ἔκραζον λέγοντα ὅτι Σὺ εἶ ὁ υἱὸς τοῦ θεοῦ. The use of λέγοντα here preceded by ὅταν (followed by the indicative), shows the evangelist thinking in terms of repeated occasions similar to the one he is describing. The N.E.B. translates: 'The unclean spirits,...*would* fall.'[5]

---

[1] Neirynck: 'Exposition and Discourse', pp. 114ff.; 'Narrative and Discourse', pp. 112–14; 'Oratio Obliqua and Oratio Recta', pp. 63–71.

[2] P. 142, n. 9: 'this ὅτι when introducing direct speech is equivalent to our colon (:); it is very common in Mark and John perhaps owing to the influence of Aramaic, which uses di (Hebrew ki) in the same way; e.g. Jo. 10, 36'.   [3] P. 8.

[4] For 1¹⁵ see Taylor, p. 165: 'The message of Jesus described in 1. 15 is a summary of what Jesus proclaimed.'

[5] Burkill, pp. 65–6, quotes C. H. Turner's analysis of ὅταν: 14/20R 'repeated action quite excluded'. Here Mark is using the imperfect tense and his use of tenses is quite often precise (see Taylor, p. 52; Swete, p. 47).

(ii) Direct and Indirect Speech

$1^{40\,1}$ is constructed in a most curious way with the subject and opening clause, καὶ ἔρχεται πρὸς αὐτόν, probably added to the source, but the asyndeton in γονυπετῶν λέγων αὐτῷ ὅτι is even for Mark rather shocking. The repetition of πρὸς αὐτόν...π. αὐτόν...λέγων αὐτῷ, when αὐτός is used three times in a short clause, can most kindly be excused on the grounds that the participles are possibly hiding the original parataxis. The rendering of the actual words used in a graphic indirect statement is, however, perfectly good Greek. $2^{12\,2}$ starts the sentence well with ὥστε + infinitive, and then after λέγοντας ὅτι the actual chorus οὕτως οὐδέποτε εἴδαμεν reproduces the words of all. Such a mode of expression, as Zerwick remarks, helps to produce 'the much-praised liveliness and plasticity of the narrative which especially distinguishes the gospel of Mark, at least over long stretches.'[3] 3^{22} also reports the actual words spoken. 'He has Beezeboul; in (by) the ruler of demons he expels demons.' 10^{32} uses λέγω ὅτι after the redactor has summarised first in an indirect statement, which is then further explained in greater detail after ὅτι in direct speech: ἤρξατο αὐτοῖς[4] λέγειν τὰ μέλλοντα αὐτῷ συμβαίνειν, ὅτι ἰδοὺ[5] ἀναβαίνομεν εἰς Ἱεροσόλυμα, καὶ ὁ υἱὸς τοῦ ἀνθρώπου παραδοθήσεται τοῖς ἀρχιερεῦσιν...[6] Here ὅτι is a long way from λέγειν. Matthew places the indirect speech in a shortened form earlier in the sentence, while Luke omits it entirely. Matthew adds to the 'I am' in 13^{6} (ἐπὶ τῷ ὀνόματί μου λέγοντες ὅτι Ἐγώ εἰμι, καὶ...) that which in Mark is understood, 'the Messiah', and so we are to see 'in my name' as one of the few places in $13^{5-8,\,24-7}$ where a Christian hand is to be discovered.[7] In

[1] See p. 120 for two or more parts., also to be found in this verse.

[2] N.B. also εὐθύς, p. 92.

[3] Unters. zum Markus-Stil, p. 24. See also Neirynck, pp. 122-4, 'Direct Discourse preceded by Qualifying Verb'. Examples given are: $1^{14,\,15}$R, 1^{23}R, 24, 1^{25}, 1^{27}R, 1^{40}R, 1^{43-4}R, 2^{12}R, 4^{2}R, 39, 5^{12}, 5^{23}R, 6^{2}R, 45, 50, $7^{6,\,37}$R, 8^{27}R, 33R, 9^{11}R, 25, 31R, 10^{26}R, $10^{32,\,33}$R, 47R, 11^{17}R, 12^{18}R, 14^{33}R, 34, 35-6, 57-8R, 60, $14^{61,\,68}$, $15^{4,\,18}$R, 29R, 31R.

[4] See ἄρχομαι also on p. 81.

[5] See E. J. Pryke, 'ΙΔΕ and ΙΔΟΥ', N.T.S. 14, no. 3 (April 1968), 418-24.

[6] P. 145 app. R. Vocab.　　　　　[7] Taylor, p. 639.

14[58(2)], 'Some stood up and gave false evidence against him to this effect (λέγοντες ὅτι) we heard him say (λέγοντος ὅτι), "I will pull down..."' In fact, direct speech is used not only for the false witnesses, but also for the Lord's words as reported by them.

(iii) *Impersonals*

Common to these instances would appear to be a desire to make a scene more vivid, or actually to build up a vivid atmosphere. But in 6[14-16] and 8[28] the results are grammatically and syntactically deplorable. In 6[14-16] the disjunctive between Herod and the main subject, and the subject of the parenthetical statement causes great confusion, while in 8[28] the construction is ungrammatical.[1] This would seem to reflect not an original obscurity of the tradition which Mark has not clarified, but a certain overloading which is the result of the evangelist's own literary efforts, and his predilection for λέγω ὅτι.

(iv) *Explanatory*

On 5[28] Taylor[2] writes: 'The explanation is added by Mark or in the tradition he followed', and is in fact one of these 'inner thoughts' of the actors, speaking aloud for the reader, or hearer, to follow:[3] 'If I could only touch His clothes I would be saved.' Typical of Mark is the fact that the statement is made after we are told that the woman had touched the Lord, but, in view of the fact that the evocative prayer may have been communicated to Jesus by her thoughts, we forget the illogical placing in the Marcan outline.

(v) *Introductory formulae*

Let us first deal with the unemphatic group of formulae, all three of which use the accepted redactional ἔλεγεν αὐτοῖς.[4] 4[21]

---

[1] Taylor says that the variations in the constructions after ὅτι 'are of interest'. 'With 'Ιωάνην τὸν Βαπτιστήν (so also Mk. and Lk.) sc. λέγουσιν οἱ ἄνθρωποί σε εἶναι. On this the second ὅτι followed by the indicative depends' (p. 376).

[2] P. 290. See also p. 128.   [3] See p. 77, n. 2.

[4] 2[27a], 4[3a, 11, 21a], 7[9a], 9[1] = 7 times. καὶ λέγει αὐτοῖς: 2[5a, 10c, 17a], 4[13a], 7[18], 10[23, 27], 14[27].

comes in a small section, 4^{21-5}, in between the 'Interpretation of the Sower' and the three seed parables. It is unusual for the redactor to add ὅτι to the phrase κ. ἔ. α. 9^{1} starts with the unemphatic formula followed by the emphatic introduction, coming at the end of the latter. 9^{31}, the second of the Passion prophecies, commences with διδάσκειν:[1] ἐδίδασκεν γὰρ τοὺς μαθητὰς αὐτοῦ followed by καὶ ἔλεγεν αὐτοῖς ὅτι ὁ υἱὸς τοῦ ἀν....

The eight emphatic formulae, sc. ἀμὴν λέγω ὑμῖν, might well be crucial texts for an understanding of the redactional theology of the evangelist: the sin against the Holy Spirit (3^{28}); the Kingdom of God and eschatology (9^{1}, 13^{30}); the return of Elijah in the person of the Baptist (9^{13}); the receiving of Jesus' followers 'in His name' (9^{41}), the importance of faith (11^{23}); the need for total commitment to one's religion (12^{43}); the betrayal by Judas (14^{18}).

2^{17} is perhaps explained by the fact that the words of the scribes were reported to Jesus, for ἀκούσας in this context hardly means that He overheard them there in the company of the people who had castigated Him for consorting with sinners.[2] ἔλεγεν δὲ ὅτι in 7^{20} marks a resumption in the argument about eating unclean foods after the parenthesis in 7^{19b}. 7^{20} is, as Taylor says, a repetition of 7^{15}.[3] 14^{27} like 14^{58} contains two ὅτι sayings, the first the phrase of Jesus, and the second a quotation.

Possible conversion of S to R

In the light of the above we may look at the remaining nine examples marked as S. 1^{37} is described by Taylor as 'so characteristically Markan',[4] while Pesch[5] links it up with the accepted R verses 1^{39}, 1^{45}, and regards 1^{37} as 'certain' R, partly because of its 'exaggerated' 'all seek thee'. Schweizer[6] thinks that Mark has extensively revised his sources, adding 'all' in v. 32, and it would seem that Pesch and Kertelge[7] think that

[1] 15/17R.
[2] Taylor, p. 207: 'ἀκούσας indicates either that Jesus actually heard the scribes speak or that their words were reported to Him. The latter is the better interpretation, since it is not probable that the scribes were present at the meal.'
[3] P. 345.
[4] P. 183.
[5] P. 57.
[6] P. 56.
[7] Kertelge, p. 33.

'all' has been added here as well. Thus it would seem right to move 1³⁷ from S to R.

In 5²³ both Lambrecht[1] and Pesch regard the λέγω ὅτι usage as Marcan redactional style, while Kertelge in analysing the redaction in 5²¹⁻⁴³[2] notes the use of παρακαλεῖν[3] as an echo of the previous use in 5¹⁰,¹²,¹⁷,¹⁸.

The whole verse has two of the syntactical uses examined here, and also significant R vocabulary are θυγάτριον† and σῴζειν. Since the latter implies a more theological meaning than simply healing the body, and the following verse is very obviously R, thus the opening of 5²³ should be transferred to R, and very probably the whole verse.

6⁴ was regarded by R. H. Lightfoot[4] as of great interest, and betraying editorial interpretation. A number of commentators[5] detect either a complete Marcan compilation, as Wendling, or at least editorial work in the opening verses of the chapter, while Kertelge is convinced of the Marcan underlining of δύναμις and σοφία, and their Hellenistic connection. Sundwall would regard the catchword προφήτης as already linking the passage with 6¹⁴⁻¹⁶, but most moderns think that part of 6¹⁴⁻¹⁶ is very clearly R. The opening introductory phrase καὶ ἔλεγεν αὐτοῖς is a well-recognised Marcan introductory phrase to the saying, which Bultmann points out may have been developed from a popular saying.

The form-critics do not fail to stress the contradictions in the whole passage of 6¹⁻⁶ (especially telling is the footnote of R. H. Lightfoot[6] here), so the opening phrase must be regarded as R, with the whole verse much under suspicion as editorial.

6³⁵ᵃ⁷ is also probably redactional on account of its genitive absolute, +λέγω ὅτι. Redactional vocabulary includes ἤδη, ὥρα, πολλά. In view of its position as the opening verse of the feeding miracle, and the bridge from the transitional 6³⁰⁻⁴, 6³⁵ᵃ becomes R.

14²⁵ᵃ is a saying 'loosely attached', but the opening ἀμὴν

---

[1] Lambrecht, p. 95. [2] Pp. 110–20.
[3] P. 112. [4] Pp. 182ff.
[5] Cf. Kertelge, p. 122, n. 488; Bultmann, pp. 75, 102; Dibelius, p. 110; Pesch, p. 59; against Burkill, n. 48, p. 138. [6] P. 188, n. 2.
[7] Best, pp. 5, 26; Schreiber, p. 169; Trocmé, pp. 39, 128, 142, 163; against Bultmann, p. 66, contrasting 6³⁵ with 8¹.

λέγω ὑμῖν ὅτι is probably not just guaranteed as an authentic saying of the Lord, but part of the evangelist's underlining what in his opinion is an important saying of the Lord. Note also the double negative and the very unusual use of ὅταν, a very clear indication of R style. The modern commentators seem to be quite certain of 14[25] as R.[1]

14[71] contains ἄρχομαι + two infinitives of swearing, while 14[69-70] has πάλιν twice, in the secondary material in the Passion story, which may be Marcan work, incorporating new material into the old Passion narrative. Both 14[69] and 14[71] will be considered for transference from S to R in the next section.

12[6] is in the centre of 12[1-12], the parable of the 'Wicked Husbandmen', and with its υἱὸν ἀγαπητόν is possibly S. 6[18][2] shows other redactional features in its imperfect, ἔλεγεν being used as a perfect, plus a typically Marcan use of γάρ explanatory in 6[18, 20], with genitive absolutes in 6[21, 22]. Out of the nine S, six are to be converted to R, while of the three remaining, only one is categorically S.

(f) ἄρχομαι + infinitive

R: 1[45], 2[23], 4[1], 5[20], 6[2, 7, 34, 55], 8[11, 31, 32], 10[28, 32, 41, 47], 11[15], 12[1], 13[5], 14[19, 33] = 20 times
S: 5[17], 14[65, 69, 71], 15[8, 18] = 6 times
Conversion of S into R: 5[17], 14[65, 69, 71], 15[8, 18] = 6 times

ἄρχομαι is often – but not always – a redundant auxiliary. About half of the source and redactional examples are probably pleonastic, but it should not be taken for granted that this is true of all of them, for some are best treated as meant literally. Out of twenty R examples, half[3] of them are so rendered in the N.E.B., but of this number, three[4] seem uncertain. A study of Marcan usage would encourage us to regard ἄρχομαι + inf. as a contributive factor to the dynamic style of the writer.[5] Just as

---

[1] Kertelge, pp. 144–5; Pesch, pp. 69, 92, 101, 119, 149, 152, 183; Schweizer, p. 305; Taylor, p. 547.
[2] Schreiber, p. 181; Taylor, p. 312.
[3] 1[45], 2[23], 4[1], 6[2], 8[31-2], 10[32, 47], 11[15], 13[5] = 10 times.
[4] 1[45], 10[32], 11[15].
[5] J. W. Hunkin, 'Pleonastic ἄρχομαι in the New Testament', *J.T.S.* 25 (July 1924), 395: 'It would, therefore, appear that the extreme frequency

with εὐθύς and πάλιν we have connecting links which may have had their origin in Semitic speech,[1] so it would appear that Mark has taken them over and used them stylistically to good effect. 'Immediately', 'again', 'He began', are some of the evangelist's tools for creating this tension between the divine will and the evil forces struggling against the work of the Kingdom of God. In His teaching,[2] healing, and casting out evil spirits, Jesus has to begin again when impeded, He has to carry on, and recommence the struggle when the crowd tire Him out,[3] or the scribes try to destroy His authority.

(i) ἄρχομαι *with verbs of speaking*

In 1[45], according to the grammatical sense[4] (ὁ δέ) no sooner had the leper been restricted from speaking about his cure and cleansing by Jesus' command to silence than 'he began to proclaim much, and spread abroad the word...' 5[20] is a similar context to 1[45]. καὶ ἀπῆλθεν καὶ ἤρξατο κηρύσσειν ἐν τῇ Δεκαπόλει...'The man went away and began to proclaim in the Decapolis' seems to be what Mark intended us to read.

In four[5] examples the redactor uses ἤρξατο + διδάσκειν, the latter like κηρύσσειν being a much used word, high on the frequency vocabulary test.[6] Three[7] out of four of these usages of διδάσκειν are translated by 'began' in the N.E.B., 6[34], the

with which ἄρχομαι with an infinitive is used by St. Mark is to be attributed partly to the anecdotal character of the narrative he had to record, and partly to his well known non-literary style...yet its presence adds a certain movement and vividness to the narrative.'

[1] ἄρχομαι + διδάσκειν 4 times; κηρύσσειν 2 times (4[1], 6[2,34], 8[31]; 1[45], 5[20]).
[2] See p. 69.   [3] 6[55].
[4] Taylor, p. 190. Allen, p. 64: 'The whole verse probably refers to Christ.' But the use of ὁ δέ meaning a change of subject demands the leper and not Jesus. See M. E. Thrall, *Greek Particles in the New Testament – Tools and Studies*, vol. 3 (Leiden, 1962), where she challenges formidably Zerwick's 'psychologising' theory of Mark's use of δέ, p. 52: 'Secondly, Zerwick fails to take into consideration the fact that the use of the definite article as a demonstrative pronoun *ipso facto* necessitates its combination with δέ and therefore the use of δέ rather than καί as the connective. Mark is particularly fond of this idiom, and uses it some 38 times.'
[5] 4[1], 6[2,34], 8[31]. Pesch, p. 106: 'Die sprachliche Verbindung ἤρξατο λέγειν verrät deutlich die Hand des Evangelisten und dessen mehr umgangssprachlichen Stil.'
[6] See p. 137.   [7] 4[1], 6[2], 8[31].

Feeding of the Five Thousand, being regarded as pleonastic. In the example 4¹ the teaching by the lake-side was impeded by a great crowd, in 6² the preaching in the synagogue caused offence, while after the injunction to silence in 8³⁰, the first of the prophecies of the Passion (8³¹) caused an outburst by Peter, who resisted the idea of a suffering Messiah. 'And now for the first time He told them' (8³¹).

Amongst the verbs of speaking preceded by ἄρχομαι the evangelist employs λέγειν six times.[1] 10²⁸ and 13⁵ are regarded as pleonastic by the N.E.B. translators. Both texts are introductory phrases to sayings, 13⁵ being hypotactic in syntax while 10²⁸ is asyndetic and paratactic.[2] 10³², also dealt with under λέγω ὅτι, is the third prophecy of the Passion, and relates to 8³¹⁻², the first prophecy, where the literal translation seems reasonable. The second prophecy does not use ἄρχομαι. If we understand 10³² literally, i.e. that 'He began to tell them what was to happen to Him', then the first in 8³¹ seems rather strange.

(ii) ἄρχομαι + 2 infinitives

The remaining two[3] examples of ἄρχομαι + λέγειν are used in conjunction with a second infinitive. Commenting on 14¹⁹, Lagrange[4] suggests that ἤρξαντο λυπεῖσθαι καὶ λέγειν is to be understood literally, but the rendering 'one by one they asked Him' does not seem less satisfactory than 'they began to ask Him'. Again, whether 'He began to be horror-struck and distressed' (14³³) is so much better than 'He was horror-struck...' is far from obvious.[5] Whereas in the last two examples the writer has employed direct speech after the infinitive without even a participle + ὅτι, in 14³³, the third case of a double infinitive, he does use the h.p. (λέγει) καὶ λέγει αὐτοῖς...

---

[1] 10²⁸R, 32R, 47R, 13⁵R, 14¹⁹R, 69S. See Pesch, p. 106, nn. 189, 190, where he regards ἄρ. λέγειν as clearly the colloquial style of the evangelist. ἄρχομαι he calls a 'Septuagintism, and typically Markan'. See also Lambrecht, p. 93.　　　　　　　　　　　　　　[2] ἤρξατο λέγειν ὁ Πέτρος αὐτῷ.

[3] 10⁴⁷, 14¹⁹.　　　　　　　　　　　　　　[4] Lagrange, p. xciii.

[5] See p. 226, n. 10, where if we followed Torrey and Moule, perhaps we might translate *'from the start'* he was horrorstruck and distressed'. Again, in 10⁴⁷ 'he shouted at once, and kept on shouting'. In 14¹⁹, 'they were distressed from the outset, and kept on asking him individually' (?).

(iii) ἄρχομαι *with verbs of action*

Out of the seven[1] verbs of action employed by the evangelist with ἄρχομαι three[2] are translated literally by the N.E.B. As some scholars here assert Aramaic influence coming through sources or the bilingual background of the author, it is relevant to note that only two[3] of these seven texts are paratactic in design, while four[4] are constructed with reduced parataxis, and one is obviously a literary sentence, with the infinitive a long way from its auxiliary: καὶ ἤρξαντο ἐπὶ τοῖς κραβάττοις τοὺς κακῶς ἔχοντας περιφέρειν ὅπου ἤκουον ὅτι ἐστίν (6⁵⁵). The latter example, even if it is pleonastic, demonstrates that the author employs ἄρχομαι as an auxiliary, even when he is composing, or paraphrasing, sources. Thus we may seek for the origin of the redundancy in Semitic languages, and argue its presence when source material is under review, but in redaction, the influence of the Septuagint compels the author to think in his first language, Aramaic, when he is trying to write in his second, Greek. In any case, the tendency to use the main verb linked to a double infinitive seems half way to the final stage of its employment as a real auxiliary, and thus pleonastically. However, it would seem unwise to assume, as some do, that because the auxiliary was redundant in Aramaic, it would necessarily be the same in Greek.[5] If we are to think with N. Turner[6] not only of koine Greek, but also of Biblical Greek, which had a strong influence on the koine, then a hybrid language with a mixed and confused tendency is more likely than just Aramaic

---

[1] 2^{23}, $6^{7, 55}$, $8^{11, 32}$, 10^{41}, 11^{15}.   [2] 2^{23}, 8^{32}, 11^{15}.

[3] 6^7, 8^{11}.   [4] 2^{23}, 8^{32}, 10^{41}, 11^{15}.

[5] Doudna, pp. 51–3, 111–17. See pp. 116–17:

'Pleonastic ἄρχομαι may have more than one status. Where it occurs in translation it is to be viewed as a secondary Semitism; where in free composition, it may be a Semitism of thought. The possibility of its belonging to the colloquial usage of the koine must be admitted as well; the frequency in Mark may be due to his non-literary style.'

[6] Moulton, vol. 3, pp. 4–5: 'Biblical Greek is a unique language with a unity and character of its own... When the LXX was established its idioms powerfully influenced free compositions of Biblical Greek.' See also E. P. Sanders, *The Tendencies of the Synoptic Tradition*, Society for New Testament Studies Monograph Series (Cambridge, 1969), ch. 4, 'Diminishing Semitism as a possible tendency of the Tradition', pp. 190–255.

influences. In other words, the most tenable theory would seem that sometimes, as with εὐθύς, πάλιν, so also with ἄρχομαι, the redundancy is reversed, and that which was previously nominal becomes literal and active. In addition, Taylor remarks on Mark's good use of tenses, which would make it unlikely that he uses ἄρχομαι without any thought.

After examining Taylor's statement with particular reference to ἄρχομαι + διδάσκειν and κηρύσσειν the redactor's careful and wide use of tenses would seem to be a correct estimate of Mark's handling of the verb. Out of the seventeen uses of διδάσκειν seven[1] are in the aorist, two periphrastic + participle,[2] four[3] ἄρχομαι + inf., three[4] as a hypotactic participle, and one[5] the present. In the case of κηρύσσειν one employs the aorist,[6] one the subjunctive,[7] and one the future,[8] one is periphrastic,[9] and there are two instances each of the following – ἄρχομαι + inf.,[10] the participle,[11] the infinitive,[12] and the imperfect.[13] In 4¹ ἄρχομαι + inf. (διδάσκειν) is used, followed by the aorist of the same verb in 4², while 6³⁰ (aor.) and 6³⁴ (ἤρξατο) are both from a M.L.C. and S.S.P. Such an examination should warn us to be careful not to assume too quickly that ἤρξατο is an auxiliary or pleonastic.

Professor Moule makes an interesting observation about ἄρχεσθαι 'being used in a comprehensive sense, embracing not only beginning but continuance and end'.[14] In view of the fact that the redactor–editor normally uses his tenses with some discrimination, and that ἄρχεσθαι is used with a high number of verbs of speaking, teaching, and at least once with ἐκβάλλειν (11¹⁵), ἀποστέλλειν (6⁷), and περιφέρειν (6⁵⁵), he may be

---

[1] 1²¹R, 2¹³R, 4²R, 6³⁰R, 9³¹R, 10¹R, 11¹⁷R = 7 times.
[2] 1²²R, 14⁴⁹R.   [3] 4¹R, 6⁶R, ³⁴R, 8³¹R = 4 times.
[4] 5⁶R, 7⁷, 12³⁵R = 3 times (1 quot.).
[5] 12¹⁴.   [6] 6¹².   [7] 14⁹.
[8] 1³⁸.   [9] 1³⁹.   [10] 1⁴⁵, 5²⁰.
[11] 1⁴,¹⁴.   [12] 3¹⁴, 13¹⁰.   [13] 1⁷S, 7³⁶.
[14] Commenting on Torrey's article in *Harvard Theological Studies* 1 (1916), 25ff., which traces the use of ἄρχεσθαι to Aramaic meaning 'from', Moule notes the special peculiarity of Acts 1²¹,²², 10³⁷, Luke 24⁴⁷ also Acts 1¹: πάντων...ὧν ἤρξατο ὁ Ἰησοῦς ποιεῖν τε καὶ διδάσκειν, ἄχρι ἧς ἡμέρας – i.e. a finite verb to express an adverbial idea. 'From the beginning': in Luke 24²⁷ the full meaning might be 'he expounded to them Moses (where he began) and then from all the prophets (with which he continued)' and in Acts 1¹, 'all that Jesus did, from the beginning until...' (Moule, pp. 181f.).

endeavouring to convey something along the lines of the following. Jesus began to teach, but He was interrupted by the concourse, and had to begin again in a boat as a protection from the pressing crowd. Sometimes the opposing forces of the unbelieving questioner, sometimes the popularity and success make the task difficult because of numbers and sheer exhaustion – thus both combined to delay the constant teaching ministry of Jesus, but in spite of all He indefatigably tries to carry out the mission for which He was sent. ἀποστέλλειν in 6⁷ is combined with ἄρχομαι in the 'Mission to the Twelve', περιφέρειν (6⁵⁵) of the sick leaving Jesus without respite in their anxiety to be healed. In other words, Jesus was in demand as preacher, missioner, exorcist, and healer, and although interrupted, and impeded, once He began, He continued, the work until it was accomplished.

Possible conversion of S into R

Of the six source examples[1] with ἄρχομαι five come from the Passion narrative. 5¹⁷ rather stands alone. 5¹⁸⁻¹⁹ is described by Taylor:[2] 'The vocabulary and style are clearly Markan.' 5²⁰ with its ἄρχομαι + κηρύσσειν at the end of a pericope, and a topographical statement, has been marked as R, but it is similar to 5¹⁷ in its use of ἄρχομαι + inf. (ἀπελθεῖν): καὶ ἤρξαντο παρακαλεῖν αὐτὸν ἀπελθεῖν ἀπὸ τῶν ὁρίων αὐτῶν (5¹⁷); καὶ ἀπῆλθεν καὶ ἤρξατο κηρύσσειν ἐν... (5²⁰). 5¹⁷ and 5¹⁸ are possible R from S extracted from the linguistic criterion, whereas 5²⁰ has already been earmarked as R from a literary-linguistic point of view. A good number of commentators, including R. H. Lightfoot,[3] Kertelge,[4] Schreiber,[5] and Trocmé, to name some of the most important, raise the question of the ending of the exorcism at 5¹⁵, with 5¹⁶⁻¹⁷ as a journey 'necessary to bring Jesus back to the other side of the lake, where the third and greatest act of power, the raising of Jairus' daughter, is to be performed, and verses 16 and 17 supply the motive for this'.[6] As both ἀπέρχεσθαι and ὅριον are special R vocabulary, and Kertelge has already drawn our attention to παρακαλεῖν, the transference of 5¹⁷ to R seems very reasonable.

---

[1] 5¹⁷, 14⁶⁵,⁶⁹,⁷¹, 15⁸,¹⁸   [2] P. 284.
[3] Pp. 88ff.   [4] P. 103.   [5] Pp. 166, 177.
[6] Lightfoot, p. 88.

14^65,69,71 and 15^18,8 do not belong to Taylor's 'A' (primitive, Roman, non-Semitic basic account), but to 'B', the secondary, Semitic and Petrine account. ἄρχομαι + inf. is regarded by Taylor as a 'semitism'.[1] His hypothesis is that the 'Denial' (14^54,66-72) and the 'Mockery by the Soldiers' (15^16-20) were intercalated by Mark into the early Roman account which was short and similar to that envisaged by Jeremias and Bultmann, being confined to the arrest, condemnation, the Departure to the Cross, and the Crucifixion.[2] Best is of a similar opinion. Of this particular section he writes: 'Verses 53–72 are again a sandwich of which the central portion is the trial before the High Priest and the first and third parts concern the failure of Peter when put to the test of loyalty; this again suggests a Markan arrangement'.[3]

14^65 and 15^18 are closely related, as they are two of the three mockings which Best and others consider secondary to the main Passion narrative. Best writes: 'There follows the account of the mocking by the soldiers, xv 16–20a, the theme of which repeats that of xiv 65 and appears again in xv 29–32... It is probable that Mark has added each of these accounts of the mocking to the original Passion narrative.'[4] In 14^65 ἤρξαντο is used an an auxiliary to four infinitives, plus four uses of αὐτός.

14^65 is almost certainly partly quoting Is. 50^6 (LXX), and may be one of those texts where the Old Testament is influencing

---

[1] Sanders, *Synoptic Tradition*, p. 255. He warns us that the presence of 'semitisms', asyndeton, the use of the historic present, do not by themselves prove relative or absolute antiquity. 'Although the conclusion that Semitic syntax and grammar do not necessarily prove a tradition to be either relatively or absolutely early doubtless goes against the current of a great deal of modern scholarship, this chapter offers us no other surprises.' He puts the emphasis on 'redaction' or, as in the case of the historic present, on personal preference. Quoting Dalman: 'Mark's fondness for the present tense is an individual trait, like his constant use of εὐθέως.' According to some, it is to be traced to his sources.

[2] Taylor, app. J, pp. 653–64, 'The Construction of the Passion and Resurrection Narrative', esp. pp. 653, 659

[3] Best, p. 94: 'It is unlikely that the denial of Peter formed a part of the original Passion narrative, but some form of the trial must have appeared in order to show the innocence of Jesus and to make clear the grounds of his condemnation.'

[4] Best, p. 96, cites Taylor; Bultmann, pp. 271, 284, etc. P. Winter, *On the Trial of Jesus* (Berlin, 1961), pp. 21f. is in support.

the evangelist and/or his sources. κολαφίζειν, ῥαπίσμασιν, are found only here in the Gospel. The LXX text may have supplied: τὰς δὲ σιαγόνας μου εἰς ῥαπίσματα, τὸ δὲ πρόσωπόν μου. Burkill considers that '14³⁻⁹, ¹²⁻¹⁶, ⁵⁵⁻⁶⁵ were perhaps first introduced to their present contexts by the evangelist himself.' Note also the importance of mockery here and the emphasis on 'prophecy'. Thus, as 14⁶⁵ is the last verse of an intercalated section, on literary grounds it would seem to be R, and strong linguistic grounds corroborate the judgement.[1]

14⁶⁹ and 14⁷⁰ both have the Marcan πάλιν. 14⁷¹,[2] with its double infinitive following ἄρχομαι, contains also a ὅτι followed by direct speech and, like 14⁶⁹, is listed as a possible S to be converted to R in λέγω ὅτι.[3]

15⁸ contains the favoured Marcan ὄχλος, ἀναβαίνειν, ἄρχομαι, καθώς and, as it is not part of the earliest account, it may well betray a redactional hand,[4] according to Taylor. In 15¹⁸ ἄρχομαι is used with ἀσπάζεσθαι (redactional in 9¹⁵), while Taylor also cites ἐμπτύω 10³⁴, 14⁶⁵, τύπτω, κάλαμος 15³⁶. 'Into this description Mark has introduced references to blows and spitting, which recalls the mishandling of Jesus by the high priests' attendants in xiv.65... We must conclude that there was a combination of mimicry and abuse, as Mark records, or that the story has been influenced by xiv.65.'[5]

Thus we may deduce that 14⁶⁹, ⁷¹ are confirmed as R on the grounds of the ἄρχομαι + inf. and the λέγω ὅτι tests. The remaining four texts would also seem on literary and linguistic grounds to have a reasonably strong claim to graduate from S to R.

So far in this chapter the method has proceeded in the main by considering traits which have recommended themselves as Marcan on statistical grounds – thus we have attempted to use these as a possible means of detecting redaction, or confirming

[1] See also Best, pp. 42, 96-7, 149; Bultmann, p. 281; Burkill, pp. 220, 294; Lightfoot, p. 146; Lambrecht, p. 23; Schreiber, pp. 205, 226.
[2] Dibelius, pp. 183, 202; Lightfoot, pp. 101, 127; Lambrecht refers to 14⁶⁸, ⁷² as exhibiting R style, p. 246; Taylor, p. 575. N.B. παιδίσκη occurs only in 14⁶⁹ and 14⁶⁶; and παρεστῶσι in 14⁴⁷, ⁶⁹, ⁷⁰ and 4²⁹ (in Old Testament quotation), 15³⁵, ³⁹; Pesch, p. 146; Schreiber, p. 209.
[3] See p. 79. Vocabulary: ἀναθεματίζειν occurs only here and ὀμνύειν here and in 6²³ᵃ, which might also be R if πολλά is correct text.
[4] Taylor, pp. 581, 586, 663.   [5] P. 586.

the estimate previously made on literary and form-critical lines. The few verses which were not already marked as editorial and temporarily placed in the 'source' category, more often than not have had to be reconsidered as potentially 'redactional' by the following guidelines of syntax: parenthesis, genitive absolute, the participle as main verb, λέγω ὅτι followed by direct speech, πολλά accusative, and ἄρχομαι + inf. The majority – and often that implies almost all – of the verses previously annotated as editorial mainly on literary–form-critical judgements have been thus confirmed as R by means of linguistic and vocabulary criteria.

In what follows in the remainder of the chapter, the statistics are *prima facie* not as impressive as those previously considered, but are sufficiently high to merit further consideration.

(g) εὐθύς AND καὶ εὐθύς

εὐθύς: R:1³ (quot.), ²⁸, 3⁶, 5²ᵃ, ⁴²⁽¹⁾, 6⁵⁴, 7²⁵ = 7 times
S: 1⁴³R, 4¹⁵, ¹⁶, ¹⁷, ²⁹R, 6²⁵, 9²⁰R, ²⁴, 14⁴⁵ = 9 times

εὐθύς is a widely known feature of Marcan usage but its function as a connecting word, and at the same time as a stylistic device which creates movement and liveliness, is subtle enough to escape the attention of many. Mark uses it forty-three times, Matthew eight times, Luke three times, and John three times, so it is an outstanding feature of the Gospel as a whole.

Black[1] suggests that 'an Aramaic expression may in fact be the word which lies behind Mark's εὐθύς'. The Aramaic conjunction suggested could be rendered: 'at that time', 'then', 'thereupon', 'from that hour'. Possible translations are therefore 'immediately', 'thereupon', 'then', or 'at that time'. The origin of εὐθύς may be in the bilingual environment of the author and his sources, but the purpose of the adverb is two-fold: (i) to serve as a literary device to increase tension, and a sense of urgency, and (ii) to fulfil the function of the story-teller's connecting link, as part of the folk-narrator's art, originating from Mark's sources in the oral period. εὐθύς by itself sixteen times would mainly serve as a literary device, but καὶ

[1] Pp. 108–12, p. 109, n. 3.

εὐθύς sometimes is like the colloquial 'and then', which is almost pleonastic.[1]

When the adverb is placed in the middle of the sentence, as it is in most of the sixteen source and redactional examples, we are free of the confusion created by καὶ εὐθύς, where it is sometimes part of the source[2] and sometimes provided by the evangelist to link up his sources. So in analysing R and S, we cannot be absolutely certain at times which is derivative. 1[3] is part of a quotation in the opening redactional section of the Gospel. 1[28] is regarded by Bultmann and Best as fairly certainly R,[3] so it is interesting to note that here parataxis is preserved and there is seeming tautology in πανταχοῦ εἰς ὅλην τὴν περίχωρον τῆς Γαλιλαίας ('everywhere – in all the region of Galilee'). 'Galilee' is a highly redactional word.[4]

A linguistic link in 1[28], 3[6], 5[2a] and 6[54] is the common use of the verb ἐξέρχομαι. So καὶ ἐξῆλθεν... (1[28]); καὶ ἐξελθόντες (3[6]); καὶ ἐξελθόντος αὐτοῦ (5[2]); κ. ἐξελθόντων αὐτῶν (6[54]). Taylor states: 'The use of ἐξελθόντες (cf. i.29, 35, 45, ii.13) belongs to Mark's narrative style.'[5] 3[6] is a strange verse both historically and linguistically, with textual variants chiefly around συμβούλιον ἐδίδουν.[6] Knox's statement that there is no parallel for the meaning 'counsel' as against 'council', and that Latin influence is to be deduced, is in the light of the Dead Sea Scrolls seen to be incorrect. Taylor in citing the Septuagint 4 Macc. 17[17] and the Hebrew סוֹד, would not have been aware of the fact that in the Qumran Hebrew, both 'counsel' and 'council' are possible meanings of סוֹד, which at least gives a traceable linguistic source for the ambiguity without resorting to Latinisms.[7] Trocmé[8]

---

[1] Pleonastic (N.E.B.): 1[3,20,21,23], 2[8], 5[42(1)] = 6 times; literal: 1[12,28,29,43], 2[12], 3[6], 5[2a,30,42(1)], 6[45,54], 8[10], 9[15], 10[52], 14[43], 15[1] = 16 times.

[2] See p. 31.

[3] Best, p. 68: 'Verse 21a, with its reference to Capernaum and v. 28, which is in general terms, may certainly be ascribed to Mark'; Bultmann, p. 341.

[4] 10/12R. Marxsen regards all but one (6[21]) reference to Galilee as R. *Introduction to the New Testament*, trans. G. Buswell (Oxford, 1968), p. 138.

[5] Pp. 223–4.

[6] The chief variant readings include ἐποίησαν, ἐποίουν, and ἐποιοῦντο.

[7] Hymns (D.S.S.) iii, 21. '"Thou didst fashion from the dust unto eternal foundation" (לסוד עולם). יְסוֹד = foundation. סוֹד has taken on the meaning of יְסוֹד' (letter from G. R. Driver, 3rd August 1962).

[8] Pp. 29, 71.

has argued that the reference to the alliance between 'Pharisees and Herodians' is redactional. The presence of ἐξελθόντες, Φαρισαῖοι and εὐθύς would also seem pointers to redactional writing. To be noted also is the Marcan positioning of αὐτόν just before the verb (ἀπολέσωσιν).[1] 5^{2a} is also marked R on account of the genitive absolute,[2] and likewise 6^{54}.[3]

5^{42} καὶ ἐξέστησαν[4] εὐθὺς ἐκστάσει[5] μεγάλη is another example of two redactional words being used with good effect, but broken up by εὐθύς.

Possible conversion of S to R: $1^{43}(?)$, $4^{29}(?)$, $9^{20}(?)$ = 3 times
To remain S: $4^{15, 16, 17}$, 6^{25}, $9^{24}(?)$, 14^{45} = 6 times
Of the remaining nine examples of εὐθύς in the middle of the sentence, three[6] need further consideration as R verses, while six[7] should probably remain as S.

$4^{15, 16, 17}$ all come from the 'Interpretation of the Sower'. Jeremias and Dodd[8] have made out a good linguistic case for regarding the latter as different in style from the paratactic parable, so that another source than that of the original parable must be postulated. The presence of εὐθύς in the centre of these sentences, and also the use of hypotactic participles, the historic present and an unusual employment of λόγος are marked features of its style. Apart from εὐθύς the style is not markedly redactional, neither is the vocabulary. In fact the Greek is too good for that of the redactor–editor, for a number of his characteristic stylistic features are Semitic in origin, and colloquial. It would seem then that $4^{15, 16, 17}$ should remain S.

14^{45} is part of Taylor's 'A' Passion narrative and so should remain as S. 6^{25} is interesting on account of its tautology: εὐθὺς μετὰ σπουδῆς ('immediately with haste'). 9^{24} opens with an asyndetic εὐθύς followed by κράξας + main clause. Probably κράξας is a modified parataxis. The only other use of ἀπιστία is in a redactional verse (6^6), so editorial work may be deduced from these pointers.

1^{43} is omitted by Matthew and Luke, states Taylor,[9] partly

---

[1] P. 120.   [2] P. 62.
[3] P. 62.   [4] 3/4R.
[5] 2/2: 5^{42}, 16^8.   [6] 1^{43}, 4^{29}, 9^{20}.
[7] $4^{15, 16, 17}$, 6^{25}, 9^{24}, 14^{45}.
[8] Jeremias, *Parables of Jesus*, pp. 78f. Dodd, *Parables of the Kingdom*, pp. 13f.
[9] P. 189.

    4-2

because of the strong emotional language[1] used in this verse, one word of which, ἐκβάλλειν,[2] is sometimes used in redactional verses. Bultmann[3] and others regard καὶ ἐμβριμησάμενος αὐτῷ εὐθὺς ἐξέβαλεν αὐτόν as Marcan additions, and certainly v. 43 is not essential to the primitive 'form'. However, the next verse is widely held to be redactional because of its command to silence. The vocabulary of v. 43, ἐκβάλλειν, εὐθύς, two uses of αὐτός, should certainly mark the verse as R. 1[43] then is at least suspect as a source verse, and it should probably be moved from S to R.

4[29] comes at the end of the parable of the 'Seed Growing Quickly', and is one of the few examples from parables which Jeremias regards as possible quotations from the scripture by Christ himself,[4] presumably partly on the grounds that the Joel text quoted is the Hebrew text and not the LXX.[5] However, εὐθύς is not in either the Hebrew or the Greek text. Black is certain that in 4[29] someone was translating from the Aramaic original, and that the peculiarities of the Greek are to be traced to the paraphrasing, or to the translator's inadequacy. The inclusion of εὐθύς depends on whether we think Mark was the translator, or if he worked over his sources. The answer to this question is dependent on how we think Mark worked with his sources. Jeremias in a long footnote suggests that Mark has built up 4[1-34] partly from a collection of three parables, adding to them the short ones in 4[21-5]. More important for our purpose he goes on to say that Mark

[1] Of ἐμβριμάομαι Taylor writes: 'Strong feeling which "boils over" and finds expression appears to be indicated.'

[2] ἐκβάλλειν is to throw out (lit. expel), more or less forcibly, e.g. to banish, to divorce (wife), to depose (king) etc. Normally this verb is used of demons. In 1[12]R it is used of Jesus. To follow v. 43 with the directions in 44 is even for Mark rather strange.

[3] Bultmann, p. 237; Burkill, pp. 82ff.; Kertelge, pp. 62–74 (against R); Schreiber, p. 163; Taylor, p. 188; Lightfoot, p. 71.

[4] Jeremias, *Parables of Jesus*, pp. 31f.

[5] *Ibid.*, p. 32:
'Thus it appears that a strong tendency prevails to elucidate by or introduce references to scripture. This does not, however, exclude the possibility that Jesus himself occasionally referred to Scripture in a parable. In at least two cases this is extremely probable: at the end of the parable of the Mustard Seed...and at the end of the parable of the seed growing of itself (Mark 4.29 cit. Joel 4.13, following the Hebrew text).'

has worked over the framework:[1] πάλιν, ἤρξατο, συνάγεται
(historic present), καὶ ἔλεγεν αὐτοῖς, διδαχή (vv. 1f) are linguistic
characteristics of Mark; he has expanded the details about the
audience in v. 10 by the addition of vv. 11f; v. 34, too, must come
from him, since the phrase χωρὶς δὲ παραβολῆς is a reference to
v. 11b. The three stages of the tradition (Jesus . . . the primitive
Church . . . Mark) are recognizable throughout the whole of Mark's
gospel, but nowhere so clearly as in Chapter 4.[2]

Clearly εὐθύς could be a Marcan improvement of the source, as
editors of journals and newspapers are wont to improve the
articles of their contributors.

9[20] is an interesting text as to its vocabulary, and the use of
participles[3] which are rather profuse. καὶ ἰδών. . . εὐθὺς συνεσπάραξεν αὐτόν, καὶ πεσὼν ἐπὶ τῆς γῆς ἐκυλίετο ἀφρίζων. The
first participle is probably used as a main verb and, suggests
Taylor,[4] may avoid being classified as anacolouthon, if we
take πεσών as a change of subject. συνσπαράσσω is not found
either in LXX or in classical Greek, κυλίομαι† is an ἅπαξ λ. in
Mark and in the N.T., and is a special word introduced either
by him or by the tradition from the Greek Bible. ἀφρίζων probably repeats καὶ ἀφρίζει in v. 18,[5] and in structure reminds one
of 6[6] καὶ περιῆγεν. . . διδάσκων, as ἰδών recalls 7[2] (the participle
used as main verb)[6] – not forgetting three participles also.[7]
Here redactional linguistic pointers seem very marked, and
confirm εὐθύς as a Marcan characteristic. This makes one
think seriously about the remaining examples, However, it
would appear wiser to conclude that 1[43], 4[29a] and 9[20] can be
changed from S to R, but that the remaining six should stay as S.

καὶ εὐθύς: R: 1[12, 20, 21, 23, 29], 2[8, 12], 5[30, 42(1)], 6[45], 8[10], 9[15],
10[52], 11[2], 14[43], 15[1] = 16 times
S: 1[10](?), [18](?), [30](?), 4[2]S, 4[5]S, 5[29]S, 6[27]S, [50](?), 7[35](?),
11[3](?), 14[72](?) = 11 times

καὶ εὐθύς is used both in source and redaction as a connecting
link between pericopes, and also as a catchword.[8] 1[12] links up

---

[1] In this verse 4[29], R vocabulary used are: ὅταν, παραδιδόναι, εὐθύς;
which is not unimpressive. See also Pesch, pp. 101, 173, 179.

[2] Jeremias, *Parables of Jesus*, pp. 78f.

[3] See p. 64.   [4] Pp. 89f.

[5] Sundwall, pp. 59f.; Kertelge, pp. 174ff.; Schweizer, p. 187.

[6] See p. 69.   [7] N.B. also ἐπὶ τῆς γῆς.   [8] Sundwall, pp. 7–8.

with 1¹⁰ (not only by κ. ε. but also by τὸ πνεῦμα) and at the same time εἰς τὴν ἔρημον in 1¹² looks forward to 1¹³ ἐν τῇ ἐρήμῳ. The source verse 1¹⁰, from which καὶ εὐθύς may well be drawn, probably should also be seriously considered as possible R from its literary quasi-chiasmus structure:

καὶ εὐθὺς ἀναβαίνων ἐκ τοῦ ὕδατος εἶδεν (1¹⁰)
καὶ εὐθὺς τὸ πνεῦμα αὐτὸν ἐκβάλλει εἰς τὴν ἔρημον (1¹²)

ἀναβαίνων ἐκ and ἐκβάλλει εἰς may be in polarity, while ὕδατος and ἔρημον form a good contrast.

1¹⁸ and 1²⁰ are similarly related, which raises the question of the redactional possibility of 1¹⁸ as well as 1²⁰.[1] 1¹⁸ reads: καὶ εὐθὺς ἀφέντες τὰ δίκτυα ἠκολούθησαν αὐτῷ.[2] 1²⁰ καὶ εὐθὺς ἐκάλεσεν αὐτούς. καὶ ἀφέντες τὸν πατέρα αὐτῶν is in this case a sophisticated repetition of ἀφέντες and ἀκολουθεῖν in 1¹⁸, linked with ἐκάλεσεν. 'Leaving the nets' anticipates 'leaving their father'; and while 'they followed him' in 1¹⁸, in 1²⁰ 'he called them' (their brothers).[3]

1²¹ᵇ,²³,²⁹ provides a repetition of συναγωγή but a pleasing variation in the preposition gives continuity and variety: καὶ εὐθύς...εἰς τὴν συναγωγήν (1²¹); καὶ εὐθὺς ἐν τῇ συναγωγῇ (1²³); κ. ε. ἐκ τῆς συναγωγῆς (1²⁹).

Both 2⁸ and 2¹² are good examples of the combination of indirect and direct speech, the second using λέγω ὅτι, the first expressing the inner thoughts of others through the question of Jesus. 5³⁰ καὶ εὐθὺς ὁ 'Ιησοῦς ἐπιγνοὺς ἐν ἑαυτῷ is very similar in its opening to 2⁸ καὶ εὐθὺς ἐπιγνοὺς ὁ 'Ιησοῦς τῷ... In the former verse the participle stylistically used as an object is also to be noted: τὴν ἐξ αὐτοῦ δύναμιν ἐξελθοῦσαν;[4] as also the position of αὐτοῦ and the repeated ἐξ.

In the case of 5⁴² the second εὐθύς is placed in the middle of

---

[1] Probably 1³⁰ presents something similar in its κατέκειτο πυρέσσουσα... καὶ ε. λέγουσιν (impers.) αὐτῷ περὶ αὐτῆς, where λέγουσιν is one of those ambiguous impersonals.

[2] κ. ε. ἀνέβλεψεν, καὶ ἠκολούθει αὐτῷ ἐν τῇ ὁδῷ (10⁵²); see also R. Pesch, 'Berufung und Sendung, Nachfolge und Mission, Eine Studie zu Mk. 1, 16–20', Zeitschrift für Katholische Theologie, 91 (1969), 1–31.

[3] See Zerwick, Unters. zum Markus-Stil, 'Chiasmus', pp. 125–6. For other possible passages he suggests 1⁵,¹⁰,³⁴, 5⁴,⁽²⁶⁾, 6¹²,⁵⁵,⁵⁶, 7⁸,¹⁹, (9¹⁹), 9⁴⁰, 11¹⁵, 12¹⁴ᵇ,⁴⁰, 13⁹, 14⁵⁸, 9⁵⁰.

[4] Part. here is separated from its adjuncts, which is normal in classical Greek. See Blass–Debrunner, p. 250.

the sentence – a nice contrast to the first, which is at the beginning – instead of repeating κ. ε. as so often. 6⁴⁵ and 8¹⁰ are topographical links, both containing μαθηταὶ αὐτοῦ, πλοῖον, ἐμβάς¹ (ἐμβῆναι). 6⁵⁴ also uses ἐπιγνόντες (2⁸, 5³⁰), while 9¹⁵ has the familiar ὄχλος and an unusual word, ἐκθαμβεῖσθαι (9¹⁵, 14³³, 16⁵), which is rare in the N.T. and is derived from the Greek Old Testament.

11²,³ are part of a narrative, linguistically close to 14¹³⁻¹⁶, both of which are thought by Taylor to have been 'composed by Mark on the basis of tradition'. 11² as Taylor observes 'contains familar Markan words',² while ἐφ᾽ ὃν οὐδεὶς οὔπω ἀνθρώπων ἐκάθισεν omitted in Matthew may be an expansion by Mark in the light of Zech. 9⁹.

11³ καὶ εὐθὺς αὐτὸν ἀποστέλλει πάλιν ὧδε is textually complicated, but is probably correct. Once again αὐτόν comes before the verb and πάλιν³ is placed at the end of the sentence.

14⁴³ᵃ, although part of Taylor's 'A' strand, is found at a break in the narrative, and thus regarded by him⁴ as an editorial phrase, καὶ εὐθύς perhaps being in the original, which Mark altered to καὶ εὐθὺς ἔτι αὐτοῦ λαλοῦντος, which is almost identical with 5³⁵R ἔτι αὐτοῦ λαλοῦντος... 15¹ᵃ, καὶ εὐθὺς πρωΐ⁵ is probably all that Mark added to his source, but one notices immediately συμβούλιον, which has been already discussed as a problem in 3⁶R.

Possible R: 1¹⁰,¹⁸,³⁰ᵇ, 6⁵⁰ᵃ, 7³⁵(?), 11³ᶜ, 14⁷² = 7 times
To remain S: 1⁴², 4⁵, 5²⁹, 6²⁷ = 4 times

1⁴² and 4⁵ᵇ because of their parataxis should remain S, the second text coming from the 'Parable of the Sower', which is as near to the Aramaic words of Christ as is humanly possible.

---

¹ 2/4 R.

² Cited by Taylor, p. 453. οἱ μαθηταὶ αὐτοῦ 2¹⁵; ὑπάγω 1⁴⁴; κώμη 6⁶; εὐθύς 1¹⁰; εἰσπορεύομαι 1²¹; δέω 3²⁷; οὔπω 4⁴⁰; καθίζω 9³⁵; κατέναντι 12⁴¹, 13³.

³ See pp. 96ff.

⁴ P. 558: 'Mark's hand is visible in εὐθύς (v. i.10) and in ἔτι αὐτοῦ λαλοῦντος (v. 35), by which the story is linked with that of Gethsemane.'

⁵ Sundwall, p. 82: 'I merely want to point out εὐθύς v. 72 since it returns in 15¹ as the response word, and at the same time confirms the direct link with this verse which is of course also established by the chronological order (v. 72 Hahnenschrei xv, i, πρωΐ vgl. Lietzmann, *Der Prozess Jesu*).'

Both $1^{10\,1}$ and 1^{18} in addition to καὶ εὐθύς have a literary chiastic construction: ἀναβαίνων and καταβαίνων; ἐκ τοῦ ὕδατος and τὸ πνεῦμα εἰς αὐτόν, σχιζομένους τοὺς οὐρανούς and ὡς περιστεράν (1^{10}); ἀφέντες and ἠκολούθησαν (1^{18}). The vocabulary test yields both ἀναβαίνειν and καταβαίνειν (1^{10}) and ἀκολουθεῖν (1^{18}).[2]

$1^{30b\,3}$ is also a possible source verse in (m), later to be considered for transference to R. In addition to καὶ εὐθύς, to be noted are the present historic and two uses of αὐτός. As Wellhausen[4] pointed out, Ch. 1 is rather heavily edited. In this early part of the Gospel, one finds such brief and sketchy pericopae that they do not really qualify for such description. In other words, the redactor–editor may well be summarising sources, and abbreviating his fuller Aramaic notes. Trocmé remarks 'a redactional note, based on a simple reminiscence'.[5]

In 5^{29} we find a primitive verb ἰάομαι, not the more frequent θεραπεύω or the ecclesiastical σῴζειν, so it should remain S. 6^{27} is more difficult, inasmuch as ἀποκεφαλίζειν $(6^{16}R)$, and ἐπιτάσσειν (1^{27}) are found elsewhere in R verses, but as the whole style of the pericope is not outstandingly redactional in its syntax, and the other verse has been left S, it has been decided to do the same with 6^{27}.

6^{50} is also later considered for transference from S to R, on account of its γάρ explanatory clause. Pesch comments on its imperative with prohibition as editorial in style, while Best considers three of the verses from this section 6^{45-52} as R (47, 48, and 52). Lambrecht in discussing 13^{6a} with its comparable λέγω ὅτι and ἐγώ εἰμι rejects the view that ἐγώ εἰμι is a recognition-formula.[6] The vocabulary used in this verse (γάρ, εὐθύς, λαλεῖν, κ. λ. α., φοβεῖσθαι) would warrant it being upgraded from S to R.

7^{35} from the 'Deaf and Dumb Man Healed' is at least important for the Marcan arrangement in its emphasis on the

---

[1] Bultmann, pp. 245–53; Lambrecht, p. 21; Marxsen, pp. 31, 33, 38; Pesch, pp. 148, 161; Schreiber, pp. 45, 48.

[2] Lambrecht, pp. 30, 56, 83; Pesch, pp. 57–8, 98; Trocmé, p. 158.

[3] Lightfoot, p. 69, n. 1.

[4] Dibelius, p. 44; Kertelge, pp. 60–2.

[5] P. 41, n. 151, pp. 103, 123.

[6] Best, p. 78; Kertelge, p. 100; Lambrecht, pp. 98–9; Pesch, pp. 110, 120; Schreiber, p. 97.

fulfilment of the Messianic prophecy from Isaiah 35[5] (LXX), but also is influenced by the redactor's obsession with the apostles' deafness and blindness to the divinity of Jesus. Most commentators consider 7[31] and 7[36] to be R, but some would regard the primitive story as ending in 7[35], with 7[37] being a Marcan conclusion influenced by the opening of Genesis and also the 'stammerer' from Isaiah. V. 34*b* is R on account of its parenthesis (a). ἀνοίγεσθαι, δεσμός, are used only here in the Gospel, while γλῶσσα is used only in this pericope. μογιλάλος is found only once in LXX from the Isaianic prophecy. λαλεῖν is a special Marcan word. Note 7[35] ἐλάλει ὀρθῶς and almost a play upon words in 7[37][1] ἀλάλους λαλεῖν.

11[3] comes from the doublet pericope 11[1–11] (cf. 14[13–16]). Already marked as R are 11[1–2a, 9a, 10, 11]. Taylor's[2] comparison of the two similar passages reveals 11[1, 2, 3, 4, 6] as closest to 14[13, 14, 16]. Note particularly 11[1, 2, 3].

11[1–6]	14[13–16]
1. ἀποστέλλει δύο τῶν	13. ἀποστέλλει δύο τῶν
μαθητῶν αὐτοῦ	μαθητῶν αὐτοῦ
2. καὶ λέγει αὐτοῖς	καὶ λέγει αὐτοῖς
ὑπάγετε εἰς τὴν κώμην . . .	ὑπάγετε εἰς τὴν πόλιν
καὶ . . . εὑρήσετε . . .	καὶ ἀπαντήσει ὑμῖν
3. εἴπατε	εἴπατε
ὁ κύριος	14. ὁ διδάσκαλος

11[3b] καὶ εὐθὺς ἀποστέλλει πάλιν ὧδε seems modelled on 14[13] and 11[1]. Schweizer seems to think that the Passion narrative has been modelled on 11[1–6]. On the contrary, as the Passion narrative is the one primitive continuous narrative into which Mark intercalated his secondary sources, the opposite seems nearer the truth. The more formative πόλιν and διδάσκαλος have been replaced by κώμην and κύριος.[3]

If we think of the narrative of 11[1–6] as historical, then κύριος

---

[1] Particularly Dibelius, pp. 72, 76, 80ff., 93; Lightfoot, p. 72; see also Schweizer, p. 154, who thinks v. 37 is a conclusion of 'a series of miracle-stories'; N.B. for less certain and opposing views Trocmé, p. 39; A. Richardson, *The Miracle Stories of the Gospels* (London, 1941), p. 82; Kertelge, pp. 157–61.   [2] P. 536.

[3] The infrequency of κύριος in Mark should make us ready to see it as 'Sir', if historical, and yet carrying in the mind of the redactor a more exalted religious meaning as well.

is enigmatic, but the influence of the redactor and the Zechariah prophecy make κύριος much nearer to κύριος in St Matthew, the lord of the Church. Mark's style is clear in 11^{3b}: καί, εὐθύς, present historic, πάλιν, ὧδε. Almost every word of this clause could be called R style. So certainly 11^{3c} and possibly 11^3 are R.[1]

14^{72} is the last verse of the powerful 14^{66-72}, where history, drama, moralism and literary skills blend. The redactor's style is visible in $14^{66, 69, 71}$. High frequency R vocabulary are εὐθύς, φωνεῖν (2 times), λέγω ὅτι. Lambrecht also comments on ἀλέκτωρ.[2] Note also the literary πρίν, but most of all Schweizer's judgement must be accepted: 'The Markan[3] expression (eu-thus)' just then 'suggests that the dramatic conclusion wherein the rooster crows immediately after the third denial (although chickens were not permitted in Jerusalem) should be attributed to Mark'.

In view of the fact that the redactor is using consciously or unconsciously a feature of his source style, the statistics cannot be as high as in the case of parenthesis and the other five guides already discussed, but the amended figures are significantly positive: εὐθύς – 10R, 6S; καὶ εὐθύς – 23R, 4S = 33R, 10S.

(h) πάλιν

R: $2^{1, 13}, 3^{1, 20}, 4^1, 5^{21}, 7^{14, 31}, 8^{1, 13}, 10^{1(2), 10, 24, 32}, 11^{27}, 14^{40} = 17$ times

S: $8^{25}, 11^3, 12^4, 14^{39, 61, 69, 70(2)}, 15^{4, 12, 13} = 11$ times

εὐθύς, πάλιν and ἄρχομαι have two points in common: they tend to be either redundant or pleonastic, and they are probably all three Semitic in origin, yet have developed a function in Greek which is not simply identical with that of its Aramaic original. As with εὐθύς the question arises what exactly the redactor is intending as the function of this conjunction.

Wellhausen and Black[4] consider the possibility of Aramaic

---

[1] Bultmann, p. 261; Lambrecht, pp. 31–6; Pesch, pp. 101, 114, 173, 200; Trocmé, pp. 117–18.   [2] P. 246.

[3] P. 328; see also Dibelius, pp. 202, 213ff.

[4] J. Wellhausen, *Einleitung in die drei ersten Evangelien*, 2nd ed. (Berlin, 1911), p. 21; Black, p. 112.

influence with an inferential meaning like 'then', 'further', 'thereupon', as against 'again'. Lagrange[1] states that πάλιν is always iterative. C. H. Turner is of the opinion that the meaning is often 'again' rather than 'next' or 'once more'.[2] Black points out that 15^{13} must be translated: 'They thereupon shouted',[3] and regards it as a test case.

All the examples except one are translated by the N.E.B. The majority of the renderings come under the iterative meaning: 'again',[4] 'once more',[5] 'on another occasion',[6] 'insisted'.[7] The classical meaning 'back' (spatial) is given six times.[8]

At least half of the redactional uses of πάλιν refer back to previous texts: 2^{13} ($1^{16, 35, 45}$), 3^1 (1^{21}), 3^{30} (3^7), 4^1 (2^{13}, 3^7), 7^{31} (7^{24}), 8^1 (7^{33}), 8^{13} (8^{10}), 10^{32} (10^{10}), 11^{27} (11^1). Approximately half of the total of the uses of πάλιν are with verbs of movement, in the main compounds of ἔρχομαι,[9] while a considerable number are with verbs of teaching or argument and dialogue.[10] A high proportion come from the Passion narrative in Ch. 14, and belong to the denials of Peter, and the trial scenes with interrogations and repeated questions. Three[11] of the instances are associated with the journeys of Jesus, four of them with His 'house', or centre of operations,[12] eight with the teaching mission,[13] only one with healing,[14] and twelve with the Cross and Passion.[15] The emphasis is on the teaching ministry and the Crucifixion.

The main function of πάλιν, therefore, is as a linking word, referring back to the previous incidents of a similar character (teaching, journeys, missions). Its function appears to be twofold: it helps to weave together the disjointed pericopae, making a 'Gospel' which moves on from stage to stage, its ultimate point being the Passion and Resurrection. In addition, the result of the constant use of a word which in the main is translated with

---

[1] P. xcviii. [2] *J.T.S.* 29 (April 1928), pp. 283–7.
[3] Pp. 112f. [4] $8^{13, 25}$, $10^{1 (1)}$, 12^4, $14^{69, 70 (2)}$, $15^{4, 12}$ = 9 times.
[5] 2^{13}, 3^{20}, $10^{1 (1)}$, 11^{27}, 14^{39} = 5 times.
[6] 3^1; 4^1, 7^{14}, 8^1 = 4 times.
[7] 10^{24}. [8] 2^1, 5^{21}, 7^{31}, 11^{13}, 15^{13}, 14^{40} = 6 times.
[9] εἰσέρχομαι: 2^1, 3^1; συνέρχ.: 3^{20}, 5^{21}; ἐξέρχ.: 2^{13}, 7^{31}; ἔρχεται: 11^{27}, 14^{40}.
[10] διδάσκειν: 4^1, 10^1; ἐπερωτᾶν: 10^{10}, 14^{61}, 15^4.
[11] 5^{21}, 7^{31}, 8^{13}. [12] 2^1, 3^{20}, $10^{1, 10}$.
[13] 2^{13}, 3^1, 4^1, 7^{14}, 8^1, $10^{1, 24, 32}$ = 8 times. [14] 8^{25}.
[15] $11^{3, 27}$, 12^4, $14^{39, 40, 61, 69, 70 (2)}$, $15^{4, 12, 13}$ = 12 times.

iterative force is to give urgency, drive and liveliness to the narrative, concentrating in particular on the itinerary and teaching mission of Jesus, and His ordeal in the trial scenes.

Passages containing πάλιν which are confirmed as R by reference to linguistic characteristics discussed elsewhere in this chapter are the following: with gen. absolute (8^1);[1] with redundant part. (8^{13});[2] with ἤρξατο + διδάσκειν (4^1);[3] with προσκαλεσάμενος (7^{14}).[4]

Possible conversion of S to R: 11^{3b}, $14^{39, 61, 69, 70(2)}$, $15^{12-13(?)}$ = 8 times

To remain S: 8^{25}, 12^4, 15^4 = 3 times

The majority of these texts are from the Passion narrative, so it will simplify matters if the three other texts are discussed first. 8^{25} and 12^4 come from pericopae which apart from the seams appear free of redaction, so they have been left as S. 14^{61} and 15^4, as part of Taylor's primitive strand ('A'), have been marked as S, but it should be stated that 15^4 is more secure than 14^{61}, for Taylor puts 14^{55-64} in brackets as these verses may well have been intercalated by Mark into a previous structure, i.e. 14^{53a}, $15^{1, 3-5, 15}$. Best comments on the unifying of ὁ Χριστός and ὁ υἱὸς τοῦ εὐλογητοῦ by Mark,[5] and a number of recent commentators regard 14^{61-2} as secondary, and influenced by later Christian theological reflection, so 14^{61} is by no means impossible as R.[6]

14^{39} comes from the Gethsemane scene, 14^{32-42}, which is thought by the critics to be an amalgam of two separate accounts,[7] and belongs to Taylor's 'B' strand. The redactor's style seems evident elsewhere in this section. To be noted are the near repetition of πάλιν ἀπελθών (14^{39}) in the next verse. καὶ πάλιν ἐλθών... (14^{40}), the parenthesis ἦσαν γάρ... αὐτῶν, the Marcan ἅπαξ λ. καταβαρυνόμενοι† (14^{40}) and the closeness in thought and language to the Transfiguration in οὐκ ᾔδεισαν

---

[1] See p. 62.
[2] See p. 100.
[3] See p. 81.
[4] 8/9R.
[5] 'Now Mark brings these two titles together', p. 95. Burkill, p. 227; Dibelius, pp. 192–3; Lambrecht, pp. 52, 98, 180, 182–4, 189, 192–3, 233, 252; Pesch, p. 227; Schreiber, p. 238; Schweizer, p. 326.
[6] Bultmann, p. 279: 'still later Mk. $14^{3-9, 32-42}$ and in all probability vv. 55–64 were inserted'.
[7] Best, p. 92; Lambrecht, p. 222; Schweizer, p. 310.

τί ἀποκριθῶσιν αὐτῷ (cf. 9⁵). R vocabulary in 14³⁹ includes πάλιν, ἀπέρχεσθαι and προσεύχεσθαι.

14⁶⁹‚⁷⁰ᵃ⁽²⁾ come from Peter's denial, 14⁶⁶⁻⁷², and as stated, are part of Taylor's 'B', which is regarded by him as secondary, and therefore bracketed. 14⁶⁹ is confirmed as R on linguistic criteria by ἤρξατο+λέγειν,[1] and also λέγω ὅτι.[2] The first πάλιν is quickly repeated with a deliberate change of tense, plus Mark's favoured ὁ δέ as demonstrative (ὁ δὲ πάλιν ἠρνεῖτο). To be noted also are ἤρξατο + two infinitives[3] + ὅτι followed by direct speech in 14⁷¹, and εὐθύς in 14⁷².[4]

15⁴‚¹²⁻¹³ᵃ come from the trial scene before Pilate (Taylor's 'B' strand). Taylor writes: 'The narrative of the Trial before Pilate (xv. 1–15) was expanded, possibly by 2, in some sense a doublet of 3–5, and by the story of Barabbas (6–14), and after the sentence the account of the Mockery by the Soldiers (xv. 16–20) was appended.'[5] Additional linguistic criteria to confirm the conversion of 15¹²⁻¹³ to R are possibly 'the explanatory comment in 15¹⁰ discussed elsewhere, common in Mark'; so Taylor.[6] Linguistically notable are ἀποκριθείς and ἔλεγεν αὐτοῖς, also 'King of the Jews', a strange title in itself,[7] and so underlined by Mark that even if it is hidden in the tradition, Mark seems to introduce it as much as possible. Almost identical with this verse is 10²⁴R ὁ δὲ Ἰησοῦς ἀποκριθεὶς λέγει αὐτοῖς.[8]

Seven instances out of eleven would seem to be possible R which makes the final statistical count: 25R 3S, which is on a par with the first six guides to linguistic usage.

(i) 'REDUNDANT' PARTICIPLE

R: 1³⁵, 7²⁴, 8¹³‚²⁸, 10¹‚²⁴‚⁵¹, 12¹²‚³⁵‚⁴², 14⁴⁰, 15² = 12 times
S: 2¹⁴, 3³³, 7²⁵, 9⁵, 11¹⁴, 12²⁶, 14⁴⁵‚⁴⁸, 15¹², 16¹ = 10 times

[1] P. 86.
[2] P. 79. Schweizer, pp. 326ff.; Lambrecht, p. 157, comments on μετά+ acc.   [3] Pp. 85ff.   [4] P. 96.
[5] P. 663. As vv. 3–5 are regarded as primary and v. 2 secondary, 15⁴ remains S.
[6] P. 582; Lambrecht, p. 241; Pesch, pp. 127, 146, 200, 235; Schweizer, pp. 334ff.
[7] Pesch, p. 235 'Jews'; cf. 7³ᶠ·, 'King of the Jews' is according to Pesch not the title of Jesus, but a 'ridiculing' title.
[8] N.B. also ἅπαξ λ. vocabulary: δύσκολος, θαμβεῖσθαι, τρυμαλιά.

The twelve R examples involve four verbs: ἀναστάς (1³⁵, 7²⁴, 10¹), ἀφείς (8¹³, 12¹²), ἀποκριθείς (10²⁴,⁵¹, 12³⁵, 15²), and ἐλθών (14⁴⁰, 12⁴²), to which we may add λέγων (8²⁸), and perhaps ten[1] examples already discussed under λέγω ὅτι, in half of which the participle seems to be redundant.[2]

As 1³⁵ emphasises the early hour of rising, ἀναστάς does not seem to be pleonastic.[3] In 7²⁴ it appears to be redundant, but as in 1³⁵ is followed by ἀπῆλθεν; 10¹ καὶ ἐκεῖθεν ἀναστὰς ἔρχεται εἰς τὰ ὅρια τῆς..., where ἀναστάς is translated by the N.E.B. 'leaving', is almost identical with the Greek of 7²⁴ ἐκεῖθεν δὲ ἀναστὰς ἀπῆλθεν εἰς τὰ ὅρια.

8¹³ and 12¹² share ἀπῆλθεν with 1³⁵ and 7²⁴. These two former examples are topographical links closing sections, and relating the isolated pericopae to each other. There seems no good reason for regarding them as redundant since they are an essential part of the rather crude and unsophisticated seams which give the 'Gospel' a framework of topography of some kind. 8¹³ is reinforced as R linguistically by its use of πάλιν, and 12¹² by parenthesis, and γάρ explanatory.[4]

12⁴² and 14⁴⁰ are not pleonastic, according to the N.E.B., and are both found in Marcan compilations. The second half of 12⁴² is a small parenthesis, and linguistically the whole section shows a certain literary flavour, according to Taylor. Examples of this are the alliteration in v. 41, πολλοὶ πλούσιοι ἔβαλλον πολλά (discussed under πολλά acc.), followed by this seeming redundant participle in v. 42, which is in fact not to be regarded as such, and the use of the present, imperfect, and aorist of βάλλω including the following: πάντες γὰρ ἐκ τοῦ περισσεύοντος αὐτοῖς ἔβαλον, αὕτη δὲ ἐκ τῆς ὑστερήσεως αὐτῆς πάντα ὅσα εἶχεν ἔβαλεν,... (12⁴⁴).

14⁴⁰ has already been discussed under πάλιν, and is placed at the opening of a sentence of which the second half is a parenthesis, accompanied by other redactional traits.[5]

The remaining four[6] examples which employ ἀποκριθείς are more likely to be really pleonastic. If one recalls that the ancients

---

[1] 1¹⁵,⁴⁰, 2¹², 3¹¹, 5³⁵, 8²⁸, 9¹¹, 13⁶, 14⁵⁷,⁵⁸ = 10 times.
[2] Literal: 1⁴⁰, 2¹², 13⁶, 14⁵⁷,⁵⁸ = 5 times; pleonastic: 1¹⁵, 3¹¹, 5³⁵, 8²⁸, 9¹¹ = 5 times.
[3] Three adverbs: πρωΐ, ἔννυχα, λίαν.   [4] See pp. 47, 127.
[5] See appendix 1, p. 147.   [6] 10²⁴,⁵¹, 12³⁵, 15².

taught by question and answer, that μαθητής[1] and διδάσκειν[2] are highly redactional words, and that the redactor was in addition probably influenced by the Greek Old Testament, such a formalised and set phraseology is not surprising in a non-literary author. 12³⁵, where διδάσκειν is employed, is still pleonastic as it begins the pericope, but another possibility emerges. If one bears in mind the last phrase of the seam in 12³⁴, καὶ οὐδεὶς οὐκετι ἐτόλμα αὐτὸν ἐπερωτῆσαι,[3] then καὶ ἀποκριθεὶς ὁ Ἰησοῦς ἔλεγεν διδάσκων ἐν τῷ ἱερῷ could be a conscious response word to ἐπερωτῆσαι and at the same time the natural pre-empting of διδάσκειν. Our evangelist does not always give a logical sequence, and it would not be the first time he anticipated!

Possible conversion of S to R: 2¹⁴, 3³³ᵃ, 7²⁵, 11¹⁴, 14⁴⁸, 15¹² = 6 times

To remain S: 9⁵, 12²⁶, 14⁴⁵, 16¹ = 4 times

2¹⁴, as Taylor and Zerwick point out, has close literary affinity with 1¹⁶⁻¹⁸. In Zerwick's comparison[4] of the two accounts, what corresponds to ἀναστάς in 1¹⁶⁻¹⁸ is καὶ εὐθύς. 2¹³ is highly redactional in vocabulary[5] and has a very simple sentence construction, plus the Marcan διδάσκειν. The N.E.B. translates ἀναστάς in 2¹⁴, for if Levi was 'sitting' it was quite in order for him to get up, but one still has the suspicion that ἀναστάς is also placed here for balance and rhythm in the sentence.

3³³ᵃ after ἀποκριθεὶς αὐτοῖς λέγει has a rhetorical question, which is probably Mark's form of indirect speech. Some form critics[6] assert that 3³⁵ has been added later, the original pericope ending at ἀδελφοί μου. Sundwall[7] draws attention to the catchwords: ἡ μήτηρ αὐτοῦ... ἰδοὺ ἡ μήτηρ σου... ἡ μήτηρ μου...

The word ἔξω (3³¹) reminds us of 4¹¹, while two participles

---

[1] 29/46R.   [2] 15/17R.   [3] 14/25R.

[4] P. 65. καὶ παράγων...εἶδεν Σίμωνα   καὶ παράγων εἶδεν Λευὶν...
καὶ Ἀνδρέαν
ἀμφιβάλλοντας ἐν τῇ θαλάσσῃ   καθήμενον ἐπὶ τὸ τελώνιον
καὶ εἶπεν αὐτοῖς ὁ Ἰησοῦς   καὶ λέγει αὐτῷ,
Δεῦτε ὀπίσω μου,   Ἀκολούθει μοι.
καὶ εὐθύς...ἠκολούθησαν   καὶ ἀναστὰς ἠκολούθησεν
αὐτῷ. (1¹⁸.)   αὐτῷ. (2¹⁴.)

[5] Kuhn, p. 89; Kertelge, p. 50, n. 56; Neirynck, p. 77; Pesch, p. 93; Schweizer, p. 64; Sundwall, p. 15; Trocmé, p. 158.

[6] Dibelius, pp. 63f.   [7] P. 23.

with the thrice used αὐτός, and καλοῦντες αὐτόν, not forgetting ἰδοὺ ἡ μήτηρ...(32) ἴδε ἡ μήτηρ and αὐτόν (34), indicate editorial and literary handiwork.[1]

7²⁵ recalls 5²².[2] The redactional linguistic characteristics ἀλλ' εὐθύς and the parenthesis in 7²⁶ have already been commented on. The way in which clauses are suspended and the facts tumble out with important details added later, and also his use of the double participle, are quite in keeping with the redactor's method and style. (N.B. εὐθύς, ἀκούειν, πνεῦμα ἀκάθαρτον, θυγάτριον are R vocabulary.)

11¹⁴ καὶ ἀποκριθεὶς εἶπεν is regarded by Taylor as plainly redundant. The previous explanatory ὁ γὰρ καιρὸς οὐκ ἦν σύκων is, as Taylor suggests, 'best ascribed to Mark himself, since such explanations are in accordance with his style'.[3] Stylistic R are double negative, ἀκούειν and μαθηταὶ αὐτοῦ.

14⁴⁸, coming from Taylor's 'B' strand, does not come within what Best calls the 'original core', vv. 43–6, and is presumably part of the 'various sayings and peripheral incidents'[4] which Mark has added to the actual arrest, i.e. 14⁴³⁻⁵². In 14⁴⁹ we find a reference to Jesus 'teaching in the temple'. Taylor notes the redundancy of ἀποκριθείς here in its context, and states that the main problem is that the question calls for another audience, which is recognised by the other evangelists.[5]

15¹²ᵃ, already transferred from S to R on account of its πάλιν,[6] comes from Taylor's 'B' strand, section 15¹⁻¹⁵, which exhibits a curious combination of what Taylor calls 'Semitisms' and 'Latinisms'.[7] δέ, πάλιν and ἔλεγεν αὐτοῖς[8] are familiar redactional

---

[1] Best, p. 117, n. 2; Lambrecht, p. 92; Schweizer, p. 83: 'There is scarcely any other passage where Mark's pen is as evident as it is here [3³¹⁻⁵]'; Trocmé, p. 66, n. 255, pp. 105ff.

[2] ἐλθοῦσα προσέπεσεν πρὸς τοὺς πόδας αὐτοῦ (7²⁵); ἰδὼν αὐτὸν πίπτει πρὸς τοὺς πόδας αὐτοῦ (5²²). Kertelge, p. 151; Schreiber, p. 171.

[3] P. 460; Pesch, pp. 73–4, 85, 92; Schreiber, pp. 134–5; Swete, p. 254; Trocmé, p. 85.   [4] Pp. 94f.

[5] P. 560. Lambrecht, p. 36, n. 1, pp. 92, 183 (N.B. μετά + gen.).

[6] See pp. 99ff.

[7] ἀποκριθεὶς λέγει, ἤρξατο + inf. and ἀποκριθεὶς κ. ἔλεγεν are classified as 'Semitisms' and τὸ ἱκανὸν ποιῆσαι + φραγελλώσας as 'Latinisms'. See Moule, pp. 171f.: 'There is the subtle problem of distinguishing between *direct* Semitisms (owing their existence to the direct impact of Hebrew or Aramaic upon the writer's vocabulary) and *indirect secondary* Semitisms mediated by the Septuagint or other translation Greek.'   [8] See p. 78.

usage, but the exact meaning of πάλιν is by no means clear, for it can mean Pilate asks the question a 'second time' or 'whereupon'.

Of the remaining four examples, 9^5 and 12^{26} do not exhibit any other markedly redactional linguistic traits. 14^{45} is in Taylor's 'A' i.e. primitive Passion account: 16^{11} because it conflicts with 15^{47} should be regarded as S, and therefore remain so marked; which leaves a total of 18R and 4S.

(j) PERIPHRASTIC TENSES

R: $1^{4, 22, 33, 39}$, $2^{6, 18}$, 5^{41}, $6^{31, 52}$, $9^{6-7(2)}$, $10^{22, 32(2)}$, $14^{40, 49}$, $15^{22, 34, 43}$, 15^{46} = 20 times

S: 1^6, 4^{38}, $5^{5, 11}$, 9^3, $13^{13, 25}$, 14^4, $15^{7, 40}$ = 10 times

Although some have argued that the periphrastic tenses are secondary Semitisms, and indicate translation Greek,[2] Luke has a higher percentage than Mark in spite of his avoidance of the Marcan passages.[3] This should make us cautious[4] about regarding the periphrastic as anything more than a sign of non-literary Greek in a writer who is very much influenced by the LXX. We have seen quite often in his redaction that he exhibits in his syntax characteristics which appear to be 'Semitisms', but which can be paralleled both in a literary writer like Luke, and also in unskilled writers of the koine, like himself.

The tense can be most expressive,[5] and is useful in emphasising the linear past tense, especially for Mark, who often uses his

[1] See p. 106, note 10.

[2] Doudna, p. 110. N.B. also Doudna, pp. 106–10; Zerwick, pp. 125–6; Black, pp. 130–2.

[3] 0.44% per page of the Souter text for Luke, and 0.42% for Mark (Doudna, p. 109, quoting W. F. Howard, 'Appendix on Semitisms in the New Testament', in Moulton, vol. 2, pt. 3, p. 452).

[4] Black, p. 130. Possibly its presence in source can be classified as secondary Semitism, but that depends on the redactional characteristics. See Sanders, *Synoptic Tradition*, p. 254, quoting Dalman: 'Mark's fondness for the present tense is an individual trait, like his constant use of εὐθέως.'

[5] Commenting on 1^{33}, Taylor, p. 181, says: 'The tense vividly describes the growing crowds.'

imperfects as aorists. Turner's suggestion that Mark's imperfect is really the periphrastic is convincing.[1]

In five[2] of the verses marked R the periphrastic tense is found in a small parenthesis (see under 'Parenthetical clauses'), three of them being translations of Aramaic phrases for the benefit of Gentile readers.[3] 6^{52} is Mark's explanation of the disciples' obtuseness, and is linguistically close to 8^{17}, which belongs to a Marcan literary construction. 14^{40} is also discussed under πάλιν, redundant participle, and γάρ explanatory.[4] 15^{43} ὃς καὶ αὐτὸς ἦν προσδεχόμενος τὴν βασιλείαν τοῦ θεοῦ is significantly explained by Taylor[5] as possibly 'Mark's addition to his source'. 15^{46}, like 15^{43}, is a clause which is singularly Marcan in content, and contains two unusual words, the first of which Matthew and Luke seem to have found offensive, while Matthew alone accepts the second.[6]

γάρ explanatory discussed at the end of this chapter accounts for a further five[7] of these periphrastic tenses. 10^{22} has been discussed under πολλά acc.,[8] and 14^{40} just recently.

Two of the examples use δέ and have a similar construction: ἦσαν δέ τινες... καθήμενοι καί (2^6) and ἦσαν δὲ ἐν τῇ ὁδῷ ἀναβαίνοντες (10^{32}). 2^{18}, generally accepted as a redactional verse, is similar to 2^6 and 10^{32}, but is preceded by καὶ ἦσαν οἱ μαθηταὶ Ἰωάννου... κ. οἱ Φ. νηστεύοντες.[9] Three[10] employ high frequency vocabulary, two of them having κηρύσσων ($1^{4,39}$). Three only use ἐγένετο, i.e. 1^4 and in the Transfiguration scene twice in the same verse. The latter uses two short γάρ clauses, which are also striking in their content:[11] Peter's not knowing what to say, for he became afraid.

Conversion of S to R: 1^6, 4^{38}, $5^{5,11}$, 9^3, 13^{13}, 14^{4a}, $15^{7,40a}$ = 9 times

To remain S: 13^{25} = 1 time

---

[1] Turner, *J.T.S.* 28 (July 1927), 351: 'When Mark wants to give the continuous sense of the imperfect, he uses ἦν with the present participle.' See also Moulton, vol. 2, pp. 226ff.; vol. 3, pp. 67, 87–9.

[2] 5^4, 6^{52} (cf. 8^{17}), 14^{40}, $15^{22,34}$.   [3] 5^{41}, $15^{22,34}$.

[4] It should probably also be considered as a parenthesis.   [5] P. 600.

[6] ἐνειλέω and λατομέω, both late verbs and ἅ. λ. (marked † in the vocabulary).

[7] 1^{22}, 6^{31}, 9^6, 10^{22}, 14^{40}. 1^{22} is also discussed under 'impersonals'; see p. 108.   [8] See p. 72.   [9] P. 140.   [10] $1^{4,39}$, 14^{49}.

[11] N.B. the repetition of the same construction in one sentence.

1⁶ reads καὶ ἦν ὁ Ἰωάννης ἐνδεδυμένος...καὶ ἐσθίων ἀκρίδας...
The participle ἐσθίων reminds one of 1³⁹ καὶ ἦν κηρύσσων...
καὶ...ἐκβάλλων.[1] Probably the latter participle, too far from
the copula, is to be regarded as the 'participle functioning as the
main verb'. On two linguistic points 1⁶ is probably redactional,
while Marxsen and others have argued the same on literary
grounds for 1¹⁻¹³.[2] 4⁴⁸, which is similar in the first half of the
verse, contains an unusual word προσκεφάλαιον marked † in
the vocabulary. The same applies to κατακόπτειν in 5⁵, while
the two participles are separated by the copula. Elsewhere[3]
from other redactional linguistic data 5¹⁴, ¹⁵, ¹⁷ have come under
review as possible R verses, 5⁸ and 5²⁰ being generally accepted
as editorial, which seems to call for a closer examination of the
whole section as possibly a Marcan literary construction, for
now 5¹¹ as well as 5⁵ may be regarded as redactional.[4] 14⁴ᵃ
ἦσαν δέ τινες ἀγανακτοῦντες πρὸς ἑαυτούς recalls 2⁶ and 10¹⁰,
and is widely accepted as an intercalated pericope in the
Passion narrative. ἀγανακτέω and πρὸς ἑαυτούς[5] are also
paralleled elsewhere in redaction. Note also how the situation is
described in indirect speech, and further explained in direct
speech (see Neirynck, pp. 45ff.).

9³, like 9⁴, employs ἐγένετο and, like 5⁵, contains specialised
LXX vocabulary, γναφεύς and στίλβοντα (marked †).[6]

The two texts from 13¹³ᵃ, ²⁵ have the periphrastic future; the
second is the more likely to be source, and free from redaction.

[1] See p. 67.
[2] I.e. (1) periphrastic tense and (2) part. used as m.v.; see also Marxsen,
pp. 17–26. See Lambrecht, p. 138; Taylor, pp. 155–6, points out the unusual vocabulary ('either hapax leg. or rare in Mk.'). He thinks that the
prophetic girdle has been 'deliberately introduced by Mark, who believes
that John belongs to the prophetic order and is Elijah, whose coming is
foretold in Mal. iii 1, iv 5 f. (cf. Mk ix 9–13)'.
[3] See p. 84. N.B. R vocab. ὄρος.
[4] Kertelge, pp. 101ff. sees the 'end-redactor' as Mark, but the composition as mainly S.
[5] Dibelius, p. 181; Lambrecht, p. 58: 'mit dem 14, 3 beginnt, zeugt von
redaktioneller Ungewandtheit'. Taylor, p. 531, refers to ἀγανακτέω 2/3R
10¹⁴,⁴¹. See also Turner, J.T.S. 29 (April 1928), p. 280, where πρὸς ἑαυτούς
in 1²⁷R, 9¹⁰S(?), 10²⁶R, 11³¹R, 12⁷S, 14⁴R, 16³S may be translated 'with
one another'.
[6] N.B. also ἐπὶ τῆς γῆς (4¹): οἷα...οὕτως (cf. 13¹⁹; see Lambrecht, pp.
162, 186; Pesch, p. 148).

Taylor[1] recalls 6^{14} when considering 13^{13a}. 13^{13b} has already been marked as R. The reason for 13^{13a} being considered as later and possibly retrospective is διὰ τὸ ὄνομά μου. The fact that ὄνομα, εἰς τέλος,[2] σωθήσεται and now the periphrastic are to be found here means that the whole verse is redactional.[3]

15^{74} and 15^{40a} are marked 'B' in Taylor's analysis, both coming at breaks in the narrative. 15^7 and 15^{40} also use δέ (cf. 2^6 and 10^{32}), and the first is regarded by Taylor as a 'parenthesis which could follow 8 or 10'.[5] An additional linguistic point is the use of the pluperfect without the augment, both here and in 15^{10} (which is already marked as R).

Taylor compares 15^{40} with 5^{11}, which has already been discussed,[6] and comments on the latter with its δέ introducing a new stage in the narrative, and he regards 15^{40} as an 'addendum'.[7] But significantly Best[8] and Bultmann[9] refer to the threefold repetition by Mark of the names of the women, Best being of the opinion that Mark is putting together 'three sections which were once separate'.[10]

On further consideration of the verses hitherto regarded as source on literary grounds, nine of the ten are to be transferred to R from S on linguistic grounds. Here we seem to have a pointer as definite as in the cases of the six linguistic features where the percentage was high.

[1] P. 510: 'The point of view is that of Mark himself when he accounts for the hostile interest of Antipas by saying φανερὸν γὰρ ἐγένετο τὸ ὄνομα αὐτοῦ (vi. 14).' See p. 127.

[2] Marxsen, pp. 108f.

[3] Lambrecht, pp. 138–44: 'In der zweiten Hälfte (v. 12–13) bleibt der Redaktor bei dem einen Thema der Verfolgung,...und mit einer Klimax v.13a gestaltet' (p. 144).

[4] 15^6 actually. Taylor, p. 580: 'Mark now introduces the story of Barabbas.'

[5] P. 581.

[6] See p. 105.

[7] Pp. 282, 598.

[8] P. 102; Dibelius, p. 190; Lambrecht, p. 18.

[9] P. 276; Pesch, p. 233; Schreiber, pp. 26–8, 44–8; Schweizer, pp. 363–4.

[10] Pp. 274f. Bultmann writes: 'Mark in three successive stories mentions by name (and with differences in detail at that!) the women who are eye-witnesses $15^{40f.,47}$ 16^1. This clearly shows that individual stories have been brought together here' (p. 276).

(k) 'IMPERSONALS'

R: $1^{21,22,29,32,45}$, 3^{21}, $5^{1,35}$, $6^{14,33,54,55}$, $9^{14,30,33}$, $10^{13,32}$, $11^{1,11,12-}$ $11^{15,19-21(2),27}$, 12^{13}, $14^{12,22,26,32}$ = 29 times

S: 1^{30}, $2^{3,18}$, $3^{2,22}$, $5^{14,15,17,38}$, 6^{43}, 7^{32}, 8^{22}, $10^{2,49}$, $13^{9,11}$, 15^{27} = 17 times

C. H. Turner's 'impersonals' in Mark may be divided into three classes: a substitute for the passive,[1] the true impersonal, i.e. denoting an amorphous crowd or unidentified person,[2] and those referring to small or larger groups following Jesus.[3] Probably only the first and second of these should properly be regarded as 'impersonals'.

Both in redactional and source passages the evangelist often avoids the passive by substituting the active third person plural. The general opinion appears to be that this type of impersonal reflects the dislike of the Aramaic language for the passive, and may be caused by the translator[4] or his non-literary style.[5] The fact that Doudna found the LXX translation Greek more tolerant of this substitute for the passive than the koine would favour his third conclusion: 'Where translation Greek is questionable (as in Mark) the overworking of the usage may be due to the laxity found in a non-literary style.'[6]

Examples of the latter usage in R and S verses amount to 7R and 8S:[7] 1^{32}R 'they brought...'; 3^{32}R 'word was brought to Him: "Your..."'; 5^{35}R 'a message came...'; 6^{14}R$^{-16(3)}$ 'people were saying...others said...others again...'; 12^{13}R 'A number...were sent'; 15^{27c} 'when it was customary to sacrifice...'

Recalling the fact that the early Christian preachers, teachers

---

[1] 1^{32}R, 2^3S, ^{18}S, 3^{32}S, 5^{35}R, 6^{14}R(3), ^{43}S, 7^{32}S, 12^{13}R, 13^9S, ^{11}S, 14^{12}R, 15^{27}S = 7R, 8S.

[2] 1^{22}R, ^{15}R, 5^{11}S, ^{15}S, 6^{33}R, ^{54}R, ^{55}R, 8^{22}S, 10^{13}R = 6R, 3S.

[3] 1^{21}R, ^{29}R, ^{30}R, ^{45}R, 3^2S, ^{21}R, 5^1R, ^{17}S, ^{38}S, 9^{14}R, ^{30}R, ^{33}R, 10^2S, ^{22}R, ^{49}S, 11^1R, ^{11}R, ^{12}R, ^{15}R, ^{19}R$^{-21(2)}$, ^{27}R, 14^{22}R, ^{26}R, ^{32}R = 20R, 5S.

[4] Black, pp. 126-8.

[5] Doudna, p. 70. Cf. Black, p. 126; Taylor, pp. 47-8, 62.

[6] Doudna, p. 70.

[7] 1^{32}R, 2^3S, ^{18}S, 3^{32}S, 5^{35}R, 6^{14}R(3), ^{43}S, 7^{32}S, 12^{13}R, 13^9S, ^{11}S, 14^{12}R, 15^{27}S.

and missionaries in the main had to rely upon their memories and that the oral tradition was handed down in communities, the considerable use by Mark of a vague 'they' or 'them' is not surprising. Black has also produced an excellent illustration from an Aramaic story of impersonals which exhibit an identical vagueness and imprecision.

They (the Romans at the gate) said to them, 'What are ye who are enemies seeking to do?' *They* (the Jews) said that even their Rabbi *they* (the Romans) did not spare. As soon as *they* (the Jews) had brought him out, *they* put him in a certain cemetery and returned to the city. As soon as *they* had returned, Rabbi Yohanan went to the forces of Vespasian.[1]

We find that this imprecision takes two forms in the Gospel: first, in the general reference to groups of people,[2] and secondly, in the itinerant mission work of Jesus,[3] where it is often uncertain who 'they' exactly are who 'come to Jerusalem', 'leave Bethany', 'come to the other side of the lake'. We can only be certain if we read it into the text; if we are content to analyse what is written, the references are oblique and often confused. In the synagogue 'the people' were astonished at His teaching (1^{22}), while at the end of the chapter we are told that 'people' kept coming to Him from all quarters (1^{45}). In the setting for the first Feeding, the Greek tells us that 'many' recognised them, but we can either infer, as does the N.E.B., that these are also the subject of εἶδαν at the beginning of the sentence, or supply a subject such as 'the people', or a 'number of persons'. 6^{54} in the Greek reads: 'When they came out of the boat, they recognised Him, they ran all over the countryside'. The second 'they' is probably the same as the third, i.e. the crowd, but is quite different from the first group, which is probably the 'disciples'. In 8^{22} we are told that 'they come to Bethsaida. And they bring a blind man, and they entreat Him to touch (cure) him.' Once again, the first group is probably the Twelve, or the disciples, while the second is an unidentified group of people trying to help a blind man.

---

[1] P. 128.   [2] 1^{22}R, 4^{5}R, 5^{14}S, 1^{5}S, 6^{33}R, 5^{4}R, 5^{5}R, 8^{22}S, 10^{13}.

[3] Jesus + 12 = 11 times; Jesus + disciples = 5 times; Jesus + 2/3/4 = 3, 2, 2; Pharisees = 1 time; Simon + others = 1 time; Jesus' relations = 1 time.

The third group of 'impersonals' Turner[1] thought could be explained by a diarist, supposing it to be Peter describing his experiences in the first person plural, 'we come', which Mark turned into 'they come' or 'came'. But we have already seen in Rabbinical stories and folk tradition a probable origin of such a way of speaking, and writing. An additional source for many of these 'impersonals' may now also be seen in redaction.

The two main reasons for this deduction are that the majority of the 'impersonals' are to be found in the 'seams', at the beginning (first or second verses) of pericopae,[2] and also in the geographical framework which has been supplied by the redactor–editor. Moreover, the ambiguity which arises from the obscurity of the impersonals occasions a high number of textual variants,[3] usually involving a change from plural to singular, at the expense of the original meaning. More often, however, the other two evangelists supply the missing subject,[4] and misunderstand Mark's intention. Quite a number of the Marcan ambiguous texts can be explained by the fact that the evangelist has taken them over from the oral tradition, but in linking pericope to pericope to form his Gospel, he has been forced to change their meaning, and so has made it difficult for the reader to be certain what exactly he does want to say.

There are at least ten instances[5] where even the most indulgent critic cannot be certain what exactly Mark intends us to understand from his Greek. In 3^2 the people who were watching to

[1] Turner, *J.T.S.* 25 (July 1924), 378–86; 26 (April 1925), 228–31. See Black, p. 127: 'Turner (following a suggestion of Godet) was convinced that these third plural verbs reflect verbs in the first person plural in Peter's Memoirs (see Turner, XXVI, p. 225f.) But there is no need to resort to such an explanation.'

[2] First or second verse pericopae: $1^{21,22}$, 1^{29-30}, 1^{32}, 2^3, 2^{18}, 3^2, 3^{21}, 3^{32}, 5^1, 5^{35}, 6^{14}, 6^{33}, 6^{54-5}, 7^{32}, 8^{22}, 9^{14}, 9^{30}, 9^{33}, 10^2, 10^{13}, 10^{32}, 11^1, 11^{12}, 11^{20}, 11^{27}, 12^{13}, 14^{12}, 14^{22}, 14^{32} = 32 times; end of pericopae: 1^{45}, 6^{43}, 11^{11}, 11^{19}, 14^{26} = 5 times.

[3] 17/46: $1^{21,22,29,32}$, 2^3, $5^{1,38}$, $6^{14,54}$, 8^{22}, $9^{14,33}$, $10^{32,49}$, $11^{1,19,27}$.

[4] Mt. 13/47: Luke 9/47. MATTHEW: Mk. 1^{22} (Mt. 7^{28}); Mk. 2^{18} (Mt. 9^{14}); Mk. 3^{32} (Mt. 12^{47}); Mk. 5^{14} (Mt. 13^{34}); Mk. 5^{17} (Mt. 8^{34}); Mk. 6^{33} (Mt. 14^{13}); Mk. 6^{54} (Mt. 14^{35}); Mk. 9^{33} (Mt. 18^1); Mk. 10^2 (Mt. 19^3); Mk. $11^{19,21}$ (Mt. 21^{20}); Mk. 12^{13} (Mt. 22^{15-16}); Mk. 14^{32} (Mt. 26^{30}). LUKE: Mk. 1^{22} (Lk. 4^{32}); Mk. 1^{45} (Lk. 5^{15}); Mk. 2^3 (Lk. 5^{18}); Mk. 2^{18} (Lk. 5^{33}); Mk. 3^2 (Lk. 6^7); Mk. 5^{17} (Lk. 8^{37}); Mk. 5^{35} (Lk. 8^{49}); Mk. 6^{33} (Lk. 9^{11}).

[5] $3^{2,21}$, 5^{17}, $6^{14,33}$, $9^{14,33}$, $10^{2,32}$, 12^{13}.

see if Jesus would heal on the sabbath day could have been either the congregation or the Pharisees. The footnote in 3^{21} in the N.E.B. shows the translator's uncertainty whether we should follow Turner and Zerwick who regard ἔλεγον γὰρ ὅτι as the impersonal rumour of Jesus' insanity, or Taylor and others who naturally take it to refer to the family. Probably both are correct. In the oral tradition it may have been impersonal, but when Mark put it down into literary form he took the risk of being misunderstood or he may in fact have misunderstood it in this way. He often uses a short γάρ clause just after an obscure statement in order to clarify it. In 5^{17} was it the spectators who asked Jesus to leave, or the people of the whole area? The imprecision in 6^{33}[1] has already been referred to, as the long parenthesis in 6^{14-16},[2] where the rumours or opinions about the ministry of Jesus are rendered by impersonals and λέγω ὅτι,[3] but at the same time they are placed in the midst of an anacolouthon which is really concerned with Herod and his opinion.

9^{14} is somewhat of a test case, for Taylor considers that the vocabulary is Markan and that 'it is clear that for the most part Mark has himself supplied this introductory passage',[4] which speaks of 'them' coming back to the disciples, when 'they saw a large crowd surrounding them'. Is the redactor using a traditional introduction and converting it so that the impersonals originally residing in ἐλθόντες and εἶδαν are now meant to refer to the persons in the previous pericope, i.e. Jesus and the three (vv. 2, 9), or are they meant to refer to the other nine apostles as well, assuming that this is what he meant by 'the disciples' (v. 14)?[5] Once again, the problem is further complicated by the variant reading, singular or plural,[6] which shows that the scribes were puzzled by the introduction. 10^2S is also instructive inasmuch as the subject supplied by some texts, 'The Pharisees (came forward and asked Him)', is consigned to a footnote in the N.E.B. and the verb regarded as impersonal. We supply 'people asked Him', or 'He was asked'. In 12^{13}, without

[1] See p. 109.   [2] See pp. 41–2.   [3] See p. 76.
[4] P. 396.   [5] Bultmann, p. 211.
[6] 'The sing. is well attested but the plural should probably be taken as the correct reading' (Taylor, p. 396; W. H. Nestle (ed.), *Novum Testamentum Graece et Latine* (Stuttgart, 1951).

a time or space reference the opening verse can be translated as in the N.E.B.: 'A number of Pharisees...were sent'; or following the previous pericope it can be assumed that the Sadducees sent them (12^{1-12}).

A similar problem faces the translator or exegete when reading the references to the followers of Jesus. In Chs. 11 and 14 there are nine[1] 'impersonals' which probably refer to the Twelve, four of them coming from Marcan literary constructions ($11^{19,20}$, $14^{22,26}$). 11^{20} reads: 'Early next morning as they passed by, they saw that the fig-tree had withered from the roots up; and Peter recalling what had happened...' The reference is probably back to 11^{12-13}, where we are told that the 'disciples' were listening, but in 11^{11} we are informed that Jesus went to Bethany with the 'Twelve'. In 14^{17}, the second pericope concerned with the Passover, we read of Jesus eating with the Twelve, but two of the three paragraphs $14^{17-21, 22-5, 26-31}$ may well have been intercalated by Mark, 14^{22-6} being a liturgical 'B' fragment, which the redactor has nicely dovetailed into the other two 'A'-strand fragments of tradition. In two of the possible 'Twelve' references, $9^{30,33}$, the group could well be the 'disciples'.

In 9^{28} Jesus' 'disciples asked Him privately'. In a fresh paragraph, 9^{30}, 'they' now left that district (cf. 8^{27}). In 9^{30} 'Jesus was teaching His disciples'. In the next pericope, He called the Twelve (9^{35}). Similarly in 14^{17} the reference to the 'Twelve' is perhaps replaced by a synonym, 'The disciples', in 14^{32}, or is the Gethsemane incident to be apportioned to a wider circle than the 'Twelve'? Probably in 5^{1}, 10^{32} and 11^{1} the reference is to the 'disciples', whatever that may mean.[2]

Sometimes Jesus takes with Him only the three apostles, Peter, James and John (5^{38}, 9^{14}). In $1^{21, 29, 30}$ the references are obscure and must be discussed. In 1^{21} we have the first section of the

[1] $11^{11,12,15,19,20,27}$, $14^{22,26,32}$ = 9 times.

[2] Bultmann, pp. 344–5.
'Indeed when Mark speaks of the μαθηταί as a group he obviously has the Twelve in mind (in all probability naively and without any reflection, even in the passages before their appointment 2^{15f} $3^{7,9}$)... But where the old tradition and the stages of the tradition before Mark speak of the μαθηταί the probability is that the Twelve were not meant, certainly not a limited circle of disciples, but a changing circle of followers, such a circle as was about Jesus in 3^{34}.'

Marcan geographical framework: 'They come to Capernaum.' Following 1²⁰ we might assume that this means Jesus, Simon, Andrew, James and John (1¹⁶⁻²⁰), but after being told in 1²⁹ that 'they' went straight to the house of Simon and Andrew, we are told that 'James and John went with them', as if James and John were not to be expected to be among the company. C. H. Turner suggests that λέγουσιν in 1³⁰, 'they told Him about her', is impersonal, but Lagrange, Taylor, and Swete think that we should understand 'οἱ περὶ τὸν Σίμωνα' as the subject.[1] One reason for the ambiguity could well be the insertion by Mark of his literary constructions concerning the 'Twelve' into a traditional pericopal material which largely concerned the 'disciples', understood in the oral Tradition in a loose sense and later by the redactor as the 'Twelve'.

In like manner the geographical outline, highly redactional in its Galilean references according to Marxsen and others, can also have caused ambiguities and confusion, especially if one recalls that the style of the writer is at times as colloquial and imprecise as that of a rustic. A high proportion of Turner's so-called 'impersonals' stand at the opening or close of pericopae, and are forms of ἔρχομαι, which suggests that a good number of them originated in the transition of the gospel to the 'Gospel', from oral to literary form, and are probably to be traced to the redaction of an editor, or editors. The commonest use of the impersonal is with some form of ἔρχομαι: 1²⁹, ⁴⁵, 2³, ¹⁸, 5¹, ¹⁴, ¹⁵⁻ 5³⁵, ³⁸, 8²², 9³⁰, ³³, 11¹², ¹³, ¹⁵, ²⁷, 14²⁶, ³²(18 times). Cf. also εἶδον (6³³, 9¹⁴, 11²⁰); ἀποστέλλει (11², 12¹³); θαμβεῖσθαι (10²⁴); (προσ)φέρω (1³², 10¹³). To quote Nineham:

After all, if Mark was to present the Lord's ministry as having been exercised in a number of different centres at all, he was bound sometimes to insert between one *pericope* and the next some indication that Jesus left one place and went to another. What better phrases for the purpose than ἐκεῖθεν ἀναστάς[2] or κἀκεῖθεν ἐξελθόντες or the like?[3]

---

[1] Taylor, p. 179; Turner, *J.T.S.* 25 (July 1924), 378, Swete, p. 23; Lagrange, p. 25.

[2] On redundant participles see p. 100.

[3] See D. E. Nineham, 'The order of events in St. Mark's Gospel – an examination of Dr. Dodd's hypothesis', in Nineham (ed.), *Studies in the Gospels*, p. 234.

Conversion of S to R: 1^{30}, 3^{32}, 5^{17}, 8^{22}, 10^{49}, $13^{9a, 11a}$, 15^{27} = 8 times

To remain S: $2^{3, 18}$, 3^2, $5^{14, 15, 38}$, 6^{43}, 7^{32}, 10^2 = 9 times[1]

1^{30b} has already been discussed under καὶ εὐθύς,[2] and although it may well be traditional material redacted it has come under the hand of the editor sufficiently to be probably classified as R. 2^3 and 2^{18} may be illuminated by a comment of Zerwick[3] on the use of the historic present:

Thus we could summarise in this way. The concepts of coming, bringing, leading, assembling, appear in Mk. at the beginning of a pericope in the present tense whenever the writer feels that they start something new (in the narrative). The same beginnings are written in the preterite if they are felt to be merely introductory or linking passages.

Thus in ἔρχονται φέροντες (2^3S) the emphasis is on the participle not on the main verb. 2^{18} is regarded by Perrin[4] as editorial, the phrase 'the disciples of the Pharisees' being an imitation of the traditional 'John's disciples' and so the sentence has been conformed to the general subject matter of Pharisees and Herodians (2^1–3^6) by Mark or some previous editor.[5] Once again we find the ambiguity arises because of a literary handling of oral material. καὶ ἔρχονται καὶ λέγουσιν could well be 'impersonals', i.e. passive and oral, but the hand of the editor is suspected in the second half of the sentence, so probably the first part should be marked as R and the second part, the impersonals, regarded as S handled by the editor.

3^{32}, from 3^{31-4}, is generally accepted as a Marcan intercalation.[6] From this short section already 3^{31}, 3^{33a} and 3^{34a} are marked R. ὄχλος is a highly used R word, also ἰδού and κάθημαι, 'possibly' R according to Lambrecht.[7] 3^2 could well be the early part of a traditional pericope which the redactor has handled in 3^1 and 3^6, while the ambiguity which Taylor[8] resolves, in opposition to Lagrange, can be accounted for by

[1] Revised statistics are therefore 37R and 9S, i.e. about 73 % of the total.
[2] See p. 94.   [3] P. 57.
[4] *Rediscovering the Teaching of Jesus* (London, 1967), p. 79.
[5] Schweizer, p. 66; Lambrecht, p. 70.   [6] See p. 12.
[7] Pp. 86, 96. Note also ἔξω (see 4^{11}).
[8] Taylor, p. 221: 'his enemies', not people in general; Lagrange, p. 57.

its inclusion in 2^1–3^6, which is concerned with Pharisees and Herodians (3^6). It therefore remains S.

$5^{14, 15, 17}$ all come from the 'Gerasene Demoniac', which is certainly a very primitive pericope, but it cannot be said that the composition is entirely free of redaction, or that its Greek style is absolutely non-literary. 5^{20} is widely held to be R. 5^8 is regarded by Taylor[1] as 'Mark's explanation', and will be discussed under γάρ clauses. 5^{15} has an unusual number of participles with the historic present constituting a 'new beginning'.[2] 5^{18} is described by Taylor as 'Marcan vocabulary and style',[3] so it is tempting to transfer $5^{14, 15, 17}$ from S to R, but 5^{14} should tentatively stay S, while 5^{17} becomes R. Its ἤρξατο + inf. is not very polished in style, but nevertheless is 'typically Marcan' – so Pesch.[4] Marcan vocabulary are ἄρχομαι, ἀπέρχεσθαι, παρακαλεῖν, ὄρος.

Turning to 5^{15}, the many participles in the sentence, the use of κάθημαι, the literary τὸν ἐσχηκότα τὸν λεγιῶνα and the R φοβεῖσθαι plus the present tenses are indicative. So although it is regarded by a good number of critics as the true end of the miracle story, it has probably been edited by the evangelist.[5]

As 15^{27} anticipates 15^{29-32}, and of 15^{25-32} all but this verse is already marked R, probably 15^{27} should be added. It is part of Taylor's 'B' strand, and also one of the Marcan intercalations.[6]

13^9 already has the opening 13^{9a}R, but παραδώσουσιν is in Mt. and Luke, so the rest of the verse must have been in S. To turn to 13^{11}, according to Lambrecht, Mark modified his sources in 13^9 and 13^{11}, thus radically placing 13^{10} in chiasmus. Thus he positions αὐτοῖς (pagan authorities) with 'all the nations', and 'as a witness' opposite to κηρυχθῆναι. 13^{9a}[7] is generally accepted as R. The source links up again in 13^{11abc}, but as 13^{11d} is omitted in Luke and altered in Matthew, with its explanatory γάρ clause it may well be R.[8]

7^{32} and 8^{22} are closely linked together from many points of view as Taylor's linguistic comparison of 7^{32-7} and 8^{22-6} con-

---

[1] P. 281. [2] So Taylor, p. 283.
[3] P. 284. [4] P. 106.
[5] Dibelius, pp. 54, 71, 76f., 80, 84, 88, 101, 292; Kertelge, p. 105; Lightfoot, pp. 88ff.
[6] Lambrecht, pp. 120–7. [7] See p. 21. [8] Lambrecht, pp. 120–36.

firms.[1] His conclusion would appear to be sound: 'Mark, there-fore, or a predecessor, deliberately uses the framework supplied by VII 32–7, but fits into it a new story suitable to his didactic purpose.'[2] 7[32], however, also comes in the pericope where the word μογιλάλος could well be considered as redactional, but should the presence also of the impersonal φέρουσιν and παρακαλοῦσιν be regarded as further indications of more in-tense redaction? However, the presence of a similar passage later, 8[22], may indicate that its source was 7[32], which is mainly S, the allusion to μογιλάλος R (emphasised by the editor) and the imper-sonals originating from the oral tradition, as Taylor suggests.[3]

Thus approximately 1/7 of our 'impersonals' are marked S, and while obviously some of the remainder (redaction) could well be S, the editor has had to overcome considerable problems handling them, creating a literary form to integrate this oral and source material with so impersonal a character.

(1) ὥστε + INFINITIVE

R: 1[27, 45], 2[2, 12], 3[10, 20], 4[1] = 7 times
S: 2[28], 4[32, 37], 9[26], 10[8], 15[5] = 6 times

In classical Greek 'Consecutive Clauses are generally expressed by the Conjunction ὥστε followed by the Infinitive (negative μή): but when stress is laid on the actual occurrence of the consequence, they are expressed by ὥστε with the Indicative (negative οὐ).'[4] According to Blass–Debrunner 'the use of the indicative after ὥστε in really dependent clauses, possible in Attic, is not genuine New Testament idiom'.[5] Of the thirteen examples used by the evangelist, eleven are followed by the accusative + infinitive construction, and the other two by the indicative (2[28]S, 10[8]S). Seven of the thirteen are found with redactional material, while six are source. The two examples of

---

[1] Pp. 368–9.   [2] P. 370.   [3] P. 369.
'To some extent the linguistic agreements may be explained by the ad-mitted tendency of Mark to repeat himself and by the ease with which popular narratives assume fixed forms in oral tradition. Such a form is the use of the impersonal plural and the frequent use of φέρω in stories of healing (cf. i.32, ii.3, ix.17, 19, 20).'
[4] North and Hillard, p. 100.   [5] P. 197.

ὥστε with the indicative are from the source verses and not from the redactional.

Three of the source examples are sayings of Jesus combined with Old Testament texts.[1] Two[2] of the three are in the indicative where we would expect the stress to be laid on the 'actual occurrence of the consequence'. The first, 2²⁸, runs: 'The Sabbath was made for the sake of man and not man for the Sabbath: therefore the Son of Man is sovereign even over the Sabbath.' The second, 10⁸, follows the quotation from Genesis 1²⁷, 2²⁴ and is translated by the N.E.B.: 'It follows that they are no longer two individuals: They are one flesh.' The stress in the first instance is on the lordship of Christ over the sabbath, and in the second on the unity or oneness of the marriage state.

Mark has not always constructed his accusative with the infinitive clauses with the greatest clarity. Three are obscure, one being almost an anacolouthon. 2² runs: καὶ συνήχθησαν πολλοὶ ὥστε μηκέτι χωρεῖν μηδὲ τὰ πρὸς τὴν θύραν. τὰ πρὸς τὴν θύραν is either an accusative of respect, or the subject of χωρεῖν. We translate either: 'so that no longer was there any room, not even in the part near the door', or 'so that no longer could the part round the door hold anybody else'. 4¹ contains, like the previous passage, συνάγειν and ὄχλος. V. 1ᵇ reads καὶ συνάγεται πρὸς αὐτὸν ὄχλος πλεῖστος ὥστε αὐτὸν εἰς πλοῖον ἐμβάντα καθῆσθαι ἐν τῇ θαλάσσῃ. The presence of αὐτόν in parallel with ἐμβάντα followed by another infinitive, complicates the sentence, which seems to mean that the crowd forced Jesus to get into a boat, 'sitting in the lake', which J. Rendel Harris explains as an Aramaism for going aboard a boat.[3] 3¹⁰ πολλοὺς γὰρ ἐθεράπευσεν, ὥστε ἐπιπίπτειν αὐτῷ ἵνα αὐτοῦ ἅψωνται ὅσοι εἶχον μάστιγας employs ὥστε + infinitive + ἵνα + ὅσοι. All the commentators seem to emphasise the fact that one of the expressions here can be paralleled in Thucydides,[4] but they ignore the fact that the Greek cannot be justified on any grammatical basis. Perhaps πολλούς is to be understood after ὥστε. The ἵνα must be final, but the main problem is still the ὥστε

---

[1] 2²⁸, 4³², 10⁸. [2] 2²⁸, 10⁸; see p. 118 also for 2²⁸.

[3] 'An Unnoticed Aramaism in St. Mark', *Expository Times* 26 (March 1915), 248ff. Thus the sentence is tautologous, if Harris is correct.

[4] Swete, p. 56, quoting Field's notes (p. 25) on Thuc. vii, 84 ἐπέπιπτόν τε ἀλλήλοις καὶ κατεπάτουν.

construction, which is explained only by the clause at the end of the sentence (ὅσοι εἶχον μάστιγας).

Three of the sentences desert the indirect speech, and change over to λέγειν, or λέγειν ὅτι.[1] Of the latter, one is source and the other redactional. To conclude with a direct statement of the effect of the miracles or teaching of Jesus seems very typical source pericopal style, and thus a symptom of the non-literary character of the material, but it is sometimes also a feature of the writer's redactional writing.

Five of the sentences come from literary constructions which are mainly summary statements of progress, and the sixth is a topographical reference.[2] The ὥστε construction is followed by the reactions of the crowd and the sick to the teaching, the exorcisms, and the healings of Jesus. In 1²⁷, where ὥστε is used, the synagogue discussed and argued about this new teaching, while in 1⁴⁵, after the proclaiming of either Jesus or the leper, Jesus had to keep to the deserts and refrain from entering the cities. In 2², 3²⁰ and 4¹ the crowd press on Jesus after His teaching or healings so that there is no room about the door of the house,[3] so that they are not able to eat,[4] and He is forced to take to a boat on the lake itself.[5] In 3¹² an additional redactional motif comes in: the idea of the healing power of His touch. 3¹⁰ anticipates 5²⁸⁻³¹ and 6⁵⁶.

One surprising feature in the Marcan usage of ὥστε is the lack of confusion with ἵνα. Whereas many of the ἵνα clauses are really consecutive, none of the ὥστε is final. Knowing the Semitic blurring of the distinction between the two,[6] the movement in Mark seems one way only.

Conversion of S to R: 2²⁸, 4³⁷⁽⁷⁾, 9²⁶ = 3 times
To remain S: 4³², 10⁸⁽⁷⁾, 15⁵ = 3 times

2²⁸ comes under peculiarities of syntax which Zerwick labels 'Sperrungen', in the case of this text between the noun 'lord' and its accompanying genitive[7] – 'of the sabbath'. He quotes Lindhammer's thesis on these 'blockages' with a significant comment: 'They [the Gospels] offer a clear proof that the split does not occur spontaneously in natural popular speech.' 2²⁸ is well balanced without the ὥστε addition, which Zerwick classifies as

---

[1] λέγειν: 1²⁷; λέγειν ὅτι: 2¹², 9²⁶.
[2] Summary statement of progress = 1²⁷,⁴⁵, 3¹⁰,²⁰, 4¹; topography = 2².
[3] 2².   [4] 3²⁰.   [5] 4¹.   [6] Moule, p. 143.   [7] Pp. 126f.

a 'blockage', namely ὥστε κύριός[1] ἐστιν ὁ υἱὸς τοῦ ἀνθρώπου καὶ τοῦ σαββάτου. 2²⁸ is also one of the two clauses which use the indicative after ὥστε, a more literary stylistic feature which we find in what appears to be source material rather than redaction. The presence of the redactional καὶ ἔλεγεν αὐτοῖς before the saying is another indication of editorial placing of vv. 27–8. Luke and Matthew have omitted Mark's καὶ τοῦ σ., and also removed the ὥστε. Schweizer points out the real possibility that vv. 23–6 were once independent of vv. 27–8. V. 27 was what Mark received, and he, or the tradition, added the saying from vv. 27–8. The presence of κύριος, a rather rare Marcan word, could be taken as a LXX translation of Yahweh, but as Best points out, the Marcan use of 'Lord' in the R passages (5¹⁹,²⁰, 7²⁸, 11³) identifies Jesus as 'Lord'. For Mark and his Church Jesus is Lord even of the Sabbath.[2]

The other instance of ὥστε followed by the indicative, 10⁸, comes from the teaching on adultery, and just before a verse which Dodd and Jeremias[3] regard as redactional. Taylor comments on the ὥστε clause as a deduction of Mark's, and as it comes just before the redactional link on to new material it is possible it is an editorial comment by Mark. There remains an element of doubt, so I have let it stay as S with a question-mark. 4³² is also concerned with scriptural quotation, but here ὥστε δύνασθαι precedes the quotation, which Jeremias regards as authentic, and to be ascribed to Jesus.

4³⁷ comes from 'The Storm on the Lake', where Bultmann speaks of editorial work in vv. 35 and 36, and the problem of separating S and R accurately.[4] 'Periphrastic tenses' gave us some indication of redactional work in 4³⁸, while the seams as usual show indications of the editor's hand. πλοῖον repeated in the sentence is a good redactional word, as also καὶ γίνεται

---

[1] In Blass–Debrunner, pp. 249, it is pointed out that κύριος is regarded as a proper name, and like a pronominal subject comes first in the sentence, but the subject here is ὁ υἱὸς not κύριος. Matthew has altered Mark to κύριος γάρ ἐστιν τοῦ σαββ. ὁ υἱὸς τ. ἀ.

[2] Cf. Kertelge, pp. 80–1, 85; Lambrecht, pp. 180, 233; Pesch, pp. 168, 206; Schweizer, p. 71.

[3] See Jeremias, *Parables of Jesus*, p. 98, n. 33: 'Mark 7.17f. εἰς οἶκον (only found in Mark in the N.T., and there always in redactional introduction), ἐπερωτᾶν, καὶ λέγει (hist. pres.); 10.10f: πάλιν, ἐπερωτᾶν, καὶ λέγει.

[4] Pp. 213–14.

at the beginning of the sentence, while ἤδη and γεμίζω can be illustrated from the other R verses.[1] The present tenses in this section help to make the writing graphic, and what Sundwall[2] classifies as 'epic' in style, so that he postulated a written source. Tentatively I think the language seems that of the redactor building up a primitive section into a livelier narrative, and so 4^{37} has been transferred to R, with a question-mark.

9^{26} begins with καί followed by two participles,[3] and then ἐγένετο (cf. 4^{37}), followed by λέγειν ὅτι ἀπέθανεν.[4] This verse has two participles, adverbial πολλά with two καί and ἐξέρχομαι: καὶ κράξας καὶ πολλὰ σπαράξας ἐξῆλθεν. 15^5 belongs to Taylor's 'A' source, and so should probably remain S, but note the δέ, the double negative and θαυμάζειν (5^{20}, 6^6).

The final count of S and R is 10R and 3S, with one of the latter possibly R.

(m) TWO OR MORE PARTICIPLES BEFORE OR AFTER THE MAIN VERB

R: $1^{14,(39),40}$, 3^{31}, 7^{25}, $8^{13,33}$, $10^{17,50}$, 12^{28}, 15^{46} = 11 times
S: $1^{26,31,41}$, 3^5, $5^{25-6,33}$, 6^{41}, $8^{6,23}$, 9^{26}, 13^{34}, $14^{23,45,67}$, $15^{1,36}$ = 16 times

An effective mastery of the participle is a basic necessity for all who essay to write Greek. In one who is possibly using Semitic sources, and who is not a master of polished syntax, the replacement of parataxis by the hypotactic participle, however crudely used, must be a sign of what Wellhausen calls 'reduced parataxis'.[5] The translator is thereby not translating literally, but

---

[1] 15^{36}.

[2] 'The beginning of the storm at sea has been worked over by Mark...It is also likely that this story, and the following one, were before Mark already in written form' (p. 29). See also p. 30: 'Like the preceding story, the Storm at Sea, this story in its epic style presupposes a written source (Pernot, p. 79).' Cf. Best, p. 105; Kertelge, pp. 91–100; Pesch, p. 178.

[3] See p. 123.

[4] Possibly this should be included in λέγω ὅτι clauses. See pp. 72ff.

[5] Black's statement on p. 64 that the hypotactic aorist participle is '*consistently absent from Mark*' is an overstatement, and conflicts with his use of Burney's statistics on the use of the aorist participle in the Gospels on p. 63:
'A survey of the occurrences of the subordinating aorist participle in the sayings of Jesus in the source Q gives for Matthew roughly one instance to the page of WH, for Luke about 2...

in paraphrasing replaces main verbs (in the Hebrew or Aramaic) by participles, for he knows that even koine Greek cannot indefinitely be burdened with endless καί followed by the main verb. In most of these twenty-seven sentences the redactor and/ or his sources employ as many as three participles, and in one case have a participle seven times in the sentence.[1] Sometimes even the experts[2] have minimised this feature of the Marcan Gospel. The style on the whole may well be described as paratactic but there is a fair number of examples of attempted and moderately successful hypotaxis which are now to be examined.

It is first important to note that nine out of eleven[3] of the redactional examples are in the beginning or ending of pericopae, whereas only half of the source verses come under this category.[4]

Secondly, six of these redactional participles come under the linguistic criteria, 'redundant participle', already discussed:[5] 7^{25} ἐλθοῦσα προσέπεσεν; 8^{13} ἐμβάς; 8^{33} ἐπιστραφεὶς καὶ ἰδών (?); 1^{15} καὶ λέγων ὅτι after κηρύσσων; 1^{40} παρακαλῶν…λέγων αὐτῷ ὅτι; 12^{28} προσελθών. There are three similar examples at present marked S: 1^{31} κ. προσελθών; 13^{34} ἀφεὶς τὴν οἰκίαν(?); 14^{45} κ. ἐλθὼν ε. προσελθών.

Thirdly, Zerwick[6] draws our attention to the absence of the dative, and the repetition of αὐτός. Examples of this are 1^{40} π. αὐτὸν κ. γ. λ. αὐτῷ, 3^{31} and 7^{25}…περὶ αὐτοῦ· ἧς εἶχεν τὸ θ. αὐτῆς π. ἀ.,…πόδας αὐτοῦ (an excellent example).[7] Note also 10^{17}, and in the source verses $1^{26,41}$, 5^{33} κ. π. αὐτῷ κ. ε. αὐτῷ,

The proportion for John given by Burney was one to a page of WH, whereas in Matthew there were 5, in *Mark about the same*, and in Luke roughly 4.' [My italics.]

It is interesting to note that Wellhausen who is quoted by Black on this page writes: 'In contrast [i.e. to the use of longer periods] very frequent is a single participle at the head of the sentence followed by the subject with the main verb.' In Wellhausen's view (*Einleitung*, p. 13) this type of construction has frequently taken the place of an original parataxis, and he points to Matthew's and Luke's editing of Mark for evidence of the further development of this process.

[1] 5^{25-6}.
[2] See p. 119, n. 5.
[3] $1^{14,39,40}$, 3^{31}, 7^{25}, $8^{13,33}$, 10^{17}, 12^{28} = 9/11.
[4] $1^{31,41}$, 5^{25-6}, 8^{23}, 9^{26}, $14^{23,67}$, 15^{1} = 8/16. But four of these are eventually converted from S to R (5^{25-6}, 9^{26}, $14^{23,67}$).
[5] See p. 121.
[6] P. 116.
[7] There is a parenthesis in 7^{26}; see p. 52.

8^{23} αὐτόν...αὐτοῦ...αὐτῷ...αὐτόν, 13^{34} (3 times), 14^{45} (2 times) and 15^{46} (2 times).

Fourthly, the asyndetic grouping of two participles without any link is to be noted in 14^{0}R κ. γονυπετῶν λέγων, 13^{1}S αὐτὴν κρατήσας, 14^{1}S κ. ὀργισθεὶς ἐκτείνας, 3^{5} κ. περιβλεψάμενος α. μ. ὁ. συλλυπού., 3^{31}, 6^{41}, $8^{6,23}$, 12^{28}, 13^{34}, ἀπόδημος ἀφείς and 14^{67}.

Fifthly, naturally two of these texts come under the genitive absolute, and link up with the hypotaxis here analysed (10^{17}, 14^{66}).

Conversion of S to R: $1^{26,31,41a}$, 3^{5a}, $5^{33,25-6}$, 6^{41}, 9^{26}, 14^{67}, $15^{1,36}$ = 11 times

To remain S: $8^{6,23}$, $13^{34(?)}$, 14^{23}, 14^{45} = 5 times

1^{26} is quite near in style to 9^{26} which has been transferred to R. Lambrecht[1] points out that in the Gospels a number of near doublets includes 1^{25-7} in parallel with 4^{39-41}, while Pesch[2] draws our attention to the evangelist's rather careful use of μέγας; so when he does use it, as here, we may consider it R handiwork. Although vv. 23–6[3] are probably a pre-Marcan source, there is clear evidence of the redactor's style in the R vocabulary: φωνεῖν, μέγας, πνεῦμα ἀκάθαρτον, ἐξέρχεσθαι, φωνή. As Wellhausen said, editorial work is marked in the first chapter, and to quote him again, the presence of Greek participles in paratactic style could be evidence of the translator[4] reducing the parataxis in his source. At the very least we would have to call 1^{26} a source verse well redacted, and probably the model for 4^{39-41} and 9^{26}. The vocabulary test, plus the double participle used as main verbs, warrant a clearer marking of the verse as R.

1^{31} (cf. 9^{17} and 5^{41}), from 1^{29-31}, receives commendation from Taylor for its careful use of tenses, the aorist participle following the main verb indicating concurrent and not antecedent action. The presence of καὶ εὐθύς,[5] impersonals,[6] catchwords[7] and two participles in the whole section suggest editorial revision of source material. R vocabulary in 1^{31} includes κρατεῖν, while

---

[1] P. 59.   [2] P. 87.   [3] So Kertelge, pp. 50–60.

[4] Dibelius, esp. p. 57: 'the present text has perhaps been worked over by the evangelist'.   [5] P. 94.   [6] P. 109.

[7] πυρέσσουσα (1^{30}) and πυρετός (1^{31}). A contrast may be suggested between κατέκειτο and διηκόνει (continuous activity)

πυρετός is used only once in Mark. αὐτός is employed three times in these short clauses. The paratactic order of καί followed by the verb or participle suggests an Aramaic source, the participle being the translator's rather crude attempt to reduce the monotony of the Semitic source style. The redactor is compressing his material when he links together a number of incidents into a working day of Jesus. 'Of course, Mark has revised the style extensively' (Schweizer[1]) would be the opinion also of Dibelius, Wellhausen, and Lightfoot.[2]

1[41] κ. ὀργισθεὶς ἐκτείνας τὴν χεῖρα αὐτοῦ ἥψατο. Once again we have to reiterate that the translator's hand is possibly betrayed by the asyndetic ἐκτείνας. One notices his fondness for emphasising the 'curative touch of Jesus' (Taylor[3]). He can hardly have invented ὀργισθείς. His probable linking of two versions of the story explains the conflict between vv. 41 and 43. The redaction here is not so marked because it is caused by paraphrasing, or reducing parataxis. In 1[41a] stylistic R include ἅπτεσθαι, two participles, two imperatives without conjunctions and the historic present.

3[5a] is singular in tone and asyndetic, and contains a specialised LXX word, συλλυπεῖσθαι, and also περιβλέπεσθαι (4/6: 3[5a, 34], 10[23], 11[11]). To be noted also is the Pauline and Hebraic idea of 'hardness of heart', which is emphasised in several redactional passages, notably the literary constructions.[4]

5[33] has already been commented on for its double use of αὐτός, while the redundancy this time is in the main verb. ἦλθεν is followed by favoured words in Mark, προσέπεσεν[5] and φοβεῖσθαι.[6] The ending phrase πᾶσαν τὴν ἀλήθειαν is referred to by Taylor as 'classical' (Plato, *Apol.* 17B) and Johannine (16[13]), but one should also say one of the few examples where indirect speech has been sustained. If it is redactional, it shows the writer succeeding in writing in a more elevated style, and yet in the same sentence writing ἦλθεν καὶ προσέπεσεν αὐτῷ καὶ εἶπεν αὐτῷ.

---

[1] P. 54. [2] P. 69, n. 1.

[3] 'It is, of course, possible that Mark has combined two versions of the same story (cf. J. Weiss, 153 n.)' (p. 185). See Burkill, pp. 82f.

[4] Schweizer, p. 74; Lambrecht, p. 182 (use of μετά+gen.); Pesch, n. 67, p. 57, quotes Easton on 3[6] as R, regarding 3[5] as too abrupt a conclusion.

[5] 3[11]R, 5[33](?), 7[25]R(?). [6] 8/12R.

5²⁵⁻⁶ is noted by most commentators for its proliferation of participles, which hardly escapes notice even after a summary glance at the text. It could never be described as stylistic Greek, however, for seven participles and only one main verb, with parenthetical statements, make up a sprawling uncontrolled sentence. There are certain linguistic points which suggest that the passage might be editorial, apart from the obvious fact that it is a seam. δώδεκα ἔτη in 5²⁵ links up with the only other reference to δώδεκα ἔτη, in 5⁴². Lagrange considers that the twelve years of illness and the twelve years of age are coincidental. Sundwall's suggestion that Mark breaks up his sources and intercalates them needs, however, to be taken more seriously. Probably originally the 'Woman with the Issue of Blood' and the 'Raising of Jairus' Daughter' could have been linked by the common catchword of 'twelve'. Mark's short γάρ clause may unconsciously reflect his recognition that these two accounts were connected, and it is the significant number of twelve which effects the connection. Two small phrases illustrate also what Zerwick calls the 'blockages', or literary structure of the passage: τὰ παρ' αὐτῆς πάντα (v. 26) and also τὰ περὶ τοῦ Ἰησοῦ (v. 27). Vocabulary in 5²⁵⁻⁶ which may be editorial includes ὠφελεῖν (7¹¹R 1/3), ὄχλος (27/38R), πάσχειν (8³¹, 9¹² 2/3), ἅπτεσθαι (7/11R). As Taylor[1] suggests, the action of the woman implies the belief in the magical powers of touch, which can be paralleled by 3¹⁰R and 6⁵⁶R. The following verse, 5²⁸, also with its γάρ[2] and λέγω ὅτι, ἔλεγον γὰρ ὅτι recalls 5⁸. Its meaning is not that of the imperfect tense but the perfect, for 'she had said' illustrates the tendency of the evangelist to write first and explain afterwards. ἐν τῷ ὄχλῳ anticipates the redactional 5³⁰.

9²⁶ has already been discussed under ὥστε + inf.[3] The presence of adverbial πολλά, plus καί + participle twice, could imply that the evangelist is translating and reducing parataxis. He has in fact produced a pleasing similarity of sound in κράξας[4]...σπαράξας[5] in spite of his 'and' twice.[6]

14⁶⁷ᵃ, 'Peter's Denial', in its syntax displays signs of the

[1] P. 290.   [2] P. 128.   [3] P. 119.
[4] 3¹¹, 11⁹, 15³⁹. See Schweizer, p. 187: 'Mark has combined these two stories.' Kertelge, pp. 176f. regards vv. 20–7 as R.   [5] 1²⁶S, 9²⁶(?).
[6] καὶ κράξας καὶ πολλὰ σπαράξας ἐξῆλθεν (25/38R).

123

translator keeping close to his sources but translating his main verbs into participles, e.g. καὶ ἰδοῦσα τὸν Πέτρον... ἐμβλέψασα αὐτῷ λέγει.[1] Vv. 66a, 69, 70a, 71a and 72 are already marked R.

15[1a][2] has been marked R, so the two participles ποιήσαντες and δήσαντες may also be the translator's rendering of the Aramaic main verbs, συμβούλιον being paralleled by 3[6], and the whole passage being well based in tradition, but acting as a bridge to link with 14[55-65]. 15[1] is in some sense a duplication and at the same time a bridge, to bring the narrative back to the original pre-Marcan trial account, and the intercalated incident.

As 15[36] is part of Taylor's 'A' strand, it would seem at first reckoning that it should be marked S and left there, but the matter is more complicated than that. Wellhausen, Taylor, and Lindars[3] are very uncertain about the tradition at this point. Lindars states that Wellhausen 'may well be right to regard v. 36a as a separate tradition' which presumably has come in from Psalm 69. Best says that the second piece of mockery 'may represent the combination of two traditions, 35, 36b and 36a; cf. Taylor'.[4] If it is Mark who is combining these two traditions in the early stages of the Passion narrative – and we know his peculiar interest in the Baptist tradition – he may well have welded v. 36a into 35, 36b as suggested, which will account for the three participles, περιθείς, δραμών, γεμίσας,[5] the asyndetic linking of them, and the absence of the dative. Turner's suggestion of v. 36a as a parenthesis makes vv. 35 and 36b run more smoothly.

6[41] is closely linked to 14[22-3] by language and theology so they should be considered together. 14[23], although part of Taylor's 'B' strand, is liturgical tradition which Mark would have handled with care.[6] The repetition of (καὶ) λαβών in 14[23] from 14[22] is not followed by the same participle εὐλογήσας, but by εὐχαριστήσας, while both have the participles with asyndeton and ἔδωκεν αὐτοῖς. Probably a Semitism and not literary skill lies behind καὶ ἔπιον ἐξ αὐτοῦ πάντες. δέ is more

---

[1] See 10[27]R. Burkill, p. 237, regards vv. 66-72 as a section.

[2] Lambrecht, pp. 22, 124, 131, 253; Pesch, p. 127.

[3] B. Lindars, *New Testament Apologetic* (London, 1961), p. 100; Taylor, pp. 594f.

[4] P. 101, n. 3.   [5] Lambrecht, p. 78.

[6] Best, pp. 144f.

generously spread in Chs. 14–16, while here one notices the paratactic καί and absence of δέ. Probably we are to take the beginning of 14²² as redactional, but the asyndetic participles may reflect the translator's reduction of parataxis as he keeps close to his source. In 6⁴¹, however, the linguistic pattern of cultic tradition is deliberately adopted, while at the opening and ending of the Feeding the redactor's hand is more visible. However, the introduction in 6³⁰⁻⁴ is heavily redactional, and the inevitable question arises of the relationship between 14²²⁻³, 8⁶, and 6⁴¹.

If there is any question of a derivative, 14²²ᶠᶠ· would seem to be the master, and the account of the Feeding of the Five Thousand would seem to show more of the redactor's style. However, the 'eucharistic' language is stronger in the Feeding of the Four Thousand than in that of the Five Thousand, and yet there is a close literary relationship at times between the two. 6⁴¹ in one aspect is notably different from 8⁶, i.e. in its use of the aorist m.v., εὐλόγησεν, and an absence of the asyndetic participles which we find in the Passion narrative and in the Feeding of the Four Thousand. Therefore 8⁶ and 14²³ remain in source and 6⁴¹ is converted to redaction.[1]

8²³ is similar, in that it belongs to a passage (8²²⁻⁶) which has a close parallel in 7³²⁻⁷. After consulting the parallel forms[2] laid out by Taylor, we find that the redactional vocabulary is much more in evidence in Ch. 7 than in Ch. 8, so it is best to leave 8²³ in source. τοῦ ὄχλου κατ' ἰδίαν may be noted, as it is a good sign of redactional language and syntax, but it is absent from 8²³.

13³⁴ comes from what Jeremias terms a conflation of three parables; the Talents (Mt. 25¹⁴), the 'Servant Entrusted with Supervision' (Mt. 24⁴⁵) and the original 'Instruction to the Doorkeeper' 13³⁴ᵇ (Luke 12³⁵⁻⁸). If he is correct, then 13³⁴ᵃ may be redactional, but 13³⁴ᵇ is source, with its favoured γρηγορῇ, followed by the repeated γρηγορεῖτε (vv. 35 and 37). It is noteworthy that the opening of 13³⁴, which precedes the conflation of the two parables, is repeated in the warning in

---

[1] Kertelge, pp. 135ff.

[2]

| 7³³ καὶ ἀπολαβόμενος. . . | 8²³ καὶ ἐπιλαβόμενος. . . |
| καὶ πτύσας ἥψατο τῆς γλώσσης αὐτοῦ | καὶ πτύσας εἰς τὰ ὄμματα αὐτοῦ |

v. 35,[1] and I suggest a clever play upon words in κύριος and καιρός: 13³³ οὐκ οἴδατε γὰρ πότε ὁ καιρός ἐστιν – 13³⁵ γρηγορεῖτε οὖν, οὐκ οἴδατε γὰρ πότε ὁ κύριος τῆς οἰκίας ἔρχεται. Here we have the four watches of the Roman night, not as in Luke, the Palestinian three.

14⁴⁵S is part of the oldest Passion narrative, and on that score is left as a source verse, but its syntax is very crude even for Mark: καὶ ἐλθὼν εὐθὺς προσελθὼν αὐτῷ λέγει, 'Ραββί. We can only surmise that the Greek is the result of too literal a translation of the Semitic original, and leave it at that.

Our total final figures are therefore 22R and 5S. The linguistic test has thereby acted as a double prong in the redactional inquiry, for the original figures were 11R and 16S.

(n) γάρ EXPLANATORY

R: 1¹⁶,²²,³⁸, 2¹⁵, 3¹⁰,²¹, 5⁸,²⁸,⁴², 6¹⁴,³¹,⁴⁸,⁵², 7³, 9⁶⁽²⁾,³¹,³⁴,⁴¹, 10²²,⁴⁵, 11¹³,¹⁸⁽²⁾,³², 12¹², 13¹¹ᵇ, 14²,⁴⁰, 15¹⁰, 16⁴,⁸⁽²⁾ = 33 times

S: 4²²,²⁵, 6¹⁷,¹⁸,²⁰,⁵⁰, 7¹⁰,²¹,²⁷, 8³⁵,³⁶,³⁷,³⁸, 9³⁹,⁴⁰,⁴⁹, 10¹⁴,²⁷, 12¹⁴, 12²³,²⁵,⁴⁴, 13¹⁹,³³,³⁵, 14⁵,⁷,⁵⁶,⁷⁰, 15¹⁴ = 30 times

At least three[2] of these clauses with γάρ are such as to have raised questions concerning the linguistic and theological intentions of the evangelist. The most celebrated is 16⁸, ἐφοβοῦντο γάρ, but the other two are not less familiar to serious students of the Gospel of Mark: 5⁴² 'for she was twelve years old', and 11¹³ 'for it was not the season of figs'. Commentators have been puzzled by all three references, and some like Bird[3] have sought more subtle Old Testament allusions of the typological variety to explain the evangelist's linguistic and conceptual methods.

All of the Marcan γάρ texts, except possibly one, can be explained in terms of M. E. Thrall's demand that the argument

[1] See Lambrecht, p. 245: 'Das ἵνα nach ἐνετείλατο ist höchstwahrscheinlich markinischer Stil; θυρωρός wie auch ἀπόδημος ist in den Synoptikern hapaxl.'

[2] 5⁴², 11¹³, 16⁸.

[3] C. H. Bird, 'Some γάρ clauses in St. Mark's Gospel', *J.T.S.*, n.s. 4 (1953), 171–87.

should be mainly a linguistic one,[1] and her further statements that 'there is no reason to suppose the existence of a general affirmatory or "assertive-allusive" sense when Jesus refers to the Scriptures without explicit quotation' and that the Marcan usage can be affirmed by Herodotus[2] and the Septuagint.[3] Such writers tend to write freely and without looking ahead. They are not masters of the 'periodic' sentence, nor do they write long clauses and suspend their main verb until the end of the sentence (as for example Demosthenes), but they make a statement without planning the logical steps of the narrative or the argument, and then explain the previous statement, or interpose a step in the narrative which they had left to the imagination of the reader.[4] Numerous examples come under this heading, but a few will illustrate what is meant. 1^{16} 'for they were fishermen' is the evangelist's recognition that he should have mentioned this earlier in the sentence. In 1^{22} we are told 'Because He taught with authority (power) the people were astonished.' 'For they were astonished because He taught with authority' is the logical order, the reverse of the Marcan sentence. In 2^{15} the many 'who followed Him' are probably the disciples but they may be the tax-gatherers.[5] In 3^{10} we are told of the crushing of Jesus by the crowd and in the γάρ clause which follows the reason given is the tremendous number of people desiring to be cured. Thirty-three[6] of the redactional examples are of this kind, needing no other explanation than that of a non-literary writer who delays important details until after the facts have tumbled out of his mind, sometimes reversing the

---

[1] M. E. Thrall, *Greek Particles in the New Testament: Linguistic and Exegetical Studies*, New Testament Tools and Studies (Leiden, 1962), pp. 41–50. See p. 41: 'The hypotheses suggested by Bird and Zerwick can be justified and maintained only if the occurrences of γάρ and δέ upon which they depend are incapable of explanation from the linguistic point of view.'

[2] Cited by Thrall, *ibid.*, p. 48. [3] *Ibid.*, p. 49.

[4] 'Writers who use γάρ frequently, as Mark does, are not always logical thinkers who develop an argument stage by stage, representing each further statement as the necessary deduction from the previous one, or who tell a story in strict, chronological sequence, with every detail in its logical position in the narrative' (Thrall, *ibid.*, p. 47).

[5] Such is the view of Thrall, *ibid.*, p. 47 but the parenthesis as Turner suggests refers immediately to the 'disciples', and not to the outcasts.

[6] $1^{16, 22, 38}$, 2^{15}, $3^{10, 21}$, $5^{8, 28}$, $6^{14, 31, 48, 52}$, 7^3, $9^{6(2), 31, 34, 41}$, $10^{22, 45}$, 11^{13}, $11^{18(2), 32}$, $12^{12, 23}$, 13^{11}, $14^{2, 40}$, 15^{10}, $16^{4, 8(2)}$ = 33 times.

logical order so that what we consider to be a logically prior statement comes second.

Secondly, γάρ in parenthesis has more than one usage. First, we find the normal parenthesis, which has been dealt with at the beginning of the chapter, there being nineteen[1] examples of γάρ being used in this way. In addition, the redactor has a curious habit of using ἔλεγεν γάρ,[2] sometimes as a perfect, in order to express a thought or narrate an action which had taken place before the incident described in the previous sentence. The N.E.B. has bracketed 5^8 and rendered the verse in the following manner: '(For Jesus was already saying to him, "Out, unclean spirit, come out of this man!").' In 5^{28} the woman speaks aloud: 'If I touch even his clothes', but in 5^{27} we have already been told that she touched Jesus. 14^2, which has aroused much discussion because of its ambiguity, is clearly meant to be the reasoning of the chief priests before the arrest.

Thirdly, γάρ is sometimes used as a catchword, and that in three ways. The first usage is traditional, and the second and third are probably redactional. Ch. 8 illustrates the traditional, where a collection of sayings is held together by catchwords, one of which is γάρ: 8^{35} ὃς γάρ..., 8^{36} τί γάρ..., 8^{37} τί γάρ..., 8^{38} ὃς γάρ... Similar examples are probably 7^{21}S, 9^{49}, 13^{22}S. In 4^{1-25}, we see instances where the evangelist himself is probably responsible for grouping together some sayings by this method:[3] 4^{22} οὐ γάρ ἐστιν, concerned with the hidden and the manifest and 4^{25} ὃς γάρ ἔχει...ὃς οὐκ ἔχει...ὃ ἔχει, dealing with the idea that success breeds greater success, are probably references back to 4^{10-12}, in its concern for the 'mystery' being revealed to some, and hidden from others. Other examples which may be either redactional, or a traditional linking of sayings in this way are 9^{40}(?), 10^{14}(?), 13^{35}R.

The third group of γάρ linking clauses are to introduce scriptural citations: 7^{10}S, 10^{27}S, 13^8S, ^{19}S.

If we consider the possible transfer of S to R, probably 4^{22} and 4^{25} are Marcan, as 4^{1-34} is generally regarded as so heavily

---

[1] 2^{15}, $3^{10, 21}$, $5^{8, 28}$, $6^{14, 31, 48}$, 7^3, $9^{6(2)}$, 11^{32}, 12^{12}, $14^{2, 40}$, 15^{10}, $16^{4, 8 (2)}$ = 19 times.   [2] $3^{21(?)}$, $5^{8,28}$, 6^{18}, 14^2.

[3] Lightfoot, p. 34; Bultmann, p. 351; μόδιος, μέτρον and μετρέω (so Lightfoot).

redactional in its seams and linking sections.[1] When we look at the Q setting of the sayings in Matthew and Luke, although they retain Mark's γάρ they omit the important εἴ τις ἔχει ὦτα ἀκούειν, ἀκουέτω. In this section, 4[1–34], which is concerned with parables, their *raison d'être*, the interpretation of one parable in particular, the sayings in this section 4[21–5] are linked by the highly redactional κ. ἔ. α. (2 times) and the catchword ἀκούειν. Mark's 4[10–12] is concerned with the importance of hearing and understanding that which is hidden, i.e. the mystery of the Kingdom. The Marcan redactional motif of the obtuseness of the apostles has special significance in the problem of the teaching of Jesus, and parables in particular.

The first three references in Ch. 6 come from the death of John Baptist. 6[18] is commented on by Taylor,[2] as follows: 'Again as in 14, 20, etc. Mark adds an explanatory note.' ἔλεγεν is similar in style to the parenthetical sentences in other passages,[3] while we recall that the first use of γάρ is in the long parenthesis 6[14–16]. 6[17][4] typically explains Herod's curious remark about Jesus being 'John raised from the dead' by going on to tell us that Herod had put John into prison, and subsequently informs us of his death. 6[18][5] also contains λέγω ὅτι, while 6[20] looks back to 6[19] καὶ οὐκ ἠδύνατο. 6[21] and 6[22] are two of the few remaining genitive absolutes[6] which are not marked R from a literary critical point of view, but were subsequently transferred from S to R. 6[18] also tells us why Herod had put John in prison, i.e. because of John's outspokenness.

6[50] comes after the genitive absolute in 6[47][6] and the parenthesis in 6[48], and is also followed by the editorial comment in 6[52]. Once again αὐτόν precedes the verb, and πάντες is emphasised by its primary position in the sentence.

7[10a] comes from 7[9–13], 'The Question of Corban', an 'isolated saying, attached in Mark's manner to vii 1–8'.[7] 7[9] introduces

---

[1] Reploh, pp. 61–2; Pesch, pp. 132, 192; Lightfoot, p. 35.
[2] P. 312. [3] See p. 49.
[4] Taylor, p. 311, reminds us that the aorists are initially pluperfects: 'The reference is to a point earlier than 14–16 and subsequent to 1.14.'
[5] See p. 79. Pesch, p. 134; Lambrecht, p. 47; cf. 12[37] ἤκουεν αὐτοῦ ἡδέως and 6[20] καὶ ἡδέως αὐτοῦ ἤκουεν.
[6] See p. 66. N.B. also 6[47] has been transferred from S to R.
[7] So Taylor, p. 339.

Jesus' saying with the familiar κ. ἔ. αὐτοῖς, while the logion is attached by Μωϋσῆς γὰρ εἶπεν to the LXX of Ex. 22¹². 7²¹⁻³ expounds the explanation in 7²⁰, which repeats 7¹⁵ᵇ. Probably 7²¹⁻³ is a 'Pauline' type of list of twelve vices which is added by Mark to his exposition. ἔσωθεν γὰρ ἐκ τῆς καρδίας may well look back to ἔξωθεν in 7¹⁵, while ἐκ τῆς καρδίας looks back to εἰς τὴν καρδίαν in 7¹⁹.

7²⁷ᵇ comes under review as a possible R verse. Many[1] commentators regard 7²⁷ᵃ as either an editorial redaction or a later revision by a scribe. From the literary analysis, 7²⁴⁻⁹, 'The Syro-Phoenician Woman's Faith', is certainly not a standard miracle story, nor a pronouncement story. Rather, according to one scholar,[2] 'the teaching enunciated in verses 1–23 is applied in verses 24–31: words become deeds'. Lohmeyer[3] sees our 7²⁷ as central to a whole section 6³⁰⁻⁸²⁶, the overall subject being 'The Bread Miracle'. ἄρτος is either the evangelist's or his pre-Marcan source catchword which binds[4] together some strange allegorising texts.

Generally acknowledged as R are 7²⁴⁻⁵. 7²⁶ᵃ is one of C. H. Turner's parenthetical clauses.[5] Vv. 29 and 27a are regarded as R by Kertelge.[6] He points out the repetition of καὶ ἔλεγεν (εἶπεν) αὐτῇ, and the R phrase, τοῦτον τὸν λόγον, and also ὕπαγε in v. 29 (see R vocabulary for ὑπάγειν).

In 7²⁷ᵃ, the text is thought to be in line with, and influenced by, the famous Romans 1¹⁶ 'first to the Jews, then to the Greeks'. πρῶτον is 3/6 R. χορτασθῆναι is found in 6⁴², 7²⁷R, 8⁴·⁸. Although only one of these texts is possibly R, 6⁴¹ is R, as also 6³⁰⁻⁵, the introduction of the 'Feeding of the Five Thousand', of which 6⁴² is a verse. 8⁴·⁸ are from the 'Feeding of the Four Thousand'. Some would therefore regard 7²⁷ as preparing us for 8¹⁻¹⁰, and the 'bread' motif being a feeding of word and sacrament, first to the Jewish mission in the first feeding, and then to the Gentiles in the second, the Syro-Phoenician's daughter being a sample of the greater mission of expansion to follow. Sundwall[7] thought that these two feedings reflected

---

[1] Taylor, p. 350, quotes Bultmann, Klostermann, Holtzmann, Weiss, Bussmann. See also Kertelge, p. 153, who quotes Burkill and E. Schweizer.
[2] T. A. Burkill, *Zeitschrift für die neutestamentliche Wissenschaft* 57 (1966), 29.
[3] *Markus*, pp. 121f.   [4] 6³¹,³²⁻⁴⁴,⁵², 7²⁻⁵,²⁷f., 8¹⁻¹⁰,¹⁴⁻²⁰.
[5] See p. 52.   [6] P. 155.
[7] See pp. 48ff.

historically the twelve and the seven serving tables in Acts. The editor's language in the two feedings is influenced by the tradition in the Passion narrative, and the choice of words gives the feeding a eucharistic tone. ἄρτος (7/20 R: 6⁸,⁴¹⁽²⁾R, ⁵²R, 7²R, ⁵,²⁷, 8¹⁴⁽²⁾R, ¹⁶R, ¹⁷R, ¹⁹R, 14²²) is a key R word, but κυνάριον is used only in this section. If the arguments and tension over the problems of the Gentile mission are the background to this *Streitgespräch*, then the Lord's acceptance of the Gentile woman, even if not authentic, illustrates the struggle which St Paul and St Stephen had before the Gentile mission became commonly acceptable. If 7²⁷ᵃ is R, as many seem to think, and 7²⁷ᵇ is authentic, then the redactor's γάρ explanatory is most natural as an explanation of 7²⁷ᵃ.[1]

9³⁹R, ⁴⁰R, from 9³⁸⁻⁴¹ 'He who is not against us is for us', is radically different in meaning from the 'Q' form in Matthew and Luke. Matthew's 10⁴² reads: καὶ ὃς ἂν ποτίσῃ and εἰς ὄνομα μαθητοῦ, which is possibly interpreting the explanatory ὑμᾶς, and ὅτι Χριστοῦ ἐστε of Mk. 9⁴¹. Both Trocmé and Reploh[2] see Marcan shaping of 9³⁸⁻⁴⁰ linking the section on to 9⁴²ᶠᶠ·, where ἕνα τῶν μικρῶν τούτων τῶν πιστευόντων are the same as those who 'are Christ's'. Trocmé reminds us that in spite of the emphasis laid by Taylor and others on the pre-Marcan use of the catchwords γάρ and 'in my name', perhaps linking a pre-Marcan collection, we cannot rule out 'certain improvements of the author'. Jesus' sharp reply to John is given a further emphasis in a word of caution to the exclusive spirit and against the rigorist exclusion of those 'who are against us', which is almost turned upside down by the Matthaean form.

Mk. 9⁴⁹⁻⁵⁰ has no exact parallel in 9⁵⁰ᶜ in Matthew and Luke, and certainly no corresponding phrase to πᾶς γὰρ πυρί. 'Salt' is the linking word for vv. 50 and 49. 'Mark has added' this section according to Schweizer,[3] and although it is clear that he is making use of older collections, his own hand is not missing in the compilations.

Horstmann[4] and Reploh[5] consider the γάρ in 8³⁵ and 8³⁶ as

---

[1] Burkill, p. 148; Horstmann, p. 124; Pesch, pp. 61-2, 130, 134; Schweizer, p. 151; Trocmé, p. 128, n. 77.

[2] Trocmé, pp. 96-7, esp. p. 97, n. 89; Reploh, pp. 148ff.; Schweizer, p. 197: 'It is likely that Mark inserted vss. 38-40 on account of the catchword "in your name".'   [3] P. 200.

[4] Pp. 43ff.   [5] Pp. 36ff.

editorial, and while most students of the Gospels would have heard of 8^{35c} as R, modern critics of redaction are much interested in 8^{38} and 9^{1ac} as editorial placing of sayings of Jesus, to fit in with the overall plan of the author. 8^{35} is thought to refer back to 8^{34}, and to relate to it, while 8^{35a} ἕνεκεν ἐμοῦ καὶ τοῦ εὐαγγελίου is widely accepted as redactional and exegetical. The general subject which links up all these texts is the word 'life' or 'soul', and as the prophecy of 8^{31} was concerned with the death of Jesus, so these sayings are concerned with the κόσμος and 'life'. Comparison with the 'Q' form of the texts reveals some interesting emphases of the evangelist and choice of vocabulary.[1] An extension similar to that of εὐαγγελίου in 8^{35} could be καὶ τοὺς ἐμοὺς λόγους in 8^{38} where ἐν τῇ γενεᾷ ταύτῃ τῇ μοιχαλίδι καὶ ἁμαρτωλῷ is not found in Matthew and Luke. As 8^{35} and 8^{38} are regarded as R for reasons other than γάρ explanatory, the whole section from 8^{31}–9^{1} must be heavily edited, especially in the first four verses. Thus we should accept 8$^{35ac,\,38ac}$ confidently and 8$^{36a,\,37a}$, with less certainty but a considerable degree of probability, as editorial.

8$^{35,\,36,\,37,\,38}$ are sayings of Jesus linked by the catchword γάρ. Taylor[2] and his contemporaries regarded the linking as pre-Marcan and designed for catechetical purposes. 8$^{27ff.}$, 'Peter's Confession', was regarded by Manson and others as a climactic point in the ministry of Jesus. The shift of emphasis in modern criticism in favour of a form-critical treatment of the Gospels disallows us from making that kind of use of the Gospel pericopes. The redactional critic of the Gospel would say that 8$^{27ff.}$ marks a climactic point in Mark's presentation of the unbelief of the apostles, and that Peter's illumination marks a breakthrough from the hitherto hidden Messiahship of Jesus. Thus 8^{31}R is the first of the redactional prophecies of the Passion which prepares the reader for the suffering Messiahship and the Passion chapters in 14–16^{8}. Peter's limited understanding of the Messiahship of Jesus is sharply rebuked by Jesus, and with the generally accepted redactional summons to 'his disciples' (8^{34a}), the disciple is summoned to 'take up his cross if he wishes to follow Jesus'. Very soon after this section, 8^{35}–9^{1}, a high point of the Gospel arrives in the Transfiguration of Jesus,

[1] Mt. 16$^{24-8}$; Luke 9$^{23-7}$.   [2] Pp. 409–10; Sundwall, p. 8.

9^{2-8}. Thus $8^{35\text{ff.}}$ from a literary point of view is transitional, and near to a major bridge passage like 37^{-12}, etc.

10^{14} comes from 10^{13-16}, the teaching on children. Even if we follow Bultmann's[1] view that 10^{15} was probably attached by a compiler to $10^{13,14,16}$, this would hardly affect 10^{14} as S. 10^{27}, however, is somewhat different. In the Nestle text γάρ is not printed in black type. I find it difficult to see exact parallels in the LXX, but Taylor and Nestle consider that Genesis, Job or Zechariah are being conflated.[2] If this is so these texts do not have γάρ, and the compiler of this section would appear to be Mark himself. Every verse in it seems to be marked as partly R so that 10^{27} may well qualify for conversion from S to R.

Three of the four texts in Ch. 12 are found in passages so far not regarded as heavily redacted, and therefore left as S. 12^{44} is quite different from these in that it has already been commented on linguistically as a verse which shows signs of literary construction, and paradoxically also tautologous[3] writing, awkwardly placed in the syntax of the sentence – both characteristic of the evangelist. πάντες γάρ is opposed to αὕτη δέ; ἐκ τοῦ περισσεύοντος is contrasted with ἐκ τῆς ὑστερήσεως while πάντα ὅσα εἶχεν is awkwardly placed near to ὅλον τὸν βίον αὐτῆς, so that we are probably sound in regarding it as R in contrast to the other three.

Ch. 13 has six examples of γάρ, but two[4] of them are doubtful textually, and so have not been included. The other four, $13^{11b,19a}$R,^{33b,35} are probably R. 13^{19} has the following comment from Taylor:[5] 'The opening words (ἔσονται γάρ) read like a homiletical comment on the preceding sayings; cf. the use of γάρ in i.22b, v. 8, vi. 52, vii. 3, xvi. 8 etc.' 13^{33b} and 13^{35b}R are obviously related if only on the grounds of repetition: οὐκ οἴδατε γάρ πότε ὁ καιρός (κύριος)... Taylor says tentatively that 13^{33} 'also anticipates, and perhaps is suggested by,' 13^{35}.[6] Neither v. 33

---

[1] Pp. 75, 81, 105.

[2] Gen. 18^{14} ἀδυνατεῖ παρὰ τῷ θεῷ ῥῆμα; Job 10^{13}, 42^2; Zech. 8^6. Schweizer, p. 209; Reploh, pp. 197ff.

[3] There are 49S and 13R examples of tautology. R: $1^{28,32,34,38,45(?)}$, $4^{1,2,33-4}$, $8^{1,17}$, $9^{2,30}$, 14^1. See Allen, pp. 12ff. S: 1^{16}, $2^{19,20,25,27}$, $3^{14-15,26}$, $4^{5,31-2,39,40}$, $5^{12,15,19,40-1}$, $6^{3,4,17-18,25,28,35}$, $7^{13,15,21,33}$, 8^{12}, $10^{22,27,30}$, 11^4, $11^{24,28-9}$, $12^{2,14,23,24,27,44}$, $13^{20,29}$, $14^{6,15,30,43,45,54,61,62,71}$.

[4] $13^{8,22}$.   [5] P. 514. Lambrecht, p. 161; Marxsen, p. 198, n. 77.

[6] Lambrecht, p. 246; Jeremias, *Parables of Jesus*, pp. 55f.

nor v. 35 is to be found in the parallels in Matthew and Luke. We have here a fusion of two parables. 13^{34} with its 'successive participles and imperfect constructions' (so Taylor) was amongst our verses changed from S to R. All verses build up to the impressive 13^{37}, which is widely accepted as editorial.

The remaining texts to be considered come from the Passion narrative.[1] One[2] out of five is to be transferred from S to R rather hesitantly, while of the three to remain as S, two[3] display some signs of redactional style. 14^{7a} resembled 12^{44} in its γάρ and δέ clauses contrasted, which are possibly consciously inverted: πάντοτε γὰρ τοὺς πτωχοὺς ἔχετε μεθ᾽ ἑαυτῶν...ἐμὲ δὲ οὐ πάντοτε ἔχετε (14^7). As they both ($14^{5, 7}$) come from the Marcan intercalation they might well be editorial. However, the redaction should be heavier after v. 7, and the periphrastic tenses were evident in 14^4, so it might well be that the two verses with γάρ here show linguistic signs of further redaction.

14^{56a} is clearly a parallel tradition with 14^{57-9}, which has been placed in redaction. The first ἐψευδομαρτύρουν κατ᾽ αὐτοῦ may be the source for the same in 14^{57} so it remains S, while 14^{70} with καὶ γὰρ Γαλιλαῖος εἶ may well have been of great interest to the editor on account of its Galilean reference, but such a statement is hardly likely to be R alone. However, the Greek καὶ γάρ can be paralleled with 2 Thess. 3^{10}. Swete suggests that the words mean 'For, besides other considerations...' 14^{70a} has been transferred from S to R, so this strengthens the possibility of 14^{70c} being the same.

15^{14b}, the remaining text, comes from Taylor's 'B' strand, and is part of an intercalated section which has revealed some unsuspected redaction: the parenthesis in 15^{10}, πάλιν, redundant ἀποκριθείς and ἔλεγεν α. in 15^{12}, πάλιν again in 15^{13}, and ἔ. α. again in 15^{14} – now γάρ as well.

Conversion of S to R: $4^{22a, 25a}$, $6^{17, 18, 20, 50}$, $7^{10, 21a, 27b}$, $8^{35, 36, 37, 38}$, $9^{39, 40, 49}$, 10^{27}, 12^{44ac}, $13^{19, 33, 35}$, $14^{5, 7}$, 15^{14} = 24 times
To remain S: 10^{14}, $12^{14, 23, 25}$, $14^{56, 70}$ = 6 times

The final figures which emerge after a careful examination of individual texts, in the light of the total linguistic and literary investigation are, therefore, 24 redactional and 6 to remain in source of the previous 30, marked as R solely on the basis of literary criteria and a primary investigation into S and R. This

---

[1] $14^{5, 7, 56, 70}$, 15^{14}.   [2] 15^{14}.   [3] $14^{5, 7}$.

makes a reassessed figure of 57R and 6S, which leaves only 6 instances of clauses with γάρ which are S out of a total of 63.

FINAL STATISTICS OF THE LINGUISTIC TESTS

	Syntax	Final statistics	By linguistic method
(a)	Parenthetical clauses	28/29	—
(b)	Genitive absolute	29/29	5/5 converted from S to R
(c)	Participle as a main verb	5/5	1/5 from S to R
(d)	πολλά accusative	9/10	1/2 from S to R
(e)	λέγω ὅτι	38/41	6/9 from S to R
(f)	ἄρχομαι + infinitive	26/26	6/6 from S to R
(g)	εὐθύς	10/16	3/9 from S to R
	καὶ εὐθύς	23/27	7/11 from S to R
(h)	πάλιν	25/28	8/11 from S to R
(i)	'Redundant' participle	18/22	6/10 from S to R
(j)	Periphrastic tenses	29/30	9/10 from S to R
(k)	'Impersonals'	37/46	8/17 from S to R
(l)	ὥστε + infinitive	10/13	3/6 from S to R
(m)	Two or more participles before or after the main verb	22/27	11/16 from S to R
(n)	γάρ explanatory	57/63	24/30 from S to R

Total verses by linguistic method = 98/140

III MARCAN REDACTIONAL VOCABULARY MOST FREQUENTLY USED BY THE AUTHOR

The most frequent words are listed in alphabetical order.

From an analysis of the total vocabulary of the Gospel the proportion of R to S is denoted thus: ὄχλος 20/38 = 20R out of a total of 38. To qualify for inclusion in the analysis a word must not be used less than 5 times in the Gospel, and the percentage of the whole must not be less than 50%.

ἀγρεύειν† 1/1	διδαχή 5/5
ἀκολουθεῖν 11/18	δύσκολος† 1/1
ἀκούειν 30/43	δώδεκα 13/15
ἄλαλος† 2/3	ἐγείρειν 9/18
ἀμήν 11/13	εἰσπορεύεσθαι 4/8
ἀμφιβάλλειν 1/1	ἐκβάλλειν δαιμόνια 4/7
ἄμφοδον† 1/1	ἐκεῖ 6/11
ἀναβαίνειν 5/9	ἐκθαμβεῖσθαι† 2/4
ἀναπηδᾶν† 1/1	ἐκθαυμάζειν† 1/1
ἀνίστημι 11/16	ἐκπλήσσεσθαι 5/5
ἀπέρχεσθαι 11/22	ἐκπορεύεσθαι 6/11
ἅπτεσθαι 7/11	ἐμβαίνειν 5/5
ἄρχεσθαι 26/27	ἐναγκαλίζεσθαι† 2/2
ἀφρίζειν 1/2	ἐνειλεῖν† 1/1
βλέπειν 10/15	ἐξάπινα† 1/1
Γαλιλαία 10/12	ἐξέρχεσθαι 25/38
γάρ 57/63	ἐξουδενεῖσθαι 1/1
γινώσκειν 7/12	ἔξω 5/10
γναφεύς† 1/1	ἐπερωτᾶν 14/25
γραμματεύς 12/21	ἔρημος 8/8
γράφειν 6/10	εὐαγγέλιον 7/7
γρηγορεῖν 3/6	εὐθύς 33/43
δεῖ 4/6	ζητεῖν 6/10
διαλογίζεσθαι 6/7	ἤδη 6/8
διαστέλλεσθαι 5/5	Ἡρῴδης 8/8
διδάσκειν 15/17	θάλασσα 12/19

θαμβεῖσθαι†	3/3	ὄχλος	27/38
θυγάτριον	2/2	ὄψιος	5/5
θύρα	4/6	παιδιόθεν	1/1
Ἰάκωβος ὁ τοῦ Ζεβ.	5/11	πάλιν	25/28
ἰδού	6/7	παραβολή	12/13
ἱερόν	6/9	παραδιδόναι	13/21
Ἱεροσόλυμα	9/10	παράδοσις	3/5
Ἰωάννης ὁ Βαπτίζων	9/16	παραλαμβάνειν	5/6
Ἰωάννης ὁ τοῦ Ζεβ.	7/10	πέραν, εἰς τό	5/5
καθῆσθαι	8/11	περιβλέπεσθαι	4/6
καθώς	6/8	περιτρέχειν†	1/1
καιρός	3/5	πλοῖον	12/17
καλῶς	3/5	πνεῦμα ἀκάθαρτον	7/11
καρδία	6/11	πόλις	5/8
καταβαίνειν	4/6	πολλά	36/57
καταβαρύνεσθαι	1/1	πρασιά†	2/2
κατακόπτειν†	1/1	προάγειν	5/5
κατευλογεῖν†	1/1	προσάββατον	1/1
κατ' ἰδίαν	6/7	προσκαλεῖσθαι	8/9
κατοίκησις†	1/1	προσκεφάλαιον†	1/1
κηρύσσειν	11/12	προσκυλίειν†	1/1
κοράσιον	3/5	προσπορεύεσθαι†	1/1
κράβαττος	3/5	προφήτης	5/6
κράζειν	7/10	πρωΐ	4/5
κρατεῖν	9/15	πρῶτον	3/6
κυλίεσθαι	1/1	πῶς	8/15
κώμη	5/7	ῥάπισμα	1/1
λαλεῖν	12/19	στίλβειν†	1/1
λέγειν ὅτι	38/41	συζητεῖν	5/6
λίθος	6/8	συμπόσιον	2/2
μαθητής	35/46	συνάγειν	5/5
μηδείς	8/9	συναγωγή	6/8
μνημεῖον	3/6	συνθλίβειν†	2/2
μογιλάλος†	1/1	συνίειν	4/5
οἰκία	10/18	συνλυπεῖσθαι†	1/1
οἶκος	6/12	σῴζειν	8/14
ὄνομα	8/14	τόπος	6/9
ὅριον	4/5	τρυμαλιά†	1/1
ὅρος	8/11	υἱὸς τοῦ ἀνθρώπου	8/15
οὕτως	9/10	ὑπάγειν	8/15

ὑπολήνιον 1/1

Φαρισαῖος 11/12

φοβεῖσθαι 8/12

φωνεῖν 7/9

φωνή 4/7

Χριστός 4/7

ὥρα 6/12

ὥστε 9/13

REDACTIONAL VERSES CLASSIFIED WITH THEIR MAIN SYNTACTICAL FEATURES AND MOST FREQUENTLY USED VOCABULARY LISTED

1^{1-4}: (a), (g), (j), γράφειν, ἔρημος (2), εὐαγγέλιον, εὐθύς, ἰδού, Ἰωάννης ὁ Βαπτίζων, καθώς, κηρύσσειν, προφήτης, φωνή, Χριστός.

1^6: (g), (c), Ἰωάννης [ὁ Βαπτίζων].

1^8: πνεῦμα, δέ.

1^{9a}

1^{10}: (d), (m), ἀναβαίνειν, εὐθύς, καταβαίνειν.

1^{11a}: φωνή.

1^{12}: (g), ἐκβάλλειν, ἔρημος, εὐθύς.

1^{14-15}: (e), (m), Γαλιλαία, εὐαγγέλιον (2), Ἰωάννης [ὁ Βαπτ.], καιρός, κηρύσσειν, λέγειν ὅτι, παραδιδόναι.

1^{16ac}: (n), ἀμφιβάλλειν, Γαλιλαία, γάρ, θάλασσα (3).

1^{18}: (d), ἀκολουθεῖν, εὐθύς.

1^{20a}: (g), εὐθύς.

1^{21-2}: (g), (j), (k), (k), (n), γάρ, γραμματεύς, διδάσκειν (2), διδαχή, εἰσπορεύεσθαι, ἐκπλήσσεσθαι, εὐθύς, συναγωγή.

1^{23a}: (g), εὐθύς, συναγωγή.

1^{26}: (m), ἐξέρχεσθαι, πνεῦμα ἀκάθαρτον, φωνεῖν, φωνή.

1^{27-8}: (g), (l), Γαλιλαία, διδαχή, ἐξέρχεσθαι, εὐθύς, θαμβεῖσθαι, πνεῦμα ἀκάθαρτον, συζητεῖν, ὥστε.

1^{29a}: (g), (k), ἐξέρχεσθαι, εὐθύς, οἰκία, συναγωγή.

1^{30b}: (g), εὐθύς, λέγειν.

1^{31a}: (m), ἐγείρειν, κρατεῖν.

1^{32-4}: (b), (d), (j), (k), (m), δαιμόνια, ἐκβάλλειν, θύρα, λαλεῖν, ὄψιος, πόλις, πολλά (2).

1^{35}: (i), ἀναστῆναι, ἀπέρχεσθαι, ἐκεῖ, ἐξέρχεσθαι, ἔρημος, πρωΐ, τόπος.

1^{37-39}: (e), (c), (j), (m), (n), Γαλιλαία, γάρ, δαιμόνια, ἐκβάλλειν, ἐξέρχεσθαι, ζητεῖν, κηρύσσειν (2), λέγειν ὅτι, κώμη, πόλις, συναγωγή.

1^{40a}: (e), (m), λέγειν ὅτι.

1⁴¹ᵃ: (m), ἅπτεσθαι.

1⁴³: (g), ἐκβάλλειν, εὐθύς.

1⁴⁴ᵃ: μηδείς, ὑπάγειν.

1⁴⁵: (f), (k), (l), ἄρχεσθαι, ἐξέρχεσθαι, ἔξω, ἔρημος, κηρύσσειν, πόλις, πολλά, τόπος, ὥστε.

2¹⁻²: (c), (h), (l), ἀκούειν, θύρα, λαλεῖν, οἶκος, μηδείς, πάλιν, πολλά, συνάγειν, ὥστε.

2⁵ᵃ: (a), λέγειν.

2⁶: (j), (m), διαλογίζεσθαι, γραμματεύς, ἐκεῖ, καθῆσθαι, καρδία.

2⁸⁻⁹: (g), διαλογίζεσθαι (2), ἐγείρειν, εὐθύς, καρδία, κράβαττος, οὕτως, πνεῦμα.

2¹⁰ᶜ: (a), λέγειν.

2¹²⁻¹⁴: (e), (g), (h), (i), (l), ἀκολουθεῖν (2), ἀναστῆναι, διδάσκειν, ἐγείρειν, ἐξέρχεσθαι (2), εὐθύς, θάλασσα, καθῆσθαι, κράβαττος, λέγειν ὅτι, οὕτως, ὄχλος, πάλιν, Φαρισαῖος, ὥστε.

2¹⁵ᵃᶜ: (a), (n), ἀκολουθεῖν, γάρ, μαθητής, οἰκία, πολλά.

2¹⁶ᵃ: γραμματεύς, μαθητής, Φαρισαῖος.

2¹⁷ᵃ: (e), ἀκούειν, λέγειν ὅτι.

2¹⁸ᵃ: (j), Ἰωάννης [ὁ Βαπτίз.], μαθητής, Φαρισαῖος (2).

2²³ᵇ: (f), ἄρχεσθαι, μαθητής.

2²⁶ᵇ

2²⁷ᵃ: κ. ἔ. α.

2²⁸: (l), υἱὸς τοῦ ἀνθρώπ., ὥστε.

3¹ᵃ: (h), πάλιν, συναγωγή.

3⁵ᵃ: (m), καρδία, λέγειν, περιβλέπεσθαι, συνλυπεῖσθαι.

3⁶: (g), ἐξέρχεσθαι, εὐθύς, Φαρισαῖος.

3⁷: ἀκολουθεῖν, Γαλιλαία, θάλασσα, μαθητής.

3⁸: ἀκούειν, Ἱεροσόλυμα.

3⁹: μαθητής, ὄχλος.

3¹¹: κράζειν, λέγειν ὅτι, ὅταν, πνεῦμα ἀκάθαρτον.

3¹²: (d), πολλά.

3¹³⁻¹⁶: ἀναβαίνειν, ἀπέρχεσθαι, δώδεκα (2), ἐκβάλλειν τὰ δαιμόνια, κηρύσσειν, ὄνομα, ὄρος, προσκαλεῖσθαι.

3¹⁷ᶜ: (a), Ἰάκωβος ὁ τοῦ Ζεβ., Ἰωάννης [ὁ τοῦ Ζεβ.], ὄνομα.

3²⁰⁻¹: (e), (h), (l), (k), (n), (a), ἀκούειν, ἄρτος, γάρ, ἐξέρχεσθαι, κρατεῖν, λέγειν ὅτι, μηδέ, οἶκος, ὄχλος, πάλιν, ὥστε.

3²²ᵃ: (e), γραμματεύς, Ἱεροσόλυμα, καταβαίνειν, λέγειν ὅτι.

3²³ᵃ: ἔλεγεν αὐτοῖς, παραβολή, προσκαλεῖσθαι, πῶς.

3²⁸ᵃ: (e), ἀμήν, λέγειν ὅτι.

3^{30-33a}: (a), (k), (k), (l), (m), ἰδού, ἔξω (2), ӡητεῖν, καθῆσθαι, ὄχλος, πνεῦμα ἀκάθαρτον.

3^{34a}: (m), καθῆσθαι, μαθητής, περιβλέπεσθαι.

3^{35b}

4^{1-2}: (d), (f), (h), (l), ἄρχεσθαι, διδάσκειν (2), διδαχή, ἐμβαίνειν, θάλασσα (3), καθῆσθαι, κ. ἔ. α., ὄχλος (2), πάλιν, παραβολή, πλοῖον, πολλά, συνάγειν, ὥστε.

4^{3a}: ἀκούειν, ἐξέρχεσθαι, ἰδού.

4^9: ἀκούειν (2).

4^{10-12}: ἀκούειν (2), βλέπειν (2), παραβολή (2), δώδεκα, ἔξω, κ. ἔ. α., συνίειν.

4^{13}: παραβολή (2), πῶς.

4^{21a}: (e), κ. ἔ. α., λέγειν ὅτι.

4^{22a}: (n), γάρ.

4^{23-24a}: (n), ἀκούειν (3), κ. ἔ. α., βλέπειν.

4^{25a}: (n), γάρ.

4^{26a}: λέγειν.

4^{29a}: (g), εὐθύς, ὅταν, παραδιδόναι.

4^{30a}: λέγειν.

4^{31b}: (a), ἐπὶ τῆς γῆς.

4^{33-4}: ἀκούειν, καθώς, κατ᾽ ἰδίαν, λαλεῖν (2), μαθητής, παραβολή (2), πολλά.

4^{35-36a}: (b), εἰς τὸ πέραν, ὄψιος, ὄχλος, παραλαμβάνειν.

4^{37-8}: (l), (j), ἐγείρειν, ἤδη, μέγας, πλοῖον (2), προσκεφάλαιον, ὥστε.

4^{41} θάλασσα, μέγας, οὕτως, φοβεῖσθαι.

5^{1-2a}: (b), (g), (k), εἰς τὸ πέραν (2), ἐξέρχεσθαι, εὐθύς, θάλασσα, πλοῖον.

5^5: (j), κατακόπτειν, κράζειν, λίθος, μνημεῖον, ὄρος.

5^8: (n), ἀκάθαρτον, γάρ, ἐξέρχεσθαι, πνεῦμα.

5^{9c}: (a), ὄνομα, πολλά.

5^{11}: (j), ἐκεῖ, μέγας, ὄρος.

5^{15}: (m), καθῆσθαι, φοβεῖσθαι.

5^{17}: (f), ἀπέρχεσθαι, ἄρχεσθαι, ὄρος.

5^{18-20}: (b), ἄρχεσθαι (2), ἀπέρχεσθαι, ἐμβαίνειν, κηρύσσειν, οἶκος, πλοῖον, ὑπάγειν.

5^{21}: (b), (h), εἰς τὸ πέραν, θάλασσα, ὄχλος, πάλιν, πλοῖον, πολλά, συνάγειν.

5^{23a}: (d), θυγάτριον, λέγω ὅτι, πολλά.

5^{24}: ἀκολουθεῖν, ἀπέρχεσθαι, ὄχλος, πολλά, συνθλίβειν.

5²⁵⁻⁶: (m), δώδεκα, μηδείς, πολλά (2).

5²⁸: (n), γάρ, λέγω ὅτι, σῴζειν.

5³⁰⁻¹: (g), (m), βλέπειν, ἐξέρχεσθαι, εὐθύς, μαθητής, ὄχλος (2), συνθλίβειν.

5³³: (m), φοβεῖσθαι.

5³⁵ᵃ: (b), λαλεῖν, λέγω ὅτι.

5⁴¹ᵇ: (a), ἐγείρειν, κοράσιον.

5⁴²: (g(2)), (n), ἀναστῆναι, γάρ, δώδεκα, ἐγείρειν, εὐθύς, κοράσιον, μέγας.

5⁴³ᵃ: διαστέλλεσθαι, μηδείς, πολλά.

6¹⁻²ᵃ: (b), (f), ἀκολουθεῖν, ἀκούειν, ἄρχεσθαι, διδάσκειν, ἐκπλήσσεσθαι, ἐξέρχεσθαι, λέγειν, μαθητής, πολλά, συναγωγή.

6⁴ᵃ: κ. ἔ. α., λέγω ὅτι.

6⁶ᵃ: (c).

6⁶ᵇ⁻⁷: (f), ἄρχεσθαι, διδάσκειν, δώδεκα, κώμη, πνεῦμα ἀκάθαρτον, προσκαλεῖσθαι.

6¹⁰ᵃ: κ. ἔ. α.

6¹²⁻¹³: (d), δαιμόνια πολλά, ἐκβάλλειν, ἐξέρχεσθαι, κηρύσσειν, πολλά (2).

6¹⁴⁻¹⁶: (a), (e(3)), (k), (n), ἀκούειν (2), γάρ, ἐγείρειν (2), Ἡρῴδης (2), Ἰωάννης ὁ βαπτίζων, λέγω ὅτι (3), ὄνομα, προφήτης (2).

6¹⁷ᵃ: (n), γάρ, Ἡρῴδης, Ἰωάννης, κρατεῖν.

6¹⁸: (e), (n), γάρ, Ἡρῴδης, Ἰωάννης, λέγω ὅτι.

6²⁰ᵃᶜ: (n), ἀκούειν (2), γάρ, Ἡρῴδης, Ἰωάννης, πολλά, φοβεῖσθαι.

6²¹⁻²: (b(2)), Γαλιλαία, κοράσιον.

6²⁹: ἀκούειν, μαθητής, μνημεῖον.

6³⁰⁻³⁵ᵃ: (b), (e), (f), (j), (k), (n), ἀπέρχεσθαι, ἄρχεσθαι, γάρ, διδάσκειν, ἐκεῖ, ἐξέρχεσθαι, ἔρημος (2), ε. τ. πέραν, ἤδη, κατ' ἰδίαν (2), λέγω ὅτι, μαθητής, ὄχλος (2), πλοῖον, πόλις, πολλά, προάγειν, συνάγειν, τόπος (2), ὑπάγειν (2), ὥρα.

6⁴¹: (m), ἄρτος (2), μαθητής.

6⁴⁵: (g), ἐμβαίνειν, ε. τ. πέραν, εὐθύς, μαθητής, ὄχλος, πλοῖον, προάγειν.

6⁴⁷⁻⁸: (a), (b), (c), (n), γάρ (2), θάλασσα (2), ὄψιος, πλοῖον.

6⁵⁰ᵃ: (g), (n), γάρ, εὐθύς, λαλεῖν.

6⁵²⁻⁶: (b), (f), (g), (k(2)), (n), ἀκούειν, ἅπτεσθαι (2), ἄρτος, ἄρχεσθαι, ἐξέρχεσθαι, εὐθύς, καρδία, κράβαττος, κώμη, περιτρέχειν, πλοῖον, πόλις (2), συνίειν, σῴζειν.

7¹: (a), γραμματεύς, Ἱεροσόλυμα, συνάγειν, Φαρισαῖος.

7²ᵇ: (a), (c), μαθητής.

7³⁻⁴: (a), (d), (n), γάρ, κρατεῖν (2), παράδοσις, παραλαμβάνειν, πολλά, Φαρισαῖος, χαλκίον.

7⁵ᵃ: γραμματεύς, ἐπερωτᾶν, Φαρισαῖος.

7⁸: (a), κρατεῖν, παράδοσις.

7⁹ᵃ: καλῶς, κ. ἔ. α.

7¹⁰ᵃ: (n), γάρ.

7¹¹ᶜ: (a).

7¹³ᶜ: (d), παραδιδόναι, παράδοσις, πολλά.

7¹⁴: (h), ἀκούειν, κ. ἔ. α., ὄχλος, πάλιν, προσκαλεῖσθαι, συνίειν.

7¹⁶⁻¹⁷: ἀκούειν (2), ἐπερωτᾶν, μαθητής, οἶκος, ὄχλος, παραβολή.

7¹⁸ᵃ: οὕτως.

7¹⁹⁻²⁰ᵃ: (a), (c), (e), εἰσπορεύεσθαι, ἐκπορεύεσθαι, καρδία, λέγω ὅτι.

7²¹ᵃ: (n), γάρ, καρδία.

7²³: ἐκπορεύεσθαι.

7²⁴: (i), ἀναστῆναι, ἀπέρχεσθαι, λαλεῖν, οἰκία, ὅριον.

7²⁵: (g), (h), (i), (m), ἀκάθαρτον, ἀκούειν, εὐθύς, θυγάτριον, πνεῦμα.

7²⁶ᵃ: (a).

7²⁷ᵃᵇ: (n), ἄρτος, γάρ, πρῶτον.

7³¹⁻³²ᵃ: (h), Γαλιλαία, ἐξέρχεσθαι, θάλασσα, κωφός, μογιλάλος, ὅριον (2), πάλιν.

7³⁴ᶜ: (a), λέγειν, ὅ ἐστιν.

7³⁵⁻⁷: (a),ʼ(g), ἀκούειν, ἄλαλος, διαστέλλεσθαι (2), ἐκπλήσσεσθαι, εὐθύς, καλῶς, κηρύσσειν (2), λαλεῖν (2), λέγειν, μηδείς.

8¹: (b), (h), μαθητής, ὄχλος, πάλιν, πολλά, προσκαλεῖσθαι.

8⁹ᵇ⁻¹⁰: (g), ἐμβαίνειν, εὐθύς, μαθητής, πλοῖον.

8¹¹ᵃ: (f), ἄρχεσθαι, ἐξέρχεσθαι, συζητεῖν, Φαρισαῖος.

8¹³: (h), (i), (m), ἀπέρχεσθαι, ἐμβαίνειν, ε. τ. πέραν, πάλιν.

8¹⁴⁻¹⁶: (a), ἄρτος (2), βλέπειν, διαλογίζεσθαι, διαστέλλεσθαι, Ἡρώδης, πλοῖον, Φαρισαῖος.

8¹⁹⁻²¹: ἄρτος, δώδεκα, κ. ἔ. α., λέγω, συνίειν.

8²²ᵃ: (k).

8²⁶: κώμη, λέγω, μηδείς, οἶκος.

8²⁷⁻³³: (d), (e), (f(2)), (i), (m), ἀναστῆναι, ἄρχεσθαι (2), γραμματεύς, δεῖ, διδάσκειν, εἷς, ἐξέρχεσθαι, ἐπερωτᾶν (2), Ἰωάννης (3), κώμη, λαλεῖν, λέγω ὅτι, μαθητής, μηδείς, ὁδός, πολλά, προφήτης, υἱὸς τοῦ ἀνθρώπου, ὑπάγειν.

8³⁴ᵃ: μαθητής, ὄχλος, προσκαλεῖσθαι.

8³⁵ᵃᶜ: (n), γάρ, εὐαγγέλιον.

8³⁶ᵃ: (n), γάρ.

8³⁷ᵃ: (n), γάρ.

8³⁸ᵃᶜ: (n), γάρ.

9¹: (e), ἀμήν, κ. ἔ. α., λέγω ὅτι.

9²ᵃᵇ: Ἰάκωβος [ὁ τ. Ζ.] Ἰωάννης [ὁ τοῦ Ζεβ.], κατ᾽ ἰδίαν, ὄρος, παραλαμβάνειν.

9³: γναφεύς, ἐπὶ τῆς γῆς, οὕτως, στίλβειν.

9⁶⁻⁷ᵃ: (j(2)), (n(2)), γάρ, φωνή.

9⁹: (b), ἀναστῆναι, διαστέλλεσθαι, καταβαίνειν, μηδείς, ὄρος, ὅταν, υἱὸς τ. ἀ.

9¹²⁻¹³: (d), (e), γράφειν (2), ἐξουδενεῖσθαι, καθώς, λέγω ὅτι, μέν (2), πολλά, πρῶτον, πῶς, υἱὸς τ. ἀ.

9¹⁴⁻¹⁷ᵃ: (g), (k), γραμματεύς, εἷς, ἐκθαμβεῖσθαι, ἐπερωτᾶν (2), εὐθύς, μαθητής, ὄχλος (3), συζητεῖν (2).

9²⁰: (g), ἀφρίζειν, ἐπὶ τῆς γῆς, εὐθύς, κυλίεσθαι, πνεῦμα.

9²⁶: (l), (m), ἐξέρχεσθαι, κράζειν, λέγειν ὅτι, πολλά, ὥστε.

9²⁸ᵃ: (b), ἐπερωτᾶν, κατ᾽ ἰδίαν, μαθητής, οἶκος.

9³⁰⁻²: (e), (k), (n), ἀναστῆναι, Γαλιλαία, γάρ, διδάσκειν, ἐξέρχεσθαι, ἐπερωτᾶν, κ. ἔ. α., λέγω ὅτι, μαθητής, παραδιδόναι, υἱὸς τ. ἀ., φοβεῖσθαι.

9³³⁻⁷: (k), (n), διαλογίζεσθαι, δώδεκα, ἐναγκαλίζεσθαι, ἐπερωτᾶν, καθῆσθαι, ὁδός (2), οἰκία, ὄνομα, φωνεῖν.

9³⁸ᵃ: Ἰωάννης [ὁ τ. Ζεβ].

9³⁹ᵇ: (n), γάρ.

9⁴⁰ᵃ: (n), γάρ.

9⁴¹ᵇ: (e), (n), ἀμήν, λέγω ὅτι, ὄνομα, Χριστός.

9⁴⁹ᵃ: (n), γάρ.

9⁵⁰ᶜ

10¹: (h(2)), (i), ἀναστῆναι, διδάσκειν, ἐκεῖ, ὅριον, ὄχλος, πάλιν (2), πόλις.

10¹⁰⁻¹¹ᵃ: (h), ἐπερωτᾶν, μαθητής, οἰκία, πάλιν.

10¹³: ἅπτεσθαι, μαθητής.

10¹⁵ᵃ: ἀμήν, λέγω.

10¹⁶⁻¹⁷ᵃ: (b), (m), εἷς, ἐκπορεύεσθαι, ἐναγκαλίζεσθαι, ἐπερωτᾶν, κατευλογεῖν, προστρέχειν.

10²²ᵇ: (d), (j), (n), γάρ, πολλά.

10²³ᵃ: λέγειν, μαθητής, περιβλέπεσθαι, πῶς.

10²⁴ᵃᵇ: (h), (i), δύσκολος, θαμβεῖσθαι, μαθητής, πάλιν, πῶς.

10²⁶: ἐκπλήσσεσθαι, σώζειν.

10²⁷ᵃᶜ: (n), γάρ.

10²⁸: (f), ἀκολουθεῖν, ἄρχεσθαι, ἰδού, λέγειν.

10²⁹: ἀμήν, εὐαγγέλιον, λέγειν, οἰκία.

10³¹⁻³⁵ᵃ: (d), (f), (h), (j(2)), (k), ἀκολουθεῖν, ἀναβαίνειν, ἀναστῆναι, ἄρχεσθαι, γραμματεύς, δώδεκα, θαμβεῖσθαι (2), Ἰάκωβος [ὁ τοῦ Ζεβ.], ἰδού, Ἰεροσόλυμα (2), Ἰωάννης [ὁ τ. Ζεβ.], λέγω ὅτι, ὁδός, πάλιν, παραδιδόναι (2), παραλαμβάνειν, προάγειν, προσπορεύεσθαι, υἱὸς τ. ἀ., φοβεῖσθαι.

10⁴¹⁻⁵: (f), (n), ἀκούειν, ἄρχεσθαι, Ἰάκωβος [ὁ τοῦ Ζεβ.], Ἰωάννης [ὁ τ. Ζεβ.], μέγας, οὕτως, προσκαλεῖσθαι.

10⁴⁶⁻⁵²: (b), (f), (g), (i), (k), (m), ἀκολουθεῖν, ἀκούειν, ἀναπηδᾶν, ἄρχεσθαι, ἐγείρειν, ἐκπορεύεσθαι, εὐθύς, καθῆσθαι, κράζειν (2), λέγειν, μαθητής, ὁδός (2), ὄχλος, σώζειν, ὑπάγειν, φωνεῖν (2).

11¹⁻²ᵇ: (g), (k), εἰσπορεύεσθαι, εὐθύς, κατέναντι, Ἰεροσόλυμα, κώμη, μαθητής, ὄρος, ὑπάγειν.

11³ᶜ: (g), (h), εὐθύς, πάλιν.

11⁹⁻¹⁰: ἀκολουθεῖν, κράζειν, ὄνομα, προάγειν.

11¹¹⁻¹²: (b(2)), (k(2)), δώδεκα, ἐξέρχεσθαι (2), ἱερόν, Ἰεροσόλυμα, ὄψιος, περιβλέπεσθαι, ὥρα.

11¹³ᶜ: (n), γάρ, καιρός.

11¹⁴: (i), ἀκούειν, μαθητής, μηδείς.

11¹⁵ᵃ: (f), (k), Ἰεροσόλυμα.

11¹⁷ᵃ: διδάσκειν, γράφειν, κ. ἔ. α.

11¹⁸⁻²³ᵃ: (e), (k(2)), (n(2)), ἀκούειν, ἀμήν, γάρ (2), γραμματεύς, διδαχή, ἐκπλήσσεσθαι, ἐκπορεύεσθαι, ἔξω, ζητεῖν, λέγω ὅτι, ὅταν, ὄχλος, ὄψιος, πόλις, πρωΐ, πῶς, φοβεῖσθαι.

11²⁷: (b), (h), (k), γραμματεύς, ἱερόν, Ἰεροσόλυμα, πάλιν.

11³¹⁻²: (a), (n), διαλογίζεσθαι, γάρ, Ἰωάννης, ὄχλος, προφήτης, φοβεῖσθαι.

12¹ᵃ: (f), ἄρχεσθαι, λαλεῖν, παραβολή, ὑπολήνιον.

12¹²: (a), (i), (n), ἀπέρχεσθαι, γάρ, ζητεῖν, κρατεῖν, ὄχλος, παραβολή, φοβεῖσθαι.

12¹³: (k), ἀγρεύειν, Φαρισαῖος.

12¹⁷ᶜ: ἐκθαυμάζειν.

12¹⁸ᵃ: ἀναστῆναι, λέγειν.

12²⁸ᵃᵇ: (m), ἀκούειν, γραμματεύς, εἷς, ἐπερωτᾶν, καλῶς, συζητεῖν.

12³⁴ᶜ: ἐπερωτᾶν.

12³⁵ᵃ. (i), διδάσκειν, ἱερόν, λέγειν, πῶς.

12³⁷ᵇ: ἀκούειν, ὄχλος.

12³⁸ᵃ: διδαχή, λέγειν.

12⁴⁰ᵃ: καθῆσθαι, οἰκία.

12⁴¹⁻²: (a), (d), (i), καθῆσθαι, κατέναντι, ὄχλος, πολλά, πῶς.

12⁴³ᵃ: (e), ἀμήν, λέγειν ὅτι, μαθητής, προσκαλεῖσθαι.

12⁴⁴ᵃᶜ: (n), γάρ.

13¹: (b), εἷς, ἐκπορεύεσθαι, ἴδε, ἱερόν, λέγειν, λίθος, μαθητής.

13²⁻³: (b), βλέπειν, ἐπερωτᾶν, Ἰάκωβος, ἱερόν, Ἰωάννης (2), καθῆσθαι, κατέναντι, κατ' ἰδίαν, λίθος (2), μέγας, ὄρος.

13⁴: συντελεῖσθαι.

13⁵ᵃ: (f), ἄρχεσθαι, βλέπειν, λέγειν.

13⁶ᵇ: (e), λέγειν ὅτι, ὄνομα.

13⁷ᶜ: δεῖ.

13⁸ᶜ

13⁹ᵃ: (k), βλέπειν, δέ, παραδιδόναι.

13¹⁰: (a), δεῖ, εὐαγγέλιον, κηρύσσειν, πρῶτον.

13¹¹ᵇ: (n), γάρ, λαλεῖν, πνεῦμα.

13¹³: (j), ὄνομα, σώζειν.

13¹⁴ᵇ: (a), νοεῖν.

13¹⁹ᵃ: (n), γάρ.

13²³: βλέπειν, δέ.

13²⁴ᵇ

13²⁸ᵃ: ἤδη, ὅταν, παραβολή.

13²⁹⁻³⁰ᵃ: (e), ἀμήν, θύρα, λέγειν ὅτι, ὅταν, οὕτως.

13³³: (n), βλέπειν, γάρ, Ἰωάννης [ὁ τοῦ Ζεβ.], καιρός.

13³⁴ᵃ: οἰκία.

13³⁵ᵃ: (n), γάρ, γρηγορεῖν, οἰκία.

13³⁷: γρηγορεῖν, λέγειν.

14¹ᵃ: ζητεῖν.

14²ᵃ: (n), γάρ, λέγειν.

14³ᵃ: (b), οἰκία.

14⁴ᵃ: (j).

14⁵ᵃ: (n), γάρ.

14⁷ᵃ: (n), γάρ.

14⁸⁻⁹: ἀμήν, εὐαγγέλιον, κηρύσσειν, λαλεῖν, λέγειν.

14¹⁰: ἀπέρχεσθαι, δώδεκα, εἷς, παραδιδόναι.

14¹¹: ἀκούειν, ζητεῖν, παραδιδόναι, πῶς.

14¹²ᵃ: (k), λέγειν, μαθητής.

14¹⁷⁻²¹: (b(2)), (e), (f), ἀμήν, ἄρχεσθαι, γράφειν, δώδεκα (2), εἷς (3), καθώς, λέγειν ὅτι, μέν, ὄψιος, παραδιδόναι (2), υἱὸς τ. ἀ., ὑπάγειν.

14²²ᵃ: (b), (k).

14²⁵⁻³¹: (e(3)), (k), ἀμήν, Γαλιλαία, γράφειν, δεῖ, ἐγείρειν, ἐξέρχεσθαι, λαλεῖν, λέγειν, λέγειν ὅτι (3), ὄρος, προάγειν, φωνεῖν.

14³²ᵃ: (k), μαθητής.

14³³: (f), ἄρχεσθαι, ἐκθαμβεῖσθαι, Ἰάκωβος, Ἰωάννης, παραλαμβάνειν.

14³⁸: γρηγορεῖν, δέ, μέν, πνεῦμα.

14³⁹: (h), ἀπέρχεσθαι, πάλιν.

14⁴⁰⁻⁴³ᵃ: (b), (g), (h), (i), (j), (n), γάρ, ἐγείρειν, εὐθύς, ἰδού (2), καταβαρύνεσθαι, λαλεῖν, πάλιν, παραδιδόναι (2), παραλαμβάνειν, υἱὸς τ. ἀ., ὥρα.

14⁴⁷⁻⁵²: (a), (h), (i), (j), διδάσκειν, εἷς, ἐξέρχεσθαι, ἱερόν, κρατεῖν (2), περιβλέπεσθαι.

14⁵³ᵃ

14⁵⁷⁻⁹: (e(3)), ἀκούειν, ἀναστῆναι, λέγειν ὅτι (2), οὕτως.

14⁶¹: (h), ἐπερωτᾶν, πάλιν, Χριστός.

14⁶⁵⁻⁶⁶ᵃ: (b), (f), ἄρχεσθαι, ῥάπισμα.

14⁶⁷ᵃ: λέγειν.

14⁶⁹⁻⁷⁰ᵃ: (e), (f), (h), ἄρχεσθαι, λέγειν ὅτι, πάλιν (3).

14⁷¹ᵃ: (e), (f), ἄρχεσθαι, Χριστός.

14⁷²: (g), εὐθύς, φωνεῖν (2).

15¹ᵃ: (g), (m), γραμματεύς, εὐθύς, παραδιδόναι, πρωΐ.

15²: (i), ἐπερωτᾶν, λέγειν.

15⁷⁻⁸: (f), (j), ἀναβαίνειν, ἄρχεσθαι, καθώς, λέγειν, ὄχλος.

15¹⁰: (n), γάρ, παραδιδόναι,

15¹²⁻¹³ᵃ: (h(2)), (i), ἔ. α., πάλιν.

15¹⁴ᵇ: γάρ.

15¹⁵ᶜ: παραδιδόναι.

15¹⁶ᵇ: (a), ὅ ἐστιν.

15¹⁸: (f), ἄρχεσθαι.

15²⁰ᶜ

15²²ᵇ: (j), τόπος.

15²⁵⁻⁷: (k), ὥρα.

15²⁹⁻³²: γραμματεύς, καταβαίνειν (2), σῴζειν (3), Χριστός.

15³³: ὥρα (2).

15³⁴ᵇ: (a), (j).

15³⁶ᵃ: (m), γεμίζειν.

15^{39}: κράζειν, οὕτως.

15^{40a}: (j), δέ.

15^{42}: (b), ἤδη, ὄψιος, προσάββατον.

15^{43b} (j).

15^{46}: (j), (m), ἐνειλεῖν, θύρα, λίθος, μνημεῖον (2), προσκυλίειν.

16^{2a}: πρωΐ.

16^{4b}: (a), (n), γάρ, λίθος, μέγας.

16^{7}: ἐκεῖ, Γαλιλαία, καθώς, μαθητής, προάγειν, ὑπάγειν.

16^{8c}: (a), (n(2)), γάρ, φοβεῖσθαι.

REDACTIONAL TEXT OF MARK

The text used is that of the United Bible Societies, edited by Aland, Black, Metzger and Wikgren, 3rd ed. (1975), emended as follows:

1¹. υἱοῦ θεοῦ has good attestation, and could easily have been omitted by homoioteleuton.

1⁴. Omit καί after ἐρήμῳ.

1¹¹. ἐγένετο should be omitted, the more difficult reading being preferable. Note the possible influence of Lk. 3²² on the more polished text.

1²¹. εἰσελθών could well be an Alexandrian correction, caused partly by the confusion of εἰς and ἐν. Taylor prefers the verb ἐδίδασκεν after σάββασιν; however, the redactional usage of the position of the verb in the sentence is by no means consistently paratactic, but the verb may come at the end of the sentence (see C. H. Turner).

1²⁷. Comparing the redactional 9¹⁴,¹⁶, the unrevised text of 1²⁷ is probably ἑαυτούς and not αὐτούς. This also applies to the similar variant in 9¹⁰.

1²⁹. The plural ἐξελθόντες ἦλθον is to be preferred to the singular. Both in the synoptic Gospels and in the scribal corrections there is a marked tendency to change the plural to the singular.

1³². The more classical ἔδυ is a latter correction of the more primitive ἔδυσεν.

1³⁹. ἦλθεν has been substituted for ἦν, so Allen, Turner and Taylor. Once again the confusion of εἰς and ἐν.

1⁴⁰. Recalling the evangelist's usage re participles, sometimes without the support of the conjunction, the true reading here would seem to be π. α. καὶ γονυπετῶν λέγων αὐτῷ ὅτι, thus omitting the second καί.

1⁴¹. ὀργιοθείς is harder than σπλαγχνισθείς.

3⁷ᶠᶠ. The primitive Marcan grammar has caused a number of scribal corrections: εἰς, instead of πρός or παρά, is the most difficult reading. The favoured redactional word for the crowd is ὄχλος. Probably πολὺ πλῆθος in both 3⁷ and 3⁸ is an assimilation to the Lucan text, so read πολὺς ὄχλος. Both the singular and plural of ἀκολουθεῖν could be later attempts to redress the anacolouthon, as also πλῆθος πολύ. Thus the redactor may well have suspended the clauses ἀπό...ἀπό..., ἀπό..., until ἀκούοντες and ἦλθον.

3¹⁴ᶠᶠ·. The so-called neutral text of οὒς καὶ ἀποστόλους ὠνόμ. should almost certainly be omitted as an assimilation to Lk. 6¹³. The resultant Greek is very poor, even for Mark, and the most satisfactory solution of the problem of the original text is that the redactor once again is guilty of anacolouthon and suspended parentheses. 'First Simon' could also classify as an improvement doctrinally and grammatically, and also be influenced by the Matthaean version.

3³¹. The plural ἔρχονται is probably the original text.

3³². Omit κ. αἱ ἀδελφαί σου.

4²¹. Add ὅτι to κ. ἔ. α., as in accordance with redactional style.

4³⁶. ἀφίουσιν and not ἀφέντες would seem to be in harmony with a number of historic presents which are used in this section.

5²¹. πάλιν after εἰς τὸ πέραν, and not before. Omit ἐν τῷ πλοίῳ.

6²⁰. ἠπόρει instead of ἐποίει.

7⁴. Read ῥαντίσωνται and not βαπτίσωνται.

7¹⁶. εἴ τις ἔχει ὦτα...is similar to the placing of 4²³. Note 7¹⁴, 'Hear ye and understand.'

8¹. Add αὐτοῦ to μαθητάς, as this is a common R phrase.

10⁴⁶. Add προσαίτης after τυφλός; omit προσαιτῶν.

11³¹. Read Τί εἴπωμεν before Ἐὰν εἴπωμεν; omit [οὖν].

14⁶⁵. Read ἤρξαντό τινες ἐμπτύειν τῷ προσώπῳ αὐτοῦ, omitting αὐτῷ καὶ περικαλύπτειν αὐτοῦ τὸ πρόσωπον.

15³⁹. Add κράξας before ἐξέπνευσεν.

ΚΑΤΑ ΜΑΡΚΟΝ

*Sloping or underlined Greek type distinguishes possible S from
undisputed R*

THE PREACHING OF JOHN THE BAPTIST
(Mt. 3.1–12; Lk 3.1–9, 15–17; Jn 1.19–28)

1 Ἀρχὴ τοῦ εὐαγγελίου Ἰησοῦ Χριστοῦ υἱοῦ θεοῦ. 2 Καθὼς
γέγραπται ἐν τῷ Ἠσαΐᾳ τῷ προφήτῃ,

**Ἰδοὺ ἀποστέλλω τὸν ἄγγελόν μου πρὸ προσώπου σου,
ὃς κατασκευάσει τὴν ὁδόν σου·**
3 **φωνὴ βοῶντος ἐν τῇ ἐρήμῳ,
Ἑτοιμάσατε τὴν ὁδὸν κυρίου,
εὐθείας ποιεῖτε τὰς τρίβους αὐτοῦ –**

4 ἐγένετο Ἰωάννης ὁ βαπτίζων ἐν τῇ ἐρήμῳ κηρύσσων βάπτισμα
μετανοίας εἰς ἄφεσιν ἁμαρτιῶν... 6 καὶ ἦν ὁ Ἰωάννης ἐνδεδυμένος
τρίχας καμήλου καὶ ζώνην δερματίνην περὶ τὴν ὀσφὺν αὐτοῦ, καὶ
ἐσθίων ἀκρίδας καὶ μέλι ἄγριον... 8 ἐγὼ ἐβάπτισα ὑμᾶς ὕδατι,
αὐτὸς δὲ βαπτίσει ὑμᾶς ἐν πνεύματι ἁγίῳ.

THE BAPTISM OF JESUS
(Mt 3.13–17; Lk 3.21–22)

9 Καὶ ἐγένετο ἐν ἐκείναις ταῖς ἡμέραις... 10 καὶ εὐθὺς ἀναβαίνων
ἐκ τοῦ ὕδατος εἶδεν σχιζομένους τοὺς οὐρανοὺς καὶ τὸ πνεῦμα
ὡς περιστερὰν καταβαῖνον εἰς αὐτόν· 11 καὶ φωνὴ ἐκ τῶν
οὐρανῶν...

THE TEMPTATION OF JESUS
(Mt 4.1–11; Lk 4.1–13)

12 Καὶ εὐθὺς τὸ πνεῦμα αὐτὸν ἐκβάλλει εἰς τὴν ἔρημον.

THE BEGINNING OF THE GALILEAN MINISTRY
(Mt 4.12–17; Lk 4.14–15)

14 Μετὰ δὲ τὸ παραδοθῆναι τὸν Ἰωάννην ἦλθεν ὁ Ἰησοῦς εἰς τὴν
Γαλιλαίαν κηρύσσων τὸ εὐαγγέλιον τοῦ θεοῦ 15 καὶ λέγων ὅτι

Πεπλήρωται ὁ καιρὸς καὶ ἤγγικεν ἡ βασιλεία τοῦ θεοῦ· μετα-
νοεῖτε καὶ πιστεύετε ἐν τῷ εὐαγγελίῳ.

THE CALLING OF FOUR FISHERMEN
(Mt 4.18–22; Lk 5.1–11)

16 Καὶ παράγων παρὰ τὴν θάλασσαν τῆς Γαλιλαίας...ἀμφιβάλ-
λοντας ἐν τῇ θαλάσσῃ· ἦσαν γὰρ ἁλιεῖς...18 καὶ εὐθὺς ἀφέντες
τὰ δίκτυα ἠκολούθησαν αὐτῷ... 20 καὶ εὐθὺς ἐκάλεσεν
αὐτούς...

THE MAN WITH AN UNCLEAN SPIRIT
(Lk 4.31–37)

21 Καὶ εἰσπορεύονται εἰς Καφαρναούμ. καὶ εὐθὺς τοῖς σάββασιν
εἰς τὴν συναγωγὴν ἐδίδασκεν. 22 καὶ ἐξεπλήσσοντο ἐπὶ τῇ
διδαχῇ αὐτοῦ, ἦν γὰρ διδάσκων αὐτοὺς ὡς ἐξουσίαν ἔχων καὶ οὐχ
ὡς οἱ γραμματεῖς. 23 καὶ εὐθὺς ἦν ἐν τῇ συναγωγῇ αὐτῶν...
26 καὶ σπαράξαν αὐτὸν τὸ πνεῦμα τὸ ἀκάθαρτον καὶ φωνῆσαν
φωνῇ μεγάλῃ ἐξῆλθεν ἐξ αὐτοῦ. 27 καὶ ἐθαμβήθησαν ἅπαντες,
ὥστε συζητεῖν πρὸς ἑαυτοὺς λέγοντας, Τί ἐστιν τοῦτο; διδαχὴ
καινὴ κατ' ἐξουσίαν· καὶ τοῖς πνεύμασι τοῖς ἀκαθάρτοις ἐπιτάσσει,
καὶ ὑπακούουσιν αὐτῷ. 28 καὶ ἐξῆλθεν ἡ ἀκοὴ αὐτοῦ εὐθὺς
πανταχοῦ εἰς ὅλην τὴν περίχωρον τῆς Γαλιλαίας.

THE HEALING OF MANY PEOPLE
(Mt 8.14–17; Lk 4.38–41)

29 Καὶ εὐθὺς ἐκ τῆς συναγωγῆς ἐξελθόντες ἦλθον εἰς τὴν οἰκίαν...
30 ...καὶ εὐθὺς λέγουσιν αὐτῷ περὶ αὐτῆς. 31 καὶ προσελθὼν
ἤγειρεν αὐτὴν κρατήσας τῆς χειρός·... 32 Ὀψίας δὲ γενομένης,
ὅτε ἔδυσεν ὁ ἥλιος, ἔφερον πρὸς αὐτὸν πάντας τοὺς κακῶς ἔχοντας
καὶ τοὺς δαιμονιζομένους· 33 καὶ ἦν ὅλη ἡ πόλις ἐπισυνηγμένη
πρὸς τὴν θύραν. 34 καὶ ἐθεράπευσεν πολλοὺς κακῶς ἔχοντας
ποικίλαις νόσοις, καὶ δαιμόνια πολλὰ ἐξέβαλεν, καὶ οὐκ ἤφιεν λαλεῖν
τὰ δαιμόνια, ὅτι ᾔδεισαν αὐτόν.

A PREACHING TOUR
(Lk 4.42–44)

35 Καὶ πρωῒ ἔννυχα λίαν ἀναστὰς ἐξῆλθεν καὶ ἀπῆλθεν εἰς ἔρημον τόπον κἀκεῖ προσηύχετο... 37 καὶ εὗρον αὐτὸν καὶ λέγουσιν αὐτῷ ὅτι Πάντες ζητοῦσίν σε. 38 καὶ λέγει αὐτοῖς, Ἄγωμεν ἀλλαχοῦ εἰς τὰς ἐχομένας κωμοπόλεις, ἵνα καὶ ἐκεῖ κηρύξω· εἰς τοῦτο γὰρ ἐξῆλθον. 39 καὶ ἦν κηρύσσων εἰς τὰς συναγωγὰς αὐτῶν εἰς ὅλην τὴν Γαλιλαίαν καὶ τὰ δαιμόνια ἐκβάλλων.

THE CLEANSING OF A LEPER
(Mt 8.1–4; Lk 5.12–16)

40 Καὶ ἔρχεται πρὸς αὐτὸν λεπρὸς παρακαλῶν αὐτὸν [καὶ γονυπετῶν] λέγων αὐτῷ ὅτι... 41 καὶ ὀργισθεὶς ἐκτείνας τὴν χεῖρα αὐτοῦ ἥψατο καὶ λέγει αὐτῷ,... 43 καὶ ἐμβριμησάμενος αὐτῷ εὐθὺς ἐξέβαλεν αὐτόν, 44 καὶ λέγει αὐτῷ, Ὅρα μηδενὶ μηδὲν εἴπῃς,... 45 ὁ δὲ ἐξελθὼν ἤρξατο κηρύσσειν πολλὰ καὶ διαφημίζειν τὸν λόγον, ὥστε μηκέτι αὐτὸν δύνασθαι φανερῶς εἰς πόλιν εἰσελθεῖν, ἀλλ' ἔξω ἐπ' ἐρήμοις τόποις ἦν· καὶ ἤρχοντο πρὸς αὐτὸν πάντοθεν.

THE HEALING OF A PARALYTIC
(Mt 9.1–8; Lk 5.17–26)

2 Καὶ εἰσελθὼν πάλιν εἰς Καφαρναοὺμ δι' ἡμερῶν ἠκούσθη ὅτι ἐν οἴκῳ ἐστίν. 2 καὶ συνήχθησαν πολλοὶ ὥστε μηκέτι χωρεῖν μηδὲ τὰ πρὸς τὴν θύραν, καὶ ἐλάλει αὐτοῖς τὸν λόγον... 5 καὶ ἰδὼν ὁ Ἰησοῦς τὴν πίστιν αὐτῶν λέγει τῷ παραλυτικῷ,... 6 ἦσαν δέ τινες τῶν γραμματέων ἐκεῖ καθήμενοι καὶ διαλογιζόμενοι ἐν ταῖς καρδίαις αὐτῶν,... 8 καὶ εὐθὺς ἐπιγνοὺς ὁ Ἰησοῦς τῷ πνεύματι αὐτοῦ ὅτι οὕτως διαλογίζονται ἐν ἑαυτοῖς λέγει αὐτοῖς, Τί ταῦτα διαλογίζεσθε ἐν ταῖς καρδίαις ὑμῶν; 9 τί ἐστιν εὐκοπώτερον, εἰπεῖν τῷ παραλυτικῷ, Ἀφίενταί σου αἱ ἁμαρτίαι, ἢ εἰπεῖν, Ἔγειρε καὶ ἆρον τὸν κράβαττόν σου καὶ περιπάτει; 10 ... λέγει τῷ παραλυτικῷ, ... 12 καὶ ἠγέρθη καὶ εὐθὺς ἄρας τὸν κράβαττον ἐξῆλθεν ἔμπροσθεν πάντων, ὥστε ἐξίστασθαι πάντας καὶ δοξάζειν τὸν θεὸν λέγοντας ὅτι Οὕτως οὐδέποτε εἴδομεν.

THE CALLING OF LEVI
(Mt 9.9–13; Lk 5.27–32)

13 Καὶ ἐξῆλθεν πάλιν παρὰ τὴν θάλασσαν· καὶ πᾶς ὁ ὄχλος ἤρχετο πρὸς αὐτόν, καὶ ἐδίδασκεν αὐτούς. 14 καὶ παράγων εἶδεν Λευὶν τὸν τοῦ Ἀλφαίου καθήμενον ἐπὶ τὸ τελώνιον, καὶ λέγει αὐτῷ, Ἀκολούθει μοι. καὶ ἀναστὰς ἠκολούθησεν αὐτῷ. 15 Καὶ γίνεται κατακεῖσθαι αὐτὸν ἐν τῇ οἰκίᾳ αὐτοῦ,...ἦσαν γὰρ πολλοὶ καὶ ἠκολούθουν αὐτῷ. 16 καὶ οἱ γραμματεῖς τῶν Φαρισαί-ων,... 17 καὶ ἀκούσας ὁ Ἰησοῦς λέγει αὐτοῖς [ὅτι]...

THE QUESTION ABOUT FASTING

18 ...καὶ οἱ Φαρισαῖοι νηστεύοντες...καὶ οἱ μαθηταὶ τῶν Φαρισαίων...

PLUCKING GRAIN ON THE SABBATH
(Mt 12.1–8; Lk 6.1–5)

23 ...καὶ οἱ μαθηταὶ αὐτοῦ ἤρξαντο ὁδὸν ποιεῖν τίλλοντες τοὺς στάχυας... 26 ...ἐπὶ Ἀβιαθὰρ ἀρχιερέως... 27 καὶ ἔλεγεν αὐτοῖς... 28 ὥστε κύριός ἐστιν ὁ υἱὸς τοῦ ἀνθρώπου καὶ τοῦ σαββάτου.

THE MAN WITH A WITHERED HAND
(Mt 12.9–14; Lk 6.6–11)

3 Καὶ εἰσῆλθεν πάλιν εἰς τὴν συναγωγήν... 5 καὶ περιβλεψά-μενος αὐτοὺς μετ' ὀργῆς, συλλυπούμενος ἐπὶ τῇ πωρώσει τῆς καρδίας αὐτῶν, λέγει τῷ ἀνθρώπῳ,... 6 καὶ ἐξελθόντες οἱ Φαρισαῖοι εὐθὺς μετὰ τῶν Ἡρῳδιανῶν συμβούλιον ἐδίδουν κατ' αὐτοῦ ὅπως αὐτὸν ἀπολέσωσιν.

A MULTITUDE AT THE SEASIDE

7 Καὶ ὁ Ἰησοῦς μετὰ τῶν μαθητῶν αὐτοῦ ἀνεχώρησεν εἰς τὴν θάλασσαν. καὶ πολὺς ὄχλος ἀπὸ τῆς Γαλιλαίας...καὶ ἀπὸ τῆς Ἰουδαίας... 9 καὶ εἶπεν τοῖς μαθηταῖς αὐτοῦ ἵνα πλοιάριον

προσκαρτερῇ αὐτῷ διὰ τὸν ὄχλον ἵνα μὴ θλίβωσιν αὐτόν·... 11
καὶ τὰ πνεύματα τὰ ἀκάθαρτα, ὅταν αὐτὸν ἐθεώρουν, προσέπι-
πτον αὐτῷ καὶ ἔκραζον λέγοντα ὅτι Σὺ εἶ ὁ υἱὸς τοῦ θεοῦ. 12
καὶ πολλὰ ἐπετίμα αὐτοῖς ἵνα μὴ αὐτὸν φανερὸν ποιήσωσιν.

THE CHOOSING OF THE TWELVE
(Mt 10.1–4; Lk 6.12–16)

13 Καὶ ἀναβαίνει εἰς τὸ ὄρος καὶ προσκαλεῖται οὓς ἤθελεν αὐτός,
καὶ ἀπῆλθον πρὸς αὐτόν. 14 καὶ ἐποίησεν δώδεκα,...ἵνα ὦσιν
μετ᾽ αὐτοῦ καὶ ἵνα ἀποστέλλῃ αὐτοὺς κηρύσσειν 15 καὶ ἔχειν
ἐξουσίαν ἐκβάλλειν τὰ δαιμόνια· 16 καὶ ἐποίησεν τοὺς δώδεκα
καὶ ἐπέθηκεν ὄνομα τῷ Σίμωνι Πέτρον,... 17 ...καὶ ἐπέθηκεν
αὐτοῖς ὀνόμα[τα] Βοανηργές, ὅ ἐστιν Υἱοὶ Βροντῆς·...

JESUS AND BEELZEBUL
(Mt 12.22–32; Lk 11.14–23; 12.10)

20 Καὶ ἔρχεται εἰς οἶκον· καὶ συνέρχεται πάλιν ὄχλος, ὥστε μὴ
δύνασθαι αὐτοὺς μηδὲ ἄρτον φαγεῖν. 21 καὶ ἀκούσαντες οἱ παρ᾽
αὐτοῦ ἐξῆλθον κρατῆσαι αὐτόν, ἔλεγον γὰρ ὅτι ἐξέστη. 22 καὶ
οἱ γραμματεῖς οἱ ἀπὸ Ἱεροσολύμων καταβάντες ἔλεγον ὅτι... 23
καὶ προσκαλεσάμενος αὐτοὺς ἐν παραβολαῖς ἔλεγεν αὐτοῖς,...
28 ἀμὴν λέγω ὑμῖν ὅτι... 30 ὅτι ἔλεγον, Πνεῦμα ἀκάθαρτον
ἔχει.

THE MOTHER AND BROTHERS OF JESUS
(Mt 12.46–50; Lk 8.19–21)

31 Καὶ ἔρχονται ἡ μήτηρ αὐτοῦ καὶ οἱ ἀδελφοὶ αὐτοῦ καὶ ἔξω
στήκοντες ἀπέστειλαν πρὸς αὐτὸν καλοῦντες αὐτόν· 32 καὶ
ἐκάθητο περὶ αὐτὸν ὄχλος, καὶ λέγουσιν αὐτῷ, Ἰδοὺ ἡ μήτηρ σου
καὶ οἱ ἀδελφοί σου ἔξω ζητοῦσίν σε. 33 καὶ ἀποκριθεὶς αὐτοῖς
λέγει,... 34 καὶ περιβλεψάμενος τοὺς περὶ αὐτὸν κύκλῳ καθημέ-
νους λέγει,... 35 ...οὗτος ἀδελφός μου καὶ ἀδελφὴ καὶ μήτηρ
ἐστίν.

THE PARABLE OF THE SOWER
(Mt 13.1–9; Lk 8.4–8)

4 Καὶ πάλιν ἤρξατο διδάσκειν παρὰ τὴν θάλασσαν. καὶ συνάγεται πρὸς αὐτὸν ὄχλος πλεῖστος, ὥστε αὐτὸν εἰς πλοῖον ἐμβάντα
καθῆσθαι ἐν τῇ θαλάσσῃ, καὶ πᾶς ὁ ὄχλος πρὸς τὴν θάλασσαν
ἐπὶ τῆς γῆς ἦσαν. 2 καὶ ἐδίδασκεν αὐτοὺς ἐν παραβολαῖς πολλά,
καὶ ἔλεγεν αὐτοῖς ἐν τῇ διδαχῇ αὐτοῦ, 3 Ἀκούετε. ἰδοὺ
ἐξῆλθεν... 9 καὶ ἔλεγεν, Ὃς ἔχει ὦτα ἀκούειν ἀκουέτω.

THE PURPOSE OF THE PARABLES
(Mt 13.10–17; Lk 8.9–10)

10 Καὶ ὅτε ἐγένετο κατὰ μόνας, ἠρώτων αὐτὸν οἱ περὶ αὐτὸν
σὺν τοῖς δώδεκα τὰς παραβολάς. 11 καὶ ἔλεγεν αὐτοῖς, Ὑμῖν τὸ
μυστήριον δέδοται τῆς βασιλείας τοῦ θεοῦ· ἐκείνοις δὲ τοῖς ἔξω
ἐν παραβολαῖς τὰ πάντα γίνεται, 12 ἵνα

**βλέποντες βλέπωσιν καὶ μὴ ἴδωσιν,
καὶ ἀκούοντες ἀκούωσιν καὶ μὴ συνιῶσιν,
μήποτε ἐπιστρέψωσιν καὶ ἀφεθῇ αὐτοῖς.**

THE PARABLE OF THE SOWER EXPLAINED
(Mt 13.18–23; Lk 8.11–15)

13 Καὶ λέγει αὐτοῖς, Οὐκ οἴδατε τὴν παραβολὴν ταύτην, καὶ πῶς
πάσας τὰς παραβολὰς γνώσεσθε;

A LIGHT UNDER A BUSHEL
(Lk 8.16–18)

21 Καὶ ἔλεγεν αὐτοῖς ὅτι,... 22 οὐ γάρ ἐστιν... 23 εἴ τις ἔχει
ὦτα ἀκούειν ἀκουέτω. 24 Καὶ ἔλεγεν αὐτοῖς,... 25 ὃς γὰρ
ἔχει...

THE PARABLE OF THE GROWING SEED

26 καὶ ἔλεγεν... 29 ὅταν δὲ παραδοῖ ὁ καρπός, εὐθὺς...

THE PARABLE OF THE MUSTARD SEED
(Mt 13.31–32; Lk 13.18–19)

30 Καὶ ἔλεγεν,... 31 ...μικρότερον ὂν πάντων τῶν σπερμάτων τῶν ἐπὶ τῆς γῆς,

THE USE OF PARABLES
(Mt 13.34–35)

33 Καὶ τοιαύταις παραβολαῖς πολλαῖς ἐλάλει αὐτοῖς τὸν λόγον, καθὼς ἠδύναντο ἀκούειν· 34 χωρὶς δὲ παραβολῆς οὐκ ἐλάλει αὐτοῖς, κατ᾽ ἰδίαν δὲ τοῖς ἰδίοις μαθηταῖς ἐπέλυεν πάντα.

THE CALMING OF A STORM
(Mt 8.23–27; Lk 8.22–25)

35 Καὶ λέγει αὐτοῖς ἐν ἐκείνῃ τῇ ἡμέρᾳ ὀψίας γενομένης, Διέλθωμεν εἰς τὸ πέραν. 36 καὶ ἀφίουσιν τὸν ὄχλον...ὡς ἦν ἐν τῷ πλοίῳ,... 37 καὶ γίνεται λαῖλαψ μεγάλη ἀνέμου, καὶ τὰ κύματα ἐπέβαλλεν εἰς τὸ πλοῖον, ὥστε ἤδη γεμίζεσθαι τὸ πλοῖον. 38 καὶ αὐτὸς ἦν ἐν τῇ πρύμνῃ ἐπὶ τὸ προσκεφάλαιον καθεύδων· καὶ ἐγείρουσιν αὐτὸν καὶ λέγουσιν αὐτῷ, Διδάσκαλε, οὐ μέλει σοι ὅτι ἀπολλύμεθα;... 41 καὶ ἐφοβήθησαν φόβον μέγαν, καὶ ἔλεγον πρὸς ἀλλήλους, Τίς ἄρα οὗτός ἐστιν ὅτι καὶ ὁ ἄνεμος καὶ ἡ θάλασσα ὑπακούει αὐτῷ;

THE HEALING OF THE GERASENE DEMONIAC
(Mt 8.28–34; Lk 8.26–39)

5 Καὶ ἦλθον εἰς τὸ πέραν τῆς θαλάσσης εἰς τὴν χώραν τῶν Γερασηνῶν. 2 καὶ ἐξελθόντος αὐτοῦ ἐκ τοῦ πλοίου εὐθὺς ὑπήντησεν αὐτῷ... 5 καὶ διὰ παντὸς νυκτὸς καὶ ἡμέρας ἐν τοῖς μνήμασιν καὶ ἐν τοῖς ὄρεσιν ἦν κράζων καὶ κατακόπτων ἑαυτὸν λίθοις... 8 ἔλεγεν γὰρ αὐτῷ, Ἔξελθε τὸ πνεῦμα τὸ ἀκάθαρτον ἐκ τοῦ ἀνθρώπου. 9 καὶ ἐπηρώτα...ὅτι πολλοί ἐσμεν... 11 Ἦν δὲ ἐκεῖ πρὸς τῷ ὄρει ἀγέλη χοίρων μεγάλη βοσκομένη·... 15 καὶ ἔρχονται πρὸς τὸν Ἰησοῦν, καὶ θεωροῦσιν τὸν δαιμονιζόμενον καθήμενον ἱματισμένον καὶ σωφρονοῦντα, τὸν ἐσχηκότα τὸν λεγιῶνα, καὶ ἐφοβήθη-

σαν... 17 καὶ ἤρξαντο παρακαλεῖν αὐτὸν ἀπελθεῖν ἀπὸ τῶν ὁρίων αὐτῶν. 18 καὶ ἐμβαίνοντος αὐτοῦ εἰς τὸ πλοῖον παρεκάλει αὐτὸν ὁ δαιμονισθεὶς ἵνα μετ' αὐτοῦ ᾖ. 19 καὶ οὐκ ἀφῆκεν αὐτόν, ἀλλὰ λέγει αὐτῷ, ῞Υπαγε εἰς τὸν οἶκόν σου πρὸς τοὺς σούς, καὶ ἀπάγγειλον αὐτοῖς ὅσα ὁ κύριός σοι πεποίηκεν καὶ ἠλέησέν σε. 20 καὶ ἀπῆλθεν καὶ ἤρξατο κηρύσσειν ἐν τῇ Δεκαπόλει ὅσα ἐποίησεν αὐτῷ ὁ Ἰησοῦς, καὶ πάντες ἐθαύμαζον.

JAIRUS' DAUGHTER AND THE WOMAN WHO TOUCHED JESUS' GARMENT
(Mt 9.18–26; Lk 8.40–56)

21 Καὶ διαπεράσαντος τοῦ Ἰησοῦ εἰς τὸ πέραν πάλιν συνήχθη ὄχλος πολὺς ἐπ' αὐτόν, καὶ ἦν παρὰ τὴν θάλασσαν... 23 καὶ παρακαλεῖ αὐτὸν πολλὰ λέγων ὅτι Τὸ θυγάτριόν μου... 24 καὶ ἀπῆλθεν μετ' αὐτοῦ.

Καὶ ἠκολούθει αὐτῷ ὄχλος πολύς, καὶ συνέθλιβον αὐτόν. 25 καὶ γυνὴ οὖσα ἐν ῥύσει αἵματος δώδεκα ἔτη 26 καὶ πολλὰ παθοῦσα ὑπὸ πολλῶν ἰατρῶν καὶ δαπανήσασα τὰ παρ' αὐτῆς πάντα καὶ μηδὲν ὠφεληθεῖσα ἀλλὰ μᾶλλον εἰς τὸ χεῖρον ἐλθοῦσα,... 28 ἔλεγεν γὰρ ὅτι Ἐὰν ἅψωμαι κἂν τῶν ἱματίων αὐτοῦ σωθήσομαι... 30 καὶ εὐθὺς ὁ Ἰησοῦς ἐπιγνοὺς ἐν ἑαυτῷ τὴν ἐξ αὐτοῦ δύναμιν ἐξελθοῦσαν ἐπιστραφεὶς ἐν τῷ ὄχλῳ ἔλεγεν, Τίς μου ἥψατο τῶν ἱματίων; 31 καὶ ἔλεγον αὐτῷ οἱ μαθηταὶ αὐτοῦ, Βλέπεις τὸν ὄχλον συνθλίβοντά σε, καὶ λέγεις, Τίς μου ἥψατο... 33 ἡ δὲ γυνὴ φοβηθεῖσα καὶ τρέμουσα, εἰδυῖα ὃ γέγονεν αὐτῇ, ἦλθεν καὶ προσέπεσεν αὐτῷ καὶ εἶπεν αὐτῷ πᾶσαν τὴν ἀλήθειαν... 35 ῎Ετι αὐτοῦ λαλοῦντος ἔρχονται ἀπὸ τοῦ ἀρχισυναγώγου λέγοντες ὅτι... 41... ὅ ἐστιν μεθερμηνευόμενον Τὸ κοράσιον, σοὶ λέγω, ἔγειρε. 42 καὶ εὐθὺς ἀνέστη τὸ κοράσιον καὶ περιεπάτει, ἦν γὰρ ἐτῶν δώδεκα. καὶ ἐξέστησαν [εὐθὺς] ἐκστάσει μεγάλῃ. 43 καὶ διεστείλατο αὐτοῖς πολλὰ ἵνα μηδεὶς γνοῖ τοῦτο,...

THE REJECTION OF JESUS AT NAZARETH
(Mt 13.53–58; Lk 4.16–30)

6 Καὶ ἐξῆλθεν ἐκεῖθεν, καὶ ἔρχεται εἰς τὴν πατρίδα αὐτοῦ, καὶ ἀκολουθοῦσιν αὐτῷ οἱ μαθηταὶ αὐτοῦ. 2 καὶ γενομένου σαββάτου ἤρξατο διδάσκειν ἐν τῇ συναγωγῇ· καὶ πολλοὶ ἀκούοντες

ἐξεπλήσσοντο λέγοντες,... 4 καὶ ἔλεγεν αὐτοῖς ὁ Ἰησοῦς ὅτι
Οὐκ ἔστιν προφήτης... 6 καὶ ἐθαύμαζεν διὰ τὴν ἀπιστίαν αὐτῶν.

THE MISSION OF THE TWELVE
(Mt 10.1, 5–15; Lk 9.1–6)

Καὶ περιῆγεν τὰς κώμας κύκλῳ διδάσκων. 7 καὶ προσκαλεῖται
τοὺς δώδεκα, καὶ ἤρξατο αὐτοὺς ἀποστέλλειν δύο δύο, καὶ ἐδίδου
αὐτοῖς ἐξουσίαν τῶν πνευμάτων τῶν ἀκαθάρτων·... 10 καὶ
ἔλεγεν αὐτοῖς,... 12 Καὶ ἐξελθόντες ἐκήρυξαν ἵνα μετανοῶσιν,
13 καὶ δαιμόνια πολλὰ ἐξέβαλλον, καὶ ἤλειφον ἐλαίῳ πολλοὺς
ἀρρώστους καὶ ἐθεράπευον.

THE DEATH OF JOHN THE BAPTIST
(Mt 14.1–12; Lk 9.7–9)

14 Καὶ ἤκουσεν ὁ βασιλεὺς Ἡρῴδης, φανερὸν γὰρ ἐγένετο τὸ
ὄνομα αὐτοῦ, καὶ ἔλεγον ὅτι Ἰωάννης ὁ βαπτίζων ἐγήγερται ἐκ
νεκρῶν, καὶ διὰ τοῦτο ἐνεργοῦσιν αἱ δυνάμεις ἐν αὐτῷ. 15 ἄλλοι
δὲ ἔλεγον ὅτι Ἡλίας ἐστίν· ἄλλοι δὲ ἔλεγον ὅτι προφήτης ὡς
εἷς τῶν προφητῶν. 16 ἀκούσας δὲ ὁ Ἡρῴδης ἔλεγεν, Ὃν ἐγὼ
ἀπεκεφάλισα Ἰωάννην, οὗτος ἠγέρθη. 17 Αὐτὸς γὰρ ὁ Ἡρῴδης
ἀποστείλας ἐκράτησεν τὸν Ἰωάννην... 18 ἔλεγεν γὰρ ὁ Ἰωάννης τῷ Ἡρῴδῃ ὅτι Οὐκ ἔξεστίν σοι ἔχειν τὴν γυναῖκα τοῦ ἀδελφοῦ
σου... 20 ὁ γὰρ Ἡρῴδης ἐφοβεῖτο τὸν Ἰωάννην, *εἰδὼς αὐτὸν
ἄνδρα δίκαιον καὶ ἅγιον, καὶ συνετήρει αὐτόν, καὶ ἀκούσας αὐτοῦ
πολλὰ ἠπόρει,* καὶ ἡδέως αὐτοῦ ἤκουεν. 21 Καὶ γενομένης
ἡμέρας εὐκαίρου ὅτε Ἡρῴδης τοῖς γενεσίοις αὐτοῦ δεῖπνον
ἐποίησεν τοῖς μεγιστᾶσιν αὐτοῦ καὶ τοῖς χιλιάρχοις καὶ τοῖς
πρώτοις τῆς Γαλιλαίας, 22 καὶ εἰσελθούσης τῆς θυγατρὸς αὐτοῦ
Ἡρῳδιάδος καὶ ὀρχησαμένης, ἤρεσεν τῷ Ἡρῴδῃ καὶ τοῖς συνανακειμένοις. εἶπεν ὁ βασιλεὺς τῷ κορασίῳ, Αἴτησόν με ὃ ἐὰν θέλῃς,
καὶ δώσω σοι·... 29 καὶ ἀκούσαντες οἱ μαθηταὶ αὐτοῦ ἦλθον
καὶ ἦραν τὸ πτῶμα αὐτοῦ καὶ ἔθηκαν αὐτὸ ἐν μνημείῳ.

THE FEEDING OF THE FIVE THOUSAND
(Mt 14.13–21; Lk 9.10–17; Jn 6.1–14)

30 Καὶ συνάγονται οἱ ἀπόστολοι πρὸς τὸν Ἰησοῦν, καὶ ἀπήγ-
γειλαν αὐτῷ πάντα ὅσα ἐποίησαν καὶ ὅσα ἐδίδαξαν. 31 καὶ

λέγει αὐτοῖς, Δεῦτε ὑμεῖς αὐτοὶ κατ' ἰδίαν εἰς ἔρημον τόπον καὶ ἀναπαύσασθε ὀλίγον. ἦσαν γὰρ οἱ ἐρχόμενοι καὶ οἱ ὑπάγοντες πολλοί, καὶ οὐδὲ φαγεῖν εὐκαίρουν. 32 καὶ ἀπῆλθον ἐν τῷ πλοίῳ εἰς ἔρημον τόπον κατ' ἰδίαν. 33 καὶ εἶδον αὐτοὺς ὑπάγοντας καὶ ἐπέγνωσαν πολλοί, καὶ πεζῇ ἀπὸ πασῶν τῶν πόλεων συνέδραμον ἐκεῖ καὶ προῆλθον αὐτούς. 34 καὶ ἐξελθὼν εἶδεν πολὺν ὄχλον, καὶ ἐσπλαγχνίσθη ἐπ' αὐτοὺς ὅτι ἦσαν ὡς πρόβατα μὴ ἔχοντα ποιμένα, καὶ ἤρξατο διδάσκειν αὐτοὺς πολλά. 35 Καὶ ἤδη ὥρας πολλῆς γενομένης προσελθόντες αὐτῷ οἱ μαθηταὶ αὐτοῦ ἔλεγον ὅτι... 41 καὶ λαβὼν τοὺς πέντε ἄρτους καὶ τοὺς δύο ἰχθύας ἀναβλέψας εἰς τὸν οὐρανὸν εὐλόγησεν καὶ κατέκλασεν τοὺς ἄρτους καὶ ἐδίδου τοῖς μαθηταῖς [αὐτοῦ] ἵνα παρατιθῶσιν αὐτοῖς, καὶ τοὺς δύο ἰχθύας ἐμέρισεν πᾶσιν.

WALKING ON THE WATER
(Mt 14.22–33; Jn 6.15–21)

45 Καὶ εὐθὺς ἠνάγκασεν τοὺς μαθητὰς αὐτοῦ ἐμβῆναι εἰς τὸ πλοῖον καὶ προάγειν εἰς τὸ πέραν πρὸς Βηθσαϊδάν, ἕως αὐτὸς ἀπολύει τὸν ὄχλον... 47 καὶ ὀψίας γενομένης ἦν τὸ πλοῖον ἐν μέσῳ τῆς θαλάσσης, καὶ αὐτὸς μόνος ἐπὶ τῆς γῆς. 48 καὶ ἰδὼν αὐτοὺς βασανιζομένους ἐν τῷ ἐλαύνειν, ἦν γὰρ ὁ ἄνεμος ἐναντίος αὐτοῖς, περὶ τετάρτην φυλακὴν τῆς νυκτὸς ἔρχεται πρὸς αὐτοὺς περιπατῶν ἐπὶ τῆς θαλάσσης· καὶ ἤθελεν παρελθεῖν αὐτούς... 50 πάντες γὰρ αὐτὸν εἶδον καὶ ἐταράχθησαν. ὁ δὲ εὐθὺς ἐλάλησεν μετ' αὐτῶν,... 52 οὐ γὰρ συνῆκαν ἐπὶ τοῖς ἄρτοις, ἀλλ' ἦν αὐτῶν ἡ καρδία πεπωρωμένη.

THE HEALING OF THE SICK IN GENNESARET
(Mt 14.34–36)

53 Καὶ διαπεράσαντες ἐπὶ τὴν γῆν ἦλθον εἰς Γεννησαρὲτ καὶ προσωρμίσθησαν. 54 καὶ ἐξελθόντων αὐτῶν ἐκ τοῦ πλοίου εὐθὺς ἐπιγνόντες αὐτὸν 55 περιέδραμον ὅλην τὴν χώραν ἐκείνην καὶ ἤρξαντο ἐπὶ τοῖς κραβάττοις τοὺς κακῶς ἔχοντας περιφέρειν ὅπου ἤκουον ὅτι ἐστίν. 56 καὶ ὅπου ἂν εἰσεπορεύετο εἰς κώμας ἢ εἰς πόλεις ἢ εἰς ἀγροὺς ἐν ταῖς ἀγοραῖς ἐτίθεσαν τοὺς ἀσθενοῦντας, καὶ παρεκάλουν αὐτὸν ἵνα κἂν τοῦ κρασπέδου τοῦ ἱματίου αὐτοῦ ἅψωνται· καὶ ὅσοι ἂν ἥψαντο αὐτοῦ ἐσῴζοντο.

THE TRADITION OF THE ELDERS
(Mt 15.1–20)

7 Καὶ συνάγονται πρὸς αὐτὸν οἱ Φαρισαῖοι καί τινες τῶν γραμματέων ἐλθόντες ἀπὸ Ἱεροσολύμων 2 ...τοῦτ᾽ ἔστιν ἀνίπτοις, ... 3 – οἱ γὰρ Φαρισαῖοι καὶ πάντες οἱ Ἰουδαῖοι ἐὰν μὴ πυγμῇ νίψωνται τὰς χεῖρας οὐκ ἐσθίουσιν, κρατοῦντες τὴν παράδοσιν τῶν πρεσβυτέρων, 4 καὶ ἀπ᾽ ἀγορᾶς ἐὰν μὴ ῥαντίσωνται οὐκ ἐσθίουσιν, καὶ ἄλλα πολλά ἐστιν ἃ παρέλαβον κρατεῖν, βαπτισμοὺς ποτηρίων καὶ ξεστῶν καὶ χαλκίων [καὶ κλινῶν] – 5 καὶ ἐπερωτῶσιν αὐτὸν οἱ Φαρισαῖοι καὶ οἱ γραμματεῖς,... 8 ἀφέντες τὴν ἐντολὴν τοῦ θεοῦ κρατεῖτε τὴν παράδοσιν τῶν ἀνθρώπων. 9 Καὶ ἔλεγεν αὐτοῖς,... 10 Μωϋσῆς γὰρ εἶπεν,... 11 ...ὃ ἔστιν, Δῶρον, ὃ ἐὰν ἐξ ἐμοῦ ὠφεληθῇς,... 13 ...καὶ παρόμοια τοιαῦτα πολλὰ ποιεῖτε. 14 Καὶ προσκαλεσάμενος πάλιν τὸν ὄχλον ἔλεγεν αὐτοῖς, Ἀκούσατέ μου πάντες καὶ σύνετε... 16 εἴ τις ἔχει ὦτα ἀκούειν ἀκουέτω. 17 Καὶ ὅτε εἰσῆλθεν εἰς οἶκον ἀπὸ τοῦ ὄχλου, ἐπηρώτων αὐτὸν οἱ μαθηταὶ αὐτοῦ τὴν παραβολήν. 18 καὶ λέγει αὐτοῖς, Οὕτως καὶ ὑμεῖς ἀσύνετοί ἐστε;... 19 ὅτι οὐκ εἰσπορεύεται αὐτοῦ εἰς τὴν καρδίαν ἀλλ᾽ εἰς τὴν κοιλίαν, καὶ εἰς τὸν ἀφεδρῶνα ἐκπορεύεται; – καθαρίζων πάντα τὰ βρώματα. 20 ἔλεγεν δὲ ὅτι Τὸ... 21 ἔσωθεν γὰρ ἐκ τῆς καρδίας... 23 πάντα ταῦτα τὰ πονηρὰ ἔσωθεν ἐκπορεύεται καὶ κοινοῖ τὸν ἄνθρωπον.

THE SYRO-PHOENICIAN WOMAN'S FAITH
(Mt 15.21–28)

24 Ἐκεῖθεν δὲ ἀναστὰς ἀπῆλθεν εἰς τὰ ὅρια Τύρου. καὶ εἰσελθὼν εἰς οἰκίαν οὐδένα ἤθελεν γνῶναι, καὶ οὐκ ἠδυνήθη λαθεῖν· 25 ἀλλ᾽ εὐθὺς ἀκούσασα γυνὴ περὶ αὐτοῦ, ἧς εἶχεν τὸ θυγάτριον αὐτῆς πνεῦμα ἀκάθαρτον, ἐλθοῦσα... 26 ἡ δὲ γυνὴ ἦν Ἑλληνίς, Συροφοινίκισσα τῷ γένει·... 27 καὶ ἔλεγεν αὐτῇ, Ἄφες πρῶτον χορτασθῆναι τὰ τέκνα, οὐ γάρ ἐστιν...

A DEAF AND DUMB MAN HEALED

31 Καὶ πάλιν ἐξελθὼν ἐκ τῶν ὁρίων Τύρου ἦλθεν διὰ Σιδῶνος εἰς τὴν θάλασσαν τῆς Γαλιλαίας ἀνὰ μέσον τῶν ὁρίων Δεκαπόλεως.

32 καὶ φέρουσιν αὐτῷ κωφὸν καὶ μογιλάλον,... 34 ...ὅ ἐστιν, Διανοίχθητι. 35 καὶ εὐθέως...καὶ ἐλάλει ὀρθῶς. 36 καὶ διεστείλατο αὐτοῖς ἵνα μηδενὶ λέγωσιν· ὅσον δὲ αὐτοῖς διεστέλλετο, αὐτοὶ μᾶλλον περισσότερον ἐκήρυσσον. 37 καὶ ὑπερπερισσῶς ἐξεπλήσσοντο λέγοντες, Καλῶς πάντα πεποίηκεν· καὶ τοὺς κωφοὺς ποιεῖ ἀκούειν καὶ [τοὺς] ἀλάλους λαλεῖν.

THE FEEDING OF THE FOUR THOUSAND
(Mt 15.32–39)

8 Ἐν ἐκείναις ταῖς ἡμέραις πάλιν πολλοῦ ὄχλου ὄντος καὶ μὴ ἐχόντων τί φάγωσιν, προσκαλεσάμενος τοὺς μαθητὰς αὐτοῦ λέγει αὐτοῖς,... 9...καὶ ἀπέλυσεν αὐτούς. 10 Καὶ εὐθὺς ἐμβὰς εἰς τὸ πλοῖον μετὰ τῶν μαθητῶν αὐτοῦ ἦλθεν εἰς τὰ μέρη Δαλμανουθά.

THE DEMAND FOR A SIGN
(Mt 16.1–4)

11 Καὶ ἐξῆλθον οἱ Φαρισαῖοι καὶ ἤρξαντο συζητεῖν αὐτῷ,... 13 καὶ ἀφεὶς αὐτοὺς πάλιν ἐμβὰς ἀπῆλθεν εἰς τὸ πέραν.

THE LEAVEN OF THE PHARISEES AND OF HEROD
(Mt 16.5–12)

14 Καὶ ἐπελάθοντο λαβεῖν ἄρτους, καὶ εἰ μὴ ἕνα ἄρτον οὐκ εἶχον μεθ᾽ ἑαυτῶν ἐν τῷ πλοίῳ. 15 καὶ διεστέλλετο αὐτοῖς λέγων, Ὁρᾶτε, βλέπετε ἀπὸ τῆς ζύμης τῶν Φαρισαίων καὶ τῆς ζύμης Ἡρῴδου. 16 καὶ διελογίζοντο πρὸς ἀλλήλους ὅτι Ἄρτους οὐκ ἔχουσιν... 19 ὅτε τοὺς πέντε ἄρτους ἔκλασα εἰς τοὺς πεντακισχιλίους, πόσους κοφίνους κλασμάτων πλήρεις ἤρατε; λέγουσιν αὐτῷ, Δώδεκα. 20 Ὅτε τοὺς ἑπτὰ εἰς τοὺς τετρακισχιλίους, πόσων σπυρίδων πληρώματα κλασμάτων ἤρατε; καὶ λέγουσιν [αὐτῷ], Ἑπτά. 21 καὶ ἔλεγεν αὐτοῖς, Οὔπω συνίετε;

THE HEALING OF A BLIND MAN AT BETHSAIDA

22 Καὶ ἔρχονται εἰς Βηθσαϊδάν... 26 καὶ ἀπέστειλεν αὐτὸν εἰς οἶκον αὐτοῦ λέγων, Μηδὲ εἰς τὴν κώμην εἰσέλθῃς.

PETER'S DECLARATION ABOUT JESUS
(Mt 16.13–20; Lk 9.18–21)

27 Καὶ ἐξῆλθεν ὁ Ἰησοῦς καὶ οἱ μαθηταὶ αὐτοῦ εἰς τὰς κώμας Καισαρείας τῆς Φιλίππου· καὶ ἐν τῇ ὁδῷ ἐπηρώτα τοὺς μαθητὰς αὐτοῦ λέγων αὐτοῖς, Τίνα με λέγουσιν οἱ ἄνθρωποι εἶναι; 28 οἱ δὲ εἶπαν αὐτῷ λέγοντες [ὅτι] Ἰωάννην τὸν βαπτιστήν, καὶ ἄλλοι, Ἠλίαν, ἄλλοι δὲ ὅτι εἷς τῶν προφητῶν. 29 καὶ αὐτὸς ἐπηρώτα αὐτούς, Ὑμεῖς δὲ τίνα με λέγετε εἶναι; ἀποκριθεὶς ὁ Πέτρος λέγει αὐτῷ, Σὺ εἶ ὁ Χριστός. 30 καὶ ἐπετίμησεν αὐτοῖς ἵνα μηδενὶ λέγωσιν περὶ αὐτοῦ.

JESUS FORETELLS HIS DEATH AND RESURRECTION
(Mt 16.21–28; Lk 9.22–27)

31 Καὶ ἤρξατο διδάσκειν αὐτοὺς ὅτι δεῖ τὸν υἱὸν τοῦ ἀνθρώπου πολλὰ παθεῖν καὶ ἀποδοκιμασθῆναι ὑπὸ τῶν πρεσβυτέρων καὶ τῶν ἀρχιερέων καὶ τῶν γραμματέων καὶ ἀποκτανθῆναι καὶ μετὰ τρεῖς ἡμέρας ἀναστῆναι· 32 καὶ παρρησίᾳ τὸν λόγον ἐλάλει. καὶ προσλαβόμενος ὁ Πέτρος αὐτὸν ἤρξατο ἐπιτιμᾶν αὐτῷ. 33 ὁ δὲ ἐπιστραφεὶς καὶ ἰδὼν τοὺς μαθητὰς αὐτοῦ ἐπετίμησεν Πέτρῳ καὶ λέγει, Ὕπαγε ὀπίσω μου, Σατανᾶ, ὅτι οὐ φρονεῖς τὰ τοῦ θεοῦ ἀλλὰ τὰ τῶν ἀνθρώπων. 34 Καὶ προσκαλεσάμενος τὸν ὄχλον σὺν τοῖς μαθηταῖς αὐτοῦ εἶπεν αὐτοῖς,... 35 ὃς γὰρ ἐὰν θέλῃ... ἕνεκεν [ἐμοῦ καὶ] τοῦ εὐαγγελίου... 36 τί γὰρ ὠφελεῖ... 37 τί γὰρ δοῖ... 38 ὃς γὰρ ἐὰν ἐπαισχυνθῇ με καὶ τοὺς ἐμοὺς λόγους ἐν τῇ...ὅταν ἔλθῃ ἐν τῇ δόξῃ τοῦ πατρὸς αὐτοῦ μετὰ τῶν ἀγγέλων τῶν ἁγίων.
9 Καὶ ἔλεγεν αὐτοῖς, Ἀμὴν λέγω ὑμῖν ὅτι...ἐληλυθυῖαν ἐν δυνάμει.

THE TRANSFIGURATION OF JESUS
(Mt 17.1–13; Lk 9.28–36)

2 Καὶ μετὰ ἡμέρας ἓξ παραλαμβάνει ὁ Ἰησοῦς τὸν Πέτρον καὶ τὸν Ἰάκωβον καὶ τὸν Ἰωάννην, καὶ ἀναφέρει αὐτοὺς εἰς ὄρος ὑψηλὸν κατ' ἰδίαν μόνους.... 3 καὶ τὰ ἱμάτια αὐτοῦ ἐγένετο στίλβοντα λευκὰ λίαν οἷα γναφεὺς ἐπὶ τῆς γῆς οὐ δύναται οὕτως λευκᾶναι... 6 οὐ γὰρ ᾔδει τί ἀποκριθῇ, ἔκφοβοι γὰρ ἐγένοντο. 7 καὶ ἐγένετο νεφέλη ἐπισκιάζουσα αὐτοῖς, καὶ ἐγένετο φωνὴ ἐκ τῆς νεφέλης,...

9 Καὶ καταβαινόντων αὐτῶν ἐκ τοῦ ὄρους διεστείλατο αὐτοῖς ἵνα μηδενὶ ἃ εἶδον διηγήσωνται, εἰ μὴ ὅταν ὁ υἱὸς τοῦ ἀνθρώπου ἐκ νεκρῶν ἀναστῇ...12 ὁ δὲ ἔφη αὐτοῖς Ἠλίας μὲν ἐλθὼν πρῶτον ἀποκαθιστάνει πάντα, καὶ πῶς γέγραπται ἐπὶ τὸν υἱὸν τοῦ ἀνθρώπου ἵνα πολλὰ πάθῃ καὶ ἐξουδενηθῇ; 13 ἀλλὰ λέγω ὑμῖν ὅτι καὶ Ἠλίας ἐλήλυθεν, καὶ ἐποίησαν αὐτῷ ὅσα ἤθελον, καθὼς γέγραπται ἐπ᾽ αὐτόν.

THE HEALING OF A BOY WITH AN UNCLEAN SPIRIT
(Mt 17.14–20; Lk 9.37–43a)

14 Καὶ ἐλθόντες πρὸς τοὺς μαθητὰς εἶδον ὄχλον πολὺν περὶ αὐτοὺς καὶ γραμματεῖς συζητοῦντας πρὸς αὐτούς. 15 καὶ εὐθὺς πᾶς ὁ ὄχλος ἰδόντες αὐτὸν ἐξεθαμβήθησαν, καὶ προστρέχοντες ἠσπάζοντο αὐτόν. 16 καὶ ἐπηρώτησεν αὐτούς, Τί συζητεῖτε πρὸς αὐτούς; 17 καὶ ἀπεκρίθη αὐτῷ εἷς ἐκ τοῦ ὄχλον,... 20 καὶ ἤνεγκαν αὐτὸν πρὸς αὐτόν. καὶ ἰδὼν αὐτὸν τὸ πνεῦμα εὐθὺς συνεσπάραξεν αὐτόν, καὶ πεσὼν ἐπὶ τῆς γῆς ἐκυλίετο ἀφρίζων... 26 καὶ κράξας καὶ πολλὰ σπαράξας ἐξῆλθεν· καὶ ἐγένετο ὡσεὶ νεκρός, ὥστε τοὺς πολλοὺς λέγειν ὅτι ἀπέθανεν... 28 καὶ εἰσελθόντος αὐτοῦ εἰς οἶκον οἱ μαθηταὶ αὐτοῦ κατ᾽ ἰδίαν ἐπηρώτων αὐτόν, Ὅτι...

JESUS AGAIN FORETELLS HIS DEATH AND RESURRECTION
(Mt 17.22–23; Lk 9.43b–45)

30 Κἀκεῖθεν ἐξελθόντες παρεπορεύοντο διὰ τῆς Γαλιλαίας, καὶ οὐκ ἤθελεν ἵνα τις γνοῖ· 31 ἐδίδασκεν γὰρ τοὺς μαθητὰς αὐτοῦ καὶ ἔλεγεν αὐτοῖς ὅτι Ὁ υἱὸς τοῦ ἀνθρώπου παραδίδοται εἰς χεῖρας ἀνθρώπων, καὶ ἀποκτενοῦσιν αὐτόν, καὶ ἀποκτανθεὶς μετὰ τρεῖς ἡμέρας ἀναστήσεται. 32 οἱ δὲ ἠγνόουν τὸ ῥῆμα, καὶ ἐφοβοῦντο αὐτὸν ἐπερωτῆσαι.

WHO IS THE GREATEST?
(Mt 18.1–5; Lk 9.46–48)

33 Καὶ ἦλθον εἰς Καφαρναούμ. καὶ ἐν τῇ οἰκίᾳ γενόμενος ἐπηρώτα αὐτούς, Τί ἐν τῇ ὁδῷ διελογίζεσθε; 34 οἱ δὲ ἐσιώπων, πρὸς

ἀλλήλους γὰρ διελέχθησαν ἐν τῇ ὁδῷ τίς μείζων. 35 καὶ καθίσας
ἐφώνησεν τοὺς δώδεκα καὶ λέγει αὐτοῖς, Εἴ τις θέλει πρῶτος εἶναι
ἔσται πάντων ἔσχατος καὶ πάντων διάκονος. 36 καὶ λαβὼν παιδίον
ἔστησεν αὐτὸ ἐν μέσῳ αὐτῶν καὶ ἐναγκαλισάμενος αὐτὸ εἶπεν
αὐτοῖς, 37 Ὃς ἂν ἓν τῶν τοιούτων παιδίων δέξηται ἐπὶ τῷ
ὀνόματί μου, ἐμὲ δέχεται· καὶ ὃς ἂν ἐμὲ δέχηται, οὐκ ἐμὲ δέχεται
ἀλλὰ τὸν ἀποστείλαντά με.

HE WHO IS NOT AGAINST US IS FOR US
(Lk 9.49–50)

38 Ἔφη αὐτῷ ὁ Ἰωάννης, Διδάσκαλε,... 39 ὁ δὲ Ἰησοῦς
εἶπεν,...οὐδεὶς γάρ ἐστιν... 40 ὃς γὰρ οὐκ ἔστιν...41 ...ἐν
ὀνόματι ὅτι Χριστοῦ ἐστε, ἀμὴν λέγω ὑμῖν ὅτι... 49 πᾶς
γὰρ... 50 ...ἔχετε ἐν ἑαυτοῖς ἅλα, καὶ εἰρηνεύετε ἐν ἀλλήλοις.

TEACHING ABOUT DIVORCE
(Mt 19.1–12)

10 Καὶ ἐκεῖθεν ἀναστὰς ἔρχεται εἰς τὰ ὅρια τῆς Ἰουδαίας [καὶ]
πέραν τοῦ Ἰορδάνου, καὶ συμπορεύονται πάλιν ὄχλοι πρὸς
αὐτόν, καὶ ὡς εἰώθει πάλιν ἐδίδασκεν αὐτούς... 10 Καὶ εἰς τὴν
οἰκίαν πάλιν οἱ μαθηταὶ περὶ τούτου ἐπηρώτων αὐτόν. 11 καὶ
λέγει αὐτοῖς...

LITTLE CHILDREN BLESSED
(Mt 19.13–15; Lk 18.15–17)

13 Καὶ προσέφερον αὐτῷ παιδία ἵνα αὐτῶν ἅψηται· οἱ δὲ μαθηταὶ
ἐπετίμησαν αὐτοῖς... 15 ἀμὴν λέγω ὑμῖν,... 16 καὶ ἐναγκαλισάμενος αὐτὰ κατευλόγει τιθεὶς τὰς χεῖρας ἐπ' αὐτά.

THE RICH MAN
(Mt 19.16–30; Lk 18.18–30)

17 Καὶ ἐκπορευομένου αὐτοῦ εἰς ὁδὸν προσδραμὼν εἷς καὶ γονυπε-
τήσας αὐτὸν ἐπηρώτα αὐτόν,... 22 ...ἦν γὰρ ἔχων κτήματα
πολλά. 23 Καὶ περιβλεψάμενος ὁ Ἰησοῦς λέγει τοῖς μαθηταῖς

αὐτοῦ, Πῶς δυσκόλως... 24 οἱ δὲ μαθηταὶ ἐθαμβοῦντο ἐπὶ τοῖς
λόγοις αὐτοῦ. ὁ δὲ ᾿Ιησοῦς πάλιν ἀποκριθεὶς λέγει αὐτοῖς,
Τέκνα, πῶς δύσκολόν... 26 οἱ δὲ περισσῶς ἐξεπλήσσοντο λέγοντες πρὸς ἑαυτούς, Καὶ τίς δύναται σωθῆναι; 27 ἐμβλέψας αὐτοῖς
ὁ ᾿Ιησοῦς λέγει,... πάντα γὰρ δυνατὰ παρὰ τῷ θεῷ. 28 Ἤρξατο
λέγειν ὁ Πέτρος αὐτῷ, ᾿Ιδοὺ ἡμεῖς ἀφήκαμεν πάντα καὶ ἠκολου-
θήκαμέν σοι. 29 ἔφη ὁ ᾿Ιησοῦς, ᾿Αμὴν λέγω ὑμῖν, οὐδείς...
ἕνεκεν ἐμοῦ καὶ ἕνεκεν τοῦ εὐαγγελίου,... 31 πολλοὶ δὲ ἔσονται
πρῶτοι ἔσχατοι καὶ [οἱ] ἔσχατοι πρῶτοι.

A THIRD TIME JESUS FORETELLS HIS DEATH
AND RESURRECTION
(Mt 20.17–19, Lk 18.31–34)

32 Ἦσαν δὲ ἐν τῇ ὁδῷ ἀναβαίνοντες εἰς ῾Ιεροσόλυμα, καὶ ἦν
προάγων αὐτοὺς ὁ ᾿Ιησοῦς, καὶ ἐθαμβοῦντο, οἱ δὲ ἀκολουθοῦντες
ἐφοβοῦντο. καὶ παραλαβὼν πάλιν τοὺς δώδεκα ἤρξατο αὐτοῖς
λέγειν τὰ μέλλοντα αὐτῷ συμβαίνειν, 33 ὅτι ᾿Ιδοὺ ἀναβαίνομεν
εἰς ῾Ιεροσόλυμα, *καὶ ὁ υἱὸς τοῦ ἀνθρώπου παραδοθήσεται τοῖς ἀρχιερεῦσιν καὶ τοῖς γραμματεῦσιν, καὶ κατακρινοῦσιν αὐτὸν θανάτῳ καὶ
παραδώσουσιν αὐτὸν τοῖς ἔθνεσιν* 34 *καὶ ἐμπαίξουσιν αὐτῷ καὶ
ἐμπτύσουσιν αὐτῷ καὶ μαστιγώσουσιν αὐτὸν καὶ ἀποκτενοῦσιν, καὶ
μετὰ τρεῖς ἡμέρας ἀναστήσεται.*

THE REQUEST OF JAMES AND JOHN
(Mt 20.20–28)

35 Καὶ προσπορεύονται αὐτῷ ᾿Ιάκωβος καὶ ᾿Ιωάννης οἱ υἱοὶ
Ζεβεδαίου λέγοντες αὐτῷ,... 41 Καὶ ἀκούσαντες οἱ δέκα ἤρξαντο ἀγανακτεῖν περὶ ᾿Ιακώβου καὶ ᾿Ιωάννου. 42 καὶ προσκαλεσάμενος αὐτοὺς ὁ ᾿Ιησοῦς λέγει αὐτοῖς, Οἴδατε *ὅτι οἱ δοκοῦντες
ἄρχειν τῶν ἐθνῶν κατακυριεύουσιν αὐτῶν καὶ οἱ μεγάλοι αὐτῶν κατεξου-
σιάζουσιν αὐτῶν.* 43 οὐχ οὕτως δέ ἐστιν ἐν ὑμῖν· ἀλλ᾿ ὃς ἂν θέλῃ
μέγας γενέσθαι ἐν ὑμῖν, ἔσται ὑμῶν διάκονος, 44 καὶ ὃς ἂν θέλῃ ἐν
ὑμῖν εἶναι πρῶτος, ἔσται πάντων δοῦλος· 45 καὶ γὰρ ὁ υἱὸς τοῦ
ἀνθρώπου οὐκ ἦλθεν διακονηθῆναι ἀλλὰ διακονῆσαι καὶ δοῦναι τὴν
ψυχὴν αὐτοῦ λύτρον ἀντὶ πολλῶν.

THE HEALING OF BLIND BARTIMAEUS
(Mt 20.29–34; Lk 18.35–43)

46 Καὶ ἔρχονται εἰς Ἰεριχώ. καὶ ἐκπορευομένου αὐτοῦ ἀπὸ Ἰεριχὼ καὶ τῶν μαθητῶν αὐτοῦ καὶ ὄχλου ἱκανοῦ ὁ υἱὸς Τιμαίου Βαρτιμαῖος τυφλὸς προσαίτης ἐκάθητο παρὰ τὴν ὁδόν. 47 καὶ ἀκούσας ὅτι Ἰησοῦς ὁ Ναζαρηνός ἐστιν ἤρξατο κράζειν καὶ λέγειν, ... Υἱὲ Δαυὶδ Ἰησοῦ, ἐλέησόν με. 48 καὶ ἐπετίμων αὐτῷ πολλοὶ ἵνα σιωπήσῃ· ὁ δὲ πολλῷ μᾶλλον ἔκραζεν, Υἱὲ Δαυίδ, ἐλέησόν με. 49 καὶ στὰς ὁ Ἰησοῦς εἶπεν, Φωνήσατε αὐτόν. καὶ φωνοῦσιν τὸν τυφλὸν λέγοντες αὐτῷ Θάρσει, ἔγειρε, φωνεῖ σε. 50 ὁ δὲ ἀποβαλὼν τὸ ἱμάτιον αὐτοῦ ἀναπηδήσας ἦλθεν πρὸς τὸν Ἰησοῦν. 51 καὶ ἀποκριθεὶς αὐτῷ ὁ Ἰησοῦς εἶπεν, Τί σοι θέλεις ποιήσω; ὁ δὲ τυφλὸς εἶπεν αὐτῷ, Ραββουνι, ἵνα ἀναβλέψω. 52 καὶ ὁ Ἰησοῦς εἶπεν αὐτῷ, Ὕπαγε, ἡ πίστις σου σέσωκέν σε. καὶ εὐθὺς ἀνέβλεψεν, καὶ ἠκολούθει αὐτῷ ἐν τῇ ὁδῷ.

THE TRIUMPHAL ENTRY INTO JERUSALEM
(Mt 21.1–11; Lk 19.28–40; Jn 12.12–19)

11 Καὶ ὅτε ἐγγίζουσιν εἰς Ἱεροσόλυμα εἰς Βηθφαγὴ καὶ Βηθανίαν πρὸς τὸ Ὄρος τῶν Ἐλαιῶν, ἀποστέλλει δύο τῶν μαθητῶν αὐτοῦ 2 καὶ λέγει αὐτοῖς, Ὑπάγετε εἰς τὴν κώμην τὴν κατέναντι ὑμῶν, καὶ εὐθὺς εἰσπορευόμενοι, ... 3 ... καὶ εὐθὺς αὐτὸν ἀποστέλλει πάλιν ὧδε... 9 καὶ οἱ προάγοντες καὶ οἱ ἀκολουθοῦντες ἔκραζον,
  Ὡσαννά·
  Εὐλογημένος ὁ ἐρχόμενος ἐν ὀνόματι κυρίου·
10 Εὐλογημένη ἡ ἐρχομένη βασιλεία τοῦ πατρὸς ἡμῶν Δαυίδ·
  Ὡσαννὰ ἐν τοῖς ὑψίστοις.
11 Καὶ εἰσῆλθεν εἰς Ἱεροσόλυμα εἰς τὸ ἱερόν· καὶ περιβλεψάμενος πάντα, ὀψίας ἤδη οὔσης τῆς ὥρας, ἐξῆλθεν εἰς Βηθανίαν μετὰ τῶν δώδεκα.

THE CURSING OF THE FIG TREE
(Mt 21.18–19)

12 Καὶ τῇ ἐπαύριον ἐξελθόντων αὐτῶν ἀπὸ Βηθανίας ἐπείνασεν. 13 ...ὁ γὰρ καιρὸς οὐκ ἦν σύκων. 14 καὶ ἀποκριθεὶς εἶπεν αὐτῇ, Μηκέτι εἰς τὸν αἰῶνα ἐκ σοῦ μηδεὶς καρπὸν φάγοι. καὶ ἤκουον οἱ μαθηταὶ αὐτοῦ.

THE CLEANSING OF THE TEMPLE
(Mt 21.12–17; Lk 19.45–48; Jn 2.13–22)

15 Καὶ ἔρχονται εἰς Ἱεροσόλυμα... 17 καὶ ἐδίδασκεν καὶ ἔλεγεν αὐτοῖς, Οὐ γέγραπται ὅτι
Ὁ οἶκός μου οἶκος προσευχῆς κληθήσεται πᾶσιν τοῖς ἔθνεσιν;
ὑμεῖς δὲ πεποιήκατε αὐτὸν **σπήλαιον λῃστῶν.**
18 καὶ ἤκουσαν οἱ ἀρχιερεῖς καὶ οἱ γραμματεῖς, καὶ ἐζήτουν πῶς αὐτὸν ἀπολέσωσιν· ἐφοβοῦντο γὰρ αὐτόν, πᾶς γὰρ ὁ ὄχλος ἐξεπλήσσετο ἐπὶ τῇ διδαχῇ αὐτοῦ. 19 Καὶ ὅταν ὀψὲ ἐγένετο, ἐξεπορεύοντο ἔξω τῆς πόλεως.

THE LESSON FROM THE WITHERED FIG TREE
(Mt 21.20–22)

20 Καὶ παραπορευόμενοι πρωῒ εἶδον τὴν συκῆν ἐξηραμμένην ἐκ ῥιζῶν. 21 καὶ ἀναμνησθεὶς ὁ Πέτρος λέγει αὐτῷ, Ῥαββί, ἴδε ἡ συκῆ ἣν κατηράσω ἐξήρανται. 22 καὶ ἀποκριθεὶς ὁ Ἰησοῦς λέγει αὐτοῖς, Ἔχετε πίστιν θεοῦ, 23 ἀμὴν λέγω ὑμῖν ὅτι...

THE AUTHORITY OF JESUS QUESTIONED
(Mt 21.23–27; Lk 20.1–8)

27 Καὶ ἔρχονται πάλιν εἰς Ἱεροσόλυμα. καὶ ἐν τῷ ἱερῷ περιπατοῦντος αὐτοῦ ἔρχονται πρὸς αὐτὸν οἱ ἀρχιερεῖς καὶ οἱ γραμματεῖς καὶ οἱ πρεσβύτεροι... 31 καὶ διελογίζοντο πρὸς ἑαυτοὺς λέγοντες Τί εἴπωμεν; Ἐὰν εἴπωμεν, Ἐξ οὐρανοῦ, ἐρεῖ, Διὰ τί οὐκ ἐπιστεύσατε αὐτῷ; 32 ἀλλὰ εἴπωμεν, Ἐξ ἀνθρώπων; – ἐφοβοῦντο τὸν ὄχλον, ἅπαντες γὰρ εἶχον τὸν Ἰωάννην ὄντως ὅτι προφήτης ἦν.

THE PARABLE OF THE VINEYARD AND THE TENANTS
(Mt 21.33–46; Lk 20.9–19)

12 Καὶ ἤρξατο αὐτοῖς ἐν παραβολαῖς λαλεῖν,... 12 Καὶ ἐζήτουν αὐτὸν κρατῆσαι, καὶ ἐφοβήθησαν τὸν ὄχλον, ἔγνωσαν γὰρ ὅτι πρὸς αὐτοὺς τὴν παραβολὴν εἶπεν. καὶ ἀφέντες αὐτὸν ἀπῆλθον.

PAYING TAXES TO CAESAR
(Mt 22.15–22; Lk 20.20–26)

13 Καὶ ἀποστέλλουσιν πρὸς αὐτόν τινας τῶν Φαρισαίων καὶ τῶν Ἡρῳδιανῶν ἵνα αὐτὸν ἀγρεύσωσιν λόγῳ... 17 ...καὶ ἐξεθαύμαζον ἐπ᾽ αὐτῷ.

THE QUESTION ABOUT THE RESURRECTION
(Mt 22.23–33; Lk 20.27–40)

18 Καὶ ἔρχονται Σαδδουκαῖοι πρὸς αὐτόν, οἵτινες λέγουσιν ἀνάστασιν μὴ εἶναι,...

THE GREAT COMMANDMENT
(Mt 22.34–40; Lk 10.25–28)

28 Καὶ προσελθὼν εἷς τῶν γραμματέων ἀκούσας αὐτῶν συζητούντων, ἰδὼν ὅτι καλῶς ἀπεκρίθη αὐτοῖς, ἐπηρώτησεν αὐτόν,... 34 ...καὶ οὐδεὶς οὐκέτι ἐτόλμα αὐτὸν ἐπερωτῆσαι.

THE QUESTION ABOUT DAVID'S SON
(Mt 22.41–46; Lk 20.41–44)

35 Καὶ ἀποκριθεὶς ὁ Ἰησοῦς ἔλεγεν διδάσκων ἐν τῷ ἱερῷ, Πῶς... 37 ...καὶ [ὁ] πολὺς ὄχλος ἤκουεν αὐτοῦ ἡδέως.

THE DENOUNCING OF THE SCRIBES
(Mt 23.1–36; Lk 20.45–47)

38 Καὶ ἐν τῇ διδαχῇ αὐτοῦ ἔλεγεν, Βλέπετε... 40 οἱ κατεσθίοντες τὰς οἰκίας τῶν χηρῶν...

THE WIDOW'S OFFERING
(Lk 21.1–4)

41 Καὶ καθίσας κατέναντι τοῦ γαζοφυλακίου ἐθεώρει πῶς ὁ ὄχλος βάλλει χαλκὸν εἰς τὸ γαζοφυλάκιον· καὶ πολλοὶ πλούσιοι ἔβαλλον πολλά· 42 καὶ ἐλθοῦσα μία χήρα πτωχὴ ἔβαλεν λεπτὰ δύο, ὅ ἐστιν κοδράντης. 43 καὶ προσκαλεσάμενος τοὺς μαθητὰς αὐτοῦ εἶπεν αὐτοῖς, Ἀμὴν λέγω ὑμῖν ὅτι ἡ χήρα... 44 πάντες γὰρ... ὅλον τὸν βίον αὐτῆς.

THE DESTRUCTION OF THE TEMPLE FORETOLD
(Mt 24.1–2; Lk 21.5–6)

13 Καὶ ἐκπορευομένου αὐτοῦ ἐκ τοῦ ἱεροῦ λέγει αὐτῷ εἷς τῶν μαθητῶν αὐτοῦ, Διδάσκαλε, ἴδε ποταποὶ λίθοι καὶ ποταπαὶ οἰκοδομαί. 2 καὶ ὁ Ἰησοῦς εἶπεν αὐτῷ, Βλέπεις ταύτας τὰς μεγάλας οἰκοδομάς; οὐ μὴ ἀφεθῇ ὧδε λίθος ἐπὶ λίθον ὃς οὐ μὴ καταλυθῇ.

THE BEGINNING OF WOES
(Mt 24.3–14; Lk 21.7–19)

3 Καὶ καθημένου αὐτοῦ εἰς τὸ Ὄρος τῶν Ἐλαιῶν κατέναντι τοῦ ἱεροῦ ἐπηρώτα αὐτὸν κατ᾽ ἰδίαν Πέτρος καὶ Ἰάκωβος καὶ Ἰωάννης καὶ Ἀνδρέας, 4 Εἰπὸν ἡμῖν πότε ταῦτα ἔσται, καὶ τί τὸ σημεῖον ὅταν μέλλῃ ταῦτα συντελεῖσθαι πάντα. 5 ὁ δὲ Ἰησοῦς ἤρξατο λέγειν αὐτοῖς, Βλέπετε... 6 ...λέγοντες ὅτι Ἐγώ εἰμι,... 7 ... δεῖ γενέσθαι, ἀλλ᾽ οὔπω τὸ τέλος. 8 ...ἀρχὴ ὠδίνων ταῦτα. 9 βλέπετε δὲ ὑμεῖς ἑαυτούς· παραδώσουσιν ὑμᾶς... 10 καὶ εἰς πάντα τὰ ἔθνη πρῶτον δεῖ κηρυχθῆναι τὸ εὐαγγέλιον. 11 ...οὐ γάρ ἐστε ὑμεῖς οἱ λαλοῦντες ἀλλὰ τὸ πνεῦμα τὸ ἅγιον... 13 καὶ ἔσεσθε μισούμενοι ὑπὸ πάντων διὰ τὸ ὄνομά μου. ὁ δὲ ὑπομείνας εἰς τέλος οὗτος σωθήσεται.

THE GREAT TRIBULATION
(Mt 24.15–28; Lk 21.20–24)

14 ...ὁ ἀναγινώσκων νοείτω,... 19 ἔσονται γάρ... 23 ὑμεῖς δὲ βλέπετε· προείρηκα ὑμῖν πάντα.

THE COMING OF THE SON OF MAN
(Mt 24.29–31; Lk 21.25–28)

24 ...μετὰ τὴν θλῖψιν ἐκείνην...

THE LESSON OF THE FIG TREE
(Mt 24.32–35; Lk 21.29–33)

28 Ἀπὸ δὲ τῆς συκῆς μάθετε τὴν παραβολήν·... 29 οὕτως καὶ ὑμεῖς, ὅταν ἴδητε ταῦτα γινόμενα, γινώσκετε ὅτι ἐγγύς ἐστιν ἐπὶ θύραις. 30 ἀμὴν λέγω ὑμῖν ὅτι...

THE UNKNOWN DAY AND HOUR
(Mt 24.36-44)

33 βλέπετε ἀγρυπνεῖτε· οὐκ οἴδατε γὰρ πότε ὁ καιρός ἐστιν. 34 ὡς ἄνθρωπος ἀπόδημος ἀφεὶς τὴν οἰκίαν αὐτοῦ...ἵνα γρηγορῇ. 35 ...οὐκ οἴδατε γάρ... 37 ὃ δὲ ὑμῖν λέγω, πᾶσιν λέγω, γρηγορεῖτε.

THE PLOT TO KILL JESUS
(Mt 26.1-5; Lk 22.1-2; Jn 11.45-53)

14 Ἦν δὲ τὸ πάσχα καὶ τὰ ἄζυμα μετὰ δύο ἡμέρας... 2 ἔλεγον γάρ,...

THE ANOINTING AT BETHANY
(Mt 26.6-13; Jn 12.1-8)

3 Καὶ ὄντος αὐτοῦ ἐν Βηθανίᾳ ἐν τῇ οἰκίᾳ Σίμωνος τοῦ λεπροῦ... 4 ἦσαν δέ τινες ἀγανακτοῦντες πρὸς ἑαυτούς,... 5 ἠδύνατο γάρ... 7 πάντοτε γάρ... 8 ὃ ἔσχεν ἐποίησεν· προέλαβεν μυρίσαι τὸ σῶμά μου εἰς τὸν ἐνταφιασμόν. 9 ἀμὴν δὲ λέγω ὑμῖν ὅπου ἐὰν κηρυχθῇ τὸ εὐαγγέλιον εἰς ὅλον τὸν κόσμον, καὶ ὃ ἐποίησεν αὕτη λαληθήσεται εἰς μνημόσυνον αὐτῆς.

JUDAS' AGREEMENT TO BETRAY JESUS: THE PASSOVER
(Mt 26.14-16; Lk 22.3-6)

10 Καὶ Ἰούδας Ἰσκαριὼθ ὁ εἷς τῶν δώδεκα ἀπῆλθεν πρὸς τοὺς ἀρχιερεῖς ἵνα αὐτὸν παραδοῖ αὐτοῖς. 11 οἱ δὲ ἀκούσαντες ἐχάρησαν καὶ ἐπηγγείλαντο αὐτῷ ἀργύριον δοῦναι. καὶ ἐζήτει πῶς αὐτὸν εὐκαίρως παραδοῖ. 12 Καὶ τῇ πρώτῃ ἡμέρᾳ τῶν ἀζύμων, ὅτε τὸ πάσχα ἔθυον, λέγουσιν αὐτῷ οἱ μαθηταὶ αὐτοῦ,... 17 Καὶ ὀψίας γενομένης ἔρχεται μετὰ τῶν δώδεκα. 18 καὶ ἀνακειμένων αὐτῶν καὶ ἐσθιόντων ὁ Ἰησοῦς εἶπεν, Ἀμὴν λέγω ὑμῖν ὅτι εἷς ἐξ ὑμῶν παραδώσει με, **ὁ ἐσθίων μετ' ἐμοῦ.** 19 ἤρξαντο λυπεῖσθαι καὶ λέγειν αὐτῷ εἷς κατὰ εἷς, Μήτι ἐγώ; 20 ὁ δὲ εἶπεν

αὐτοῖς, Εἷς τῶν δώδεκα, ὁ ἐμβαπτόμενος μετ' ἐμοῦ εἰς τὸ [ἓν] τρύβλιον. 21 ὅτι ὁ μὲν υἱὸς τοῦ ἀνθρώπου ὑπάγει καθὼς γέγραπται περὶ αὐτοῦ, οὐαὶ δὲ τῷ ἀνθρώπῳ ἐκείνῳ δι' οὗ ὁ υἱὸς τοῦ ἀνθρώπου παραδίδοται· καλὸν αὐτῷ εἰ οὐκ ἐγεννήθη ὁ ἄνθρωπος ἐκεῖνος.

THE INSTITUTION OF THE LORD'S SUPPER
(Mt 26.26–30; Lk 22.15–20; 1 Cor 11.23–25)

22 Καὶ ἐσθιόντων αὐτῶν λαβών... 25 ἀμὴν λέγω ὑμῖν ὅτι οὐκέτι οὐ μὴ πίω... 26 Καὶ ὑμνήσαντες ἐξῆλθον εἰς τὸ Ὄρος τῶν Ἐλαιῶν.

PETER'S DENIAL FORETOLD
(Mt 26.31–35; Lk 22.31–34; Jn 13.36–38)

27 Καὶ λέγει αὐτοῖς ὁ Ἰησοῦς ὅτι Πάντες σκανδαλισθήσεσθε, ὅτι γέγραπται,

Πατάξω τὸν ποιμένα,
καὶ τὰ πρόβατα διασκορπισθήσονται·
28 ἀλλὰ μετὰ τὸ ἐγερθῆναί με προάξω ὑμᾶς εἰς τὴν Γαλιλαίαν. 29 ὁ δὲ Πέτρος ἔφη αὐτῷ, Εἰ καὶ πάντες σκανδαλισθήσονται, ἀλλ' οὐκ ἐγώ. 30 καὶ λέγει αὐτῷ ὁ Ἰησοῦς, Ἀμὴν λέγω σοι ὅτι σὺ *σήμερον ταύτῃ τῇ νυκτὶ πρὶν ἢ δὶς ἀλέκτορα φωνῆσαι τρίς με ἀπαρνήσῃ*. 31 ὁ δὲ ἐκπερισσῶς ἐλάλει, *Ἐὰν δέῃ με συναποθανεῖν σοι, οὐ μή σε ἀπαρνήσομαι. ὡσαύτως δὲ καὶ πάντες ἔλεγον.*

THE PRAYER IN GETHSEMANE
(Mt 26.36–46; Lk 22.39–46)

32 Καὶ ἔρχονται εἰς χωρίον οὗ τὸ *ὄνομα Γεθσημανί*, καὶ λέγει τοῖς μαθηταῖς αὐτοῦ, *Καθίσατε ὧδε ἕως προσεύξωμαι.* 33 καὶ παραλαμβάνει τὸν Πέτρον καὶ [τὸν] Ἰάκωβον καὶ [τὸν] Ἰωάννην μετ' αὐτοῦ, καὶ ἤρξατο ἐκθαμβεῖσθαι καὶ ἀδημονεῖν,... 38 γρηγορεῖτε καὶ προσεύχεσθε, ἵνα μὴ ἔλθητε εἰς πειρασμόν· τὸ μὲν πνεῦμα πρόθυμον ἡ δὲ σὰρξ ἀσθενής. 39 καὶ πάλιν ἀπελθὼν προσηύξατο τὸν αὐτὸν λόγον εἰπών. 40 καὶ πάλιν ἐλθὼν εὗρεν αὐτοὺς καθεύδοντας, ἦσαν γὰρ αὐτῶν οἱ ὀφθαλμοὶ καταβαρυνόμενοι, καὶ οὐκ ᾔδεισαν τί ἀποκριθῶσιν αὐτῷ. 41 καὶ ἔρχεται τὸ τρίτον καὶ λέγει

αὐτοῖς Καθεύδετε τὸ λοιπὸν καὶ ἀναπαύεσθε; ἀπέχει· ἦλθεν ἡ ὥρα, ἰδοὺ παραδίδοται ὁ υἱὸς τοῦ ἀνθρώπου εἰς τὰς χεῖρας τῶν ἁμαρτωλῶν. 42 ἐγείρεσθε ἄγωμεν· ἰδοὺ ὁ παραδιδούς με ἤγγικεν.

THE BETRAYAL AND ARREST OF JESUS
(Mt 26.47–56; Lk 22.47–53; Jn 18.3–12)

43 Καὶ εὐθὺς ἔτι αὐτοῦ λαλοῦντος... 47 εἷς δέ [τις] *τῶν παρεστηκότων σπασάμενος τὴν μάχαιραν ἔπαισεν τὸν δοῦλον τοῦ ἀρχιερέως καὶ ἀφεῖλεν αὐτοῦ τὸ ὠτάριον.* 48 καὶ ἀποκριθεὶς ὁ Ἰησοῦς εἶπεν αὐτοῖς, Ὡς ἐπὶ λῃστὴν ἐξήλθατε μετὰ μαχαιρῶν καὶ ξύλων συλλαβεῖν με; 49 καθ’ ἡμέραν ἤμην πρὸς ὑμᾶς ἐν τῷ ἱερῷ διδάσκων καὶ οὐκ ἐκρατήσατέ με· ἀλλ’ ἵνα πληρωθῶσιν αἱ γραφαί. 50 καὶ ἀφέντες αὐτὸν ἔφυγον πάντες.

THE YOUNG MAN WHO FLED

51 Καὶ νεανίσκος τις συνηκολούθει αὐτῷ περιβεβλημένος σινδόνα [ἐπὶ γυμνοῦ], καὶ κρατοῦσιν αὐτόν· 52 ὁ δὲ καταλιπὼν τὴν σινδόνα γυμνὸς ἔφυγεν.

JESUS BEFORE THE COUNCIL
(Mt 26.57–68; Lk 22.54–55, 63–71; Jn 18.13–14, 19–24)

53 Καὶ ἀπήγαγον τὸν Ἰησοῦν πρὸς τὸν ἀρχιερέα,... 57 καί τινες ἀναστάντες ἐψευδομαρτύρουν κατ’ αὐτοῦ λέγοντες 58 ὅτι Ἡμεῖς ἠκούσαμεν αὐτοῦ λέγοντος ὅτι Ἐγὼ καταλύσω τὸν ναὸν τοῦτον τὸν χειροποίητον καὶ διὰ τριῶν ἡμερῶν ἄλλον ἀχειροποίητον οἰκοδομήσω. 59 καὶ οὐδὲ οὕτως ἴση ἦν ἡ μαρτυρία αὐτῶν... 61 ὁ δὲ ἐσιώπα καὶ οὐκ ἀπεκρίνατο οὐδέν. πάλιν ὁ ἀρχιερεὺς ἐπηρώτα αὐτὸν καὶ λέγει αὐτῷ, Σὺ εἶ ὁ Χριστὸς ὁ υἱὸς τοῦ εὐλογητοῦ;... 65 Καὶ ἤρξαντό τινες ἐμπτύειν τῷ προσώπῳ αὐτοῦ καὶ κολαφίζειν αὐτὸν καὶ λέγειν αὐτῷ, Προφήτευσον, καὶ οἱ ὑπηρέται ῥαπίσμασιν αὐτὸν ἔλαβον.

PETER'S DENIAL OF JESUS
(Mt 26.69–75; Lk 22.56–62; Jn 18.15–18, 25–27)

66 Καὶ ὄντος τοῦ Πέτρου κάτω ἐν τῇ αὐλῇ... 67 καὶ ἰδοῦσα τὸν Πέτρον θερμαινόμενον ἐμβλέψασα αὐτῷ λέγει,... 69 καὶ ἡ παιδίσκη ἰδοῦσα αὐτὸν ἤρξατο πάλιν λέγειν τοῖς παρεστῶσιν ὅτι Οὗτος ἐξ αὐτῶν ἐστιν. 70 ὁ δὲ πάλιν ἠρνεῖτο. καὶ μετὰ μικρὸν πάλιν οἱ παρεστῶτες ἔλεγον τῷ Πέτρῳ, Ἀληθῶς ἐξ αὐτῶν εἶ, καὶ γὰρ Γαλιλαῖος εἶ. 71 ὁ δὲ ἤρξατο ἀναθεματίζειν καὶ ὀμνύναι ὅτι Οὐκ οἶδα τὸν ἄνθρωπον τοῦτον ὃν λέγετε. 72 καὶ εὐθὺς ἐκ δευτέρου ἀλέκτωρ ἐφώνησεν. καὶ ἀνεμνήσθη ὁ Πέτρος τὸ ῥῆμα ὡς εἶπεν αὐτῷ ὁ Ἰησοῦς ὅτι Πρὶν ἀλέκτορα φωνῆσαι δὶς τρίς με ἀπαρνήσῃ· καὶ ἐπιβαλὼν ἔκλαιεν.

JESUS BEFORE PILATE
(Mt 27.1–2, 11–14; Lk 23.1–5; Jn 18.28–38)

15 Καὶ εὐθὺς πρωῒ συμβούλιον ποιήσαντες οἱ ἀρχιερεῖς μετὰ τῶν πρεσβυτέρων καὶ γραμματέων καὶ ὅλον τὸ συνέδριον δήσαντες τὸν Ἰησοῦν ἀπήνεγκαν καὶ παρέδωκαν Πιλάτῳ. 2 καὶ ἐπηρώτησεν αὐτὸν ὁ Πιλᾶτος, Σὺ εἶ ὁ βασιλεὺς τῶν Ἰουδαίων; ὁ δὲ ἀποκριθεὶς αὐτῷ λέγει, Σὺ λέγεις.

JESUS SENTENCED TO DIE
(Mt 27.15–26; Lk 23.13–25; Jn 18.39–19.16)

7 ἦν δὲ ὁ λεγόμενος Βαραββᾶς μετὰ τῶν στασιαστῶν δεδεμένος οἵτινες ἐν τῇ στάσει φόνον πεποιήκεισαν. 8 καὶ ἀναβὰς ὁ ὄχλος ἤρξατο αἰτεῖσθαι καθὼς ἐποίει αὐτοῖς... 10 ἐγίνωσκεν γὰρ ὅτι διὰ φθόνον παραδεδώκεισαν αὐτὸν οἱ ἀρχιερεῖς... 12 ὁ δὲ Πιλᾶτος πάλιν ἀποκριθεὶς ἔλεγεν αὐτοῖς, Τί οὖν [θέλετε] ποιήσω [ὃν λέγετε] τὸν βασιλέα τῶν Ἰουδαίων; 13 οἱ δὲ πάλιν... 14 ...Τί γὰρ ἐποίησεν κακόν;... 15 ...καὶ παρέδωκεν τὸν Ἰησοῦν φραγελλώσας ἵνα σταυρωθῇ.

THE SOLDIERS MOCK JESUS
(Mt 27.27–31; Jn 19.2–3)

16 ...ὅ ἐστιν πραιτώριον,... 18 καὶ ἤρξαντο ἀσπάζεσθαι αὐτόν, Χαῖρε, βασιλεῦ τῶν Ἰουδαίων·... 20 ...καὶ ἐξάγουσιν αὐτὸν ἵνα σταυρώσωσιν αὐτόν.

THE CRUCIFIXION OF JESUS
(Mt 27.32–44; Lk 23.26–43; Jn 19.17–27)

22 ...τόπον, ὅ ἐστιν μεθερμηνευόμενον Κρανίου Τόπος... 25 ἦν δὲ ὥρα τρίτη καὶ ἐσταύρωσαν αὐτόν. 26 καὶ ἦν ἡ ἐπιγραφὴ τῆς αἰτίας αὐτοῦ ἐπιγεγραμμένη, Ὁ βασιλεὺς τῶν Ἰουδαίων. 27 Καὶ σὺν αὐτῷ σταυροῦσιν δύο λῃστάς, ἕνα ἐκ δεξιῶν καὶ ἕνα ἐξ εὐωνύμων αὐτοῦ... 29 Καὶ οἱ παραπορευόμενοι ἐβλασφήμουν αὐτὸν **κινοῦντες τὰς κεφαλὰς** αὐτῶν καὶ λέγοντες, Οὐὰ ὁ καταλύων τὸν ναὸν καὶ οἰκοδομῶν ἐν τρισὶν ἡμέραις, 30 σῶσον σεαυτὸν καταβὰς ἀπὸ τοῦ σταυροῦ. 31 ὁμοίως καὶ οἱ ἀρχιερεῖς ἐμπαίζοντες πρὸς ἀλλήλους μετὰ τῶν γραμματέων ἔλεγον, Ἄλλους ἔσωσεν, ἑαυτὸν οὐ δύναται σῶσαι· 32 ὁ Χριστὸς ὁ βασιλεὺς Ἰσραὴλ καταβάτω νῦν ἀπὸ τοῦ σταυροῦ, ἵνα ἴδωμεν καὶ πιστεύσωμεν. καὶ οἱ συνεσταυρωμένοι σὺν αὐτῷ ὠνείδιζον αὐτόν.

THE DEATH OF JESUS
(Mt 27.45–56; Lk 23.44–49; Jn 19.28–30)

33 Καὶ γενομένης ὥρας ἕκτης σκότος ἐγένετο ἐφ' ὅλην τὴν γῆν ἕως ὥρας ἐνάτης... 34 ...ὅ ἐστιν μεθερμηνευόμενον **Ὁ θεός μου ὁ θεός μου, εἰς τί ἐγκατέλιπές με;** ... 36 δραμὼν δέ τις [καὶ] γεμίσας σπόγγον **ὄξους** περιθεὶς καλάμῳ **ἐπότιζεν** αὐτόν, λέγων, ... 39 Ἰδὼν δὲ ὁ κεντυρίων ὁ παρεστηκὼς ἐξ ἐναντίας αὐτοῦ ὅτι οὕτως κράξας ἐξέπνευσεν εἶπεν, Ἀληθῶς οὗτος ὁ ἄνθρωπος υἱὸς θεοῦ ἦν. 40 Ἦσαν δὲ καὶ γυναῖκες ἀπὸ μακρόθεν θεωροῦσαι, ἐν αἷς...

THE BURIAL OF JESUS
(Mt 27.57–61; Lk 23.50–56; Jn 19.38–42)

42 Καὶ ἤδη ὀψίας γενομένης, ἐπεὶ ἦν παρασκευή, ὅ ἐστιν προσάββατον,... 43 ...ὃς καὶ αὐτὸς ἦν προσδεχόμενος τὴν βασιλείαν τοῦ θεοῦ,... 46 καὶ ἀγοράσας σινδόνα καθελὼν αὐτὸν ἐνείλησεν τῇ σινδόνι καὶ ἔθηκεν αὐτὸν ἐν μνημείῳ ὃ ἦν λελατομημένον ἐκ πέτρας, καὶ προσεκύλισεν λίθον ἐπὶ τὴν θύραν τοῦ μνημείου.

THE RESURRECTION OF JESUS
(Mt 28.1–8; Lk 24.1–12; Jn 20.1–10)

16 2 καὶ λίαν πρωῒ τῇ μιᾷ τῶν σαββάτων ἔρχονται... 4 ... ἦν γὰρ μέγας σφόδρα... 7 ἀλλὰ ὑπάγετε εἴπατε τοῖς μαθηταῖς αὐτοῦ καὶ τῷ Πέτρῳ ὅτι Προάγει ὑμᾶς εἰς τὴν Γαλιλαίαν· ἐκεῖ αὐτὸν ὄψεσθε, καθὼς εἶπεν ὑμῖν. 8 ...καὶ οὐδενὶ οὐδὲν εἶπαν, ἐφοβοῦντο γάρ.

SELECT BIBLIOGRAPHY

Aland, K., Black, M., Metzger, B. M. and Wikgren, A. (eds.). *The Greek New Testament*. 3rd ed., London, 1975.

Allen, W. C. *The Gospel According to Saint Mark*. London, 1915.
The Gospel according to Saint Matthew, Edinburgh, 1912.

Baltzer, K. 'The meaning of the Temple in the Lukan writings', *Harvard Theological Review* 58, no. 3 (1965), 263–77.

Bammel, E. (ed.). *The Trial of Jesus*, Studies in Biblical Theology, 2nd series, 13. London, 1970.

Barrett, C. K. *Jesus and the Gospel Tradition*. London, 1967.

Bartsch, H. W. 'Early Christian Eschatology in the Synoptic Gospels', *N.T.S.* 11, no. 4 (July 1965), 387–97.

Bauer, W. *A Greek–English Lexicon of the New Testament and other Early Christian Literature*. Trans. W. F. Arndt and F. W. Gingrich. Cambridge, 1957.
Griechisch-Deutsches Wörterbuch zu den Schriften des Neuen Testamentes und der übrigen urchristlichen Literatur. 4th rev. ed., Berlin, 1952.

Best, E. *The Temptation and the Passion: The Markan Soteriology*. Cambridge, 1965.

Black, M. *An Aramaic Approach to the Gospels and Acts*. 3rd ed., Oxford, 1967.
(ed.) *The Scrolls and Christianity*, S.P.C.K. Collections, 11. London, 1969.
Review of G. R. Driver's *Judean Scrolls* in *N.T.S.* 13, no. 1 (October 1966), 81–9.

Blass, F. and Debrunner, A. *A Greek Grammar of the New Testament*. Trans. and revision by R. W. Funk of the 9th–10th German ed. Cambridge and Chicago, 1961.

Boobyer, G. H. *St. Mark and the Transfiguration Story*. Edinburgh, 1942.
'The Eucharistic Interpretation of the Miracles of the Loaves in St. Mark's Gospel', *J.T.S.* N.S. 3 (October 1952), 161–71.

Borsch, F. H. 'Mark xiv 62 and 1 Enoch lxii 5', *N.T.S.* 14, no. 4 (July 1968), 565–7.

Bratcher, R. G. 'Mark xv, 39: the Son of God', *Expository Times* 80, no. 9 (1969), 286.

Bronson, D. B. 'Paul and Apocalyptic Judaism', *J.B.L.* 83 (September 1964), 287–92.

Bultmann, R. *The History of the Synoptic Tradition*. 2nd ed., Oxford,

1968. Trans. by J. Marsh of *Theologie des Neuen Testaments*, Tübingen, 1953.

Theology of the New Testament. Trans. K. Grobel. 2 vols, London, 1952–6.

Burkill, T. A. *Mysterious Revelation, An Examination of the Philosophy of St. Mark's Gospel*. Cornell, U.S.A., 1963.

Cadbury, H. J. *The Style and Literary Method of Luke*. Cambridge (Mass.), 1919–20.

Caird, G. B. 'Uncomfortable Words II. Shake off the Dust from Your Feet (Mk. 6¹¹)', *Expository Times* 81, no. 1 (1969), 40–3.

Cave, C. H. 'The Obedience of Unclean Spirits', *N.T.S.* 11, no. 1 (October 1964), 93–7.

'The Parables and the Scriptures', *N.T.S.* 11, no. 4 (July 1965), 374–87.

Charles, R. H. (ed.). *The Apocrypha and Pseudepigrapha of the Old Testament in English*. Oxford, 1913.

Clark, A. C. *The Primitive Text of the Gospels and Acts*. Oxford, 1914.

Conzelmann, H. *The Theology of St. Luke*. Trans. G. Buswell. London, 1960.

Coutts, J. 'Those Outside (Mk. 4, 10–12)', in *Studia Evangelica*, vol. 2, pt 1 'Texte und Untersuchungen zur Geschichte der altchristlichen Literatur', pp. 155–7. Berlin, 1964.

Cranfield, C. E. B. *The Gospel according to Saint Mark*. Cambridge, 1959.

Cross, F. L. (ed.). *Studia Evangelica*, vols. 4 and 5, Akademie-Verlag, Berlin, 1968.

Danby, H. *The Mishnah*. (English Trans.) Oxford, 1933.

Danker, F. W. 'The Literary Unity of Mark 14¹⁻²⁵', *J.B.L.* 85 (December 1966), 467–72.

Daube, D. 'The Earliest Structure of the Gospels', *N.T.S.* 5, no. 3 (April 1959), 174–87.

'Public Pronouncement and Private Explanation in the Gospels', *Expository Times* 57, no. 7 (April 1946), 175–7.

'Participle and Imperative in I Peter', in E. G. Selwyn, *The First Epistle of St. Peter*, pp. 467–88. London, 1946.

Daube, D. and Davies, W. D. (eds.). *The Background of the New Testament and its Eschatology*. Cambridge, 1956.

Davies, W. D. *Paul and Rabbinic Judaism*. London, 1948.

Dibelius, M. *From Tradition to Gospel*. Trans. B. L. Woolf. London, 1971.

Dodd, C. H. *The Parables of the Kingdom*. Rev. ed., London, 1926.

'The Framework of the Gospel Narratives' in *New Testament Studies*, pp. 1–11. Manchester, 1953.

Dodd, C. H. 'The Appearances of the Risen Christ: An Essay in Form-Criticism of the Gospels' in D. E. Nineham (ed.), *Studies in the Gospels*, pp. 9–35. Oxford, 1955.

Doudna, J. C. *The Greek of the Gospel of Mark*, J.B.L. Monograph Series 12. Philadelphia, 1961.

Dupont, J. 'La parabole du figuier qui bourgeonne', *Revue Biblique* (October 1968), 526–48.

Emerton, J. A. 'ΤΟ ΑΙΜΑ ΜΟΥ ΤΗΣ ΔΙΑΘΗΚΗΣ: The evidence of the Syriac versions', *J.T.S.* N.S. 13 (April 1962), 111–17.

'MARANATHA and EPHPHATHA', *J.T.S.* N.S. 18 (October 1967), 427–31.

'The Origin of the Son of Man Imagery', *J.T.S.* N.S. 9 (October 1958), 225–42.

'Did Jesus speak Hebrew?', *J.T.S.* N.S. 12 (October 1961), 189–202.

Eppstein, V. 'When and How the Sadducees were excommunicated', *J.B.L.* 85 (June 1966), 213–24.

Evans, C. F. 'I will go before you into Galilee', *J.T.S.* N.S. 5 (April 1954), 3–18.

The Beginning of the Gospel. London, 1968.

Farrer, A. M. *A Study in St. Mark.* London, 1951.

St. Matthew and St. Mark. London, 1954.

'An Examination of Mark xiii 10', *J.T.S.* N.S. 7 (April 1956), 75–9.

Fenton, J. C. 'Paul and Mark' in D. E. Nineham (ed.), *Studies in the Gospels*, pp. 89–112. Oxford, 1955.

Flemington, W. F. *New Testament Doctrine of Baptism.* London, 1948.

Flew, R. N. *Jesus and His Church.* London, 1938.

Gerhardsson, B. 'The Parable of the Sower and its Interpretation'. *N.T.S.* 14, no. 2 (January 1968), 165–93.

Glasson, T. F. 'Mark, xv. 39: the Son of God', *Expository Times*, 80, no. 9 (1969), 286.

Goguel, M. *The Life of Jesus.* Trans. O. Wyon. Allen and Unwin, 1933.

Grant, F. C. *The Earliest Gospel.* New York, 1943.

Grant, R. M. 'American New Testament Study 1926–1956', *J.B.L.* 87 (March 1968), 42 50.

Gray, B. *Sacrifice in the Old Testament.* Oxford, 1925.

Greek New Testament, The. See Aland *et al.*

Haenchen, E. 'Die Komposition von Mk. 8, 27–9, 1 und Par.', *N.T.* 6 (1963), 81–109.

Hainsworth, J. B. *The Flexibility of the Homeric Formula.* Oxford, 1968.

Hamilton, N. Q. 'Resurrection Tradition and the Composition of Mark', *J.B.L.* 84 (December 1965), 415–21.

Harris, J. Rendel. 'An Unnoticed Aramaism in St. Mark', *Expository Times* 26 (March 1915), 248ff.

Hatch, E. and Redpath, H. E. *A Concordance to the Septuagint.* Graz, 1954.

Hawkins, J. C. *Horae Synopticae.* Oxford, 1899.

Héring, J. *La première épître de saint Paul aux Corinthiens.* Neuchâtel–Paris, 1959.

Hiers, R. H. 'Eschatology and Methodology', *J.B.L.* 85 (June 1966), 170–84.

Hill, D. 'Δίκαιοι as a Quasi-Technical Term', *N.T.S.* 11, no. 3 (April 1965), 296–302.

Hindley, J. C. 'Towards a date for the Similitudes of Enoch. An historical approach', *N.T.S.* 14, no. 4 (July 1968), 551–65.

Holt, J. M. 'So he may run who reads it', *J.B.L.* 83 (September 1964), 298–302.

Hooker, M. D. *The Son of Man in Mark.* London, 1967.
Jesus and the Servant. London, 1959.

Horstmann, M. *Studien zur Markinischen Christologie.* Münster, 1969.

Hoskyns, E. and Davey, F. N. *The Riddle of the New Testament.* London, 1947.

Howard, W. F. 'Appendix on Semitisms in the New Testament' in J. H. Moulton and W. F. Howard, *A Grammar of New Testament Greek*, vol. 2, pt 3. Edinburgh, 1928.

Hunkin, J. W. 'Pleonastic ἄρχομαι in the New Testament', *J.T.S.* 25 (July 1924), 390ff.

Jacob, E. *Theology of the Old Testament.* London, 1958.

Jaubert, A. 'Le mercredi où Jésus fut livré', *N.T.S.* 14, no. 2 (January 1968), 145–64.
La Date de la Cène, calendrier biblique et liturgie chrétienne. Paris, 1957.

Jeremias, J. *The Parables of Jesus.* Trans. S. H. Hooke. Rev. ed., London, 1963.
The Eucharistic Words of Jesus. Trans. A. Ehrhardt. Oxford, 1955.
Jesus' Promise to the Nations. Trans. S. H. Hooke. London, 1958.

van Jersel, B. M. F. 'Die wunderbare Speisung und das Abendmahl in der synoptischen Tradition', *N.T.* 7 (1964/5), 167–94.

Johnson, A. R. *The One and the Many in the Israelite Conception of God.* Cardiff, 1942.
The Vitality of the Individual in the Thought of Ancient Israel. Cardiff, 1949.

Keck, L. E. 'The Introduction to Mark's Gospel', *N.T.S.* 12, no. 4 (July 1966), 352–70.

Kee, A. 'The question about Fasting', *N.T.* 11, no. 3 (1969), 161–73.

Kee, H. C. 'The terminology of Mark's Exorcism Stories', *N.T.S.* 14, no. 2 (January 1968), 232–46.

Kertelge, K. *Die Wunder Jesu im Markusevangelium.* München, 1970.

Kilpatrick, G. D. 'ἐπάνω: Mark xiv. 5; The Disappearance of Q; The Possessive Pronouns in the New Testament', *J.T.S.* 42 (July 1941), 181–6.

'Western Text and Original Text in the Gospels and Acts', *J.T.S.* 44 (January 1943), 24–36.

'Mark iv 29; John i 3–4 and Jerome', *J.T.S.* 46 (July–October 1945), 191–2.

The Origins of the Gospel according to St. Matthew. Oxford, 1946.

(ed.) Η ΚΑΙΝΗ ΔΙΑΘΗΚΗ. 2nd ed. with rev. critical apparatus, London, 1958.

'Mark xiii 9–10', *J.T.S.* N.S. 9 (April 1958), 81–6.

'διαλέγεσθαι and διαλογίζεσθαι in the New Testament', *J.T.S.* N.S. 11 (October 1960), 338–40.

'The Punctuation of John VII 37–38', *J.T.S.* N.S. 11 (October 1960), 340–2.

'Two Johannine idioms in the Johannine Epistles', *J.T.S.* N.S. 12 (October 1961), pp. 272–3.

'The Spirit, God, and Jesus in Acts', *J.T.S.* N.S. 15 (April 1964), 63.

'ΑΝΑΚΕΙΣΘΑΙ and ΚΑΤΑΚΕΙΣΘΑΙ in the New Testament', *J.T.S.* N.S. 17 (April 1966), 67–9.

Knox, J. *The Death of Christ: The Cross in the New Testament, History and Faith.* London, 1959.

Knox, W. L. 'The Ending of St. Mark's Gospel', *Harvard Theological Review* 35 (1942), 13–23.

The Sources of the Synoptic Gospels. Cambridge, 1953.

Kuhn, H. W. *Ältere Sammlungen im Markusevangelium.* Göttingen, 1971.

Kummel, W. G. *Introduction to the New Testament.* London, 1965.

Lagrange, M. J. *Évangile selon Saint Marc.* 5th ed., Paris, 1929.

Lake, K. *The Text of the New Testament.* 6th ed., rev. by S. New, London, 1928.

An Introduction to the New Testament. London, 1939.

Lake, K. and Foakes-Jackson, F. J. *The Beginnings of Christianity* 5 vols., London, 1920–3.

Lambrecht, J *Die Redaktion der Markus-Apokalypse.* Analecta Biblica 28, Rome, 1967.

Légasse, S. 'Jésus a-t-il annoncé la Conversion Finale d'Israël? (À propos de Marc x 23–7)', *N.T.S.* 10, no. 4 (July 1964), 480–7.

Legg, S. C. E. *Nouum Testamentum Graece secundum Textum Westcotti-Hortianum, Euangelium secundum Marcum cum apparatu critico nouo plenissimo.* Oxford, 1935.

Lightfoot, R. H. *History and Interpretation in the Gospels.* London, 1935.
Locality and Doctrine in the Gospels. London, 1938.
The Gospel Message of St. Mark. Oxford, 1950.

Lindars, B. *New Testament Apologetic.* London, 1961.

Linton, O. 'Evidences of a Second-Century Revised Edition of St. Mark's Gospel', *N.T.S.* 14, no. 3 (April 1968), 321–55.

Lohmeyer, E. *Galiläa und Jerusalem.* Göttingen, 1936.

Loisy, A. *L'évangile selon Marc.* Paris, 1912.

Longenecker, R. N. 'Some Distinctive Early Christological Motifs', *N.T.S.* 14, no. 4 (July 1968), 526–45.

Marxsen, W. *Der Evangelist Markus.* Göttingen, 1959.
Introduction to the New Testament. Trans. G. Buswell. Oxford, 1968.

Mauser, U. *Christ in the Wilderness,* Studies in Biblical Theology 39. Chatham, 1963.

Meeks, W. A. 'Galilee and Judea in the Fourth Gospel', *J.B.L.* 85 (June 1966), 159–69.

Milik, J. T. *Dix Ans de Découvertes dans le Désert de Juda.* Paris, 1957.

Montefiore, C. G. *The Synoptic Gospels, edited with an Introduction and a Commentary.* 2nd ed., London, 1927.

Moore, G. F. *Judaism.* 3 vols., Cambridge, U.S.A., 1927–30.

Morgenthaler, R. *Statistik des neutestamentlichen Wortschatzes.* Zürich–Frankfurt, 1958.

Moule, C. F. D. *An Idiom Book of New Testament Greek.* Cambridge, 1953.
Review of Kilpatrick's article in D. E. Nineham (ed.), *Studies in the Gospels,* *J.T.S.* N.S. 7 (1956), 280–2.
Review of N. Turner, *A Grammar of New Testament Greek,* ed. J. H. Moulton, vol. 3, 'Syntax', in *J.T.S.* N.S. 15 (1964), 118–21.
'St. Paul and Dualism: The Pauline Concept of Resurrection', *N.T.S.* 12, no. 2 (January 1966), 106–23.
The Phenomenon of the New Testament, Studies in Biblical Theology, 2nd series 1. London, 1967.
'Fulfilment-Words in the New Testament: Use and Abuse', *N.T.S.* 14, no. 3 (April 1968), 293–320.

Moulton, J. H. and Howard, W. F. *A Grammar of New Testament Greek.* 3rd ed. vol. 1, Edinburgh, 1906. Vol. 2, Edinburgh, 1928. Vol. 3, *see* Turner.

Moulton, J. H. and Milligan, G. *The Vocabulary of the Greek Testament illustrated from the Papyri and other non-literary sources.* London, 1930.

Moulton, W. F. and Geden, A. S. *A Concordance to the Greek Testament.* 4th ed. rev., Edinburgh, 1963.

Neill, S. *The Interpretation of the New Testament 1861–1961.* London, 1964.

Neirynck, F. *Duality in Mark, Contributions to the Study of Markan Redaction*. Bibliotheca Ephemeridum Theologicarum Lovaniensium 31. Leuven, 1972.

Nemoy, L. 'Al-Qirqisani's Account of the Jewish Sects and Christianity', *Hebrew Union College Annual* 7 (1930), 326ff.

Nestle, E. and Aland, K. *Novum Testamentum Graece*. 25th ed. London–Stuttgart, 1967.

Nevius, R. C. 'The Use of the Definite Article with "Jesus" in the Fourth Gospel', *N.T.S.* 12 (October 1965), 81–5.

Nineham, D. E. (ed.). *Studies in the Gospels: Essays in Memory of R. H. Lightfoot*. Oxford, 1955.

'The order of events in St. Mark's Gospel – an examination of Dr. Dodd's hypothesis' in *Studies in the Gospels*, pp. 223–39.

Saint Mark, Pelican Commentaries. London, 1963.

'Jesus in the Gospels' in N. Pittenger (ed.), *Christ for us today*, pp. 45–65.

O'Rourke, J. J. 'Critical Notes: A note concerning the use of ΕΙΣ and ΕΝ in Mark', *J.B.L.* 85 (September 1966), 349–51.

Otto, R. *The Kingdom of God and the Son of Man*. Trans. F. V. Filson and B. L. Woolf. London, 1938.

Parker, P. *The Gospel Before Mark*. Chicago, 1953.

Parry, M. 'Studies in the Epic Technique of Oral Verse-Making: 1. Homer and Homeric Style', *Harvard Studies in Classical Philology* 41 (1930), 73–147.

Perrin, N. *Rediscovering the Teaching of Jesus*. London, 1967.

'The Composition of Mark ix, 1', *N.T.* 11 (January 1969), 67–70.

Pesch, R. *Naherwartungen: Tradition und Redaktion in Mk 13*. Düsseldorf, 1968.

'Berufung und Sendung, Nachfolge und Mission, Eine Studie zu Mk. 1, 16–20', *Zeitschrift für Katholische Theologie* 91 (1969), 1–31.

Pryke, E. J. 'ΙΔΕ and ΙΔΟΥ', *N.T.S.* 14, no. 3 (April 1968), 418–24.

'Eschatology in the Scrolls' in Black (ed.), *S.P.C.K. Collections* 11, pp. 45–57.

'The Historical Present in S. Mark: A Study in Redaction', paper given at Oxford Fifth International Congress on Biblical Studies, 1973, and to be published in *Studia Evangelica*.

Rawlinson, A. E. J. *The Gospel according to St. Mark*. London, 1925.

Reploh, K. G. *Markus – Lehrer der Gemeinde: Eine redaktionsgeschichtliche Studie zu den Jüngerperikopen des Markus-Evangeliums*. Stuttgart, 1969.

Reynolds, S. M. 'ΠΥΓΜΗΙ (Mark 7³) as "cupped Hand"', *J.B.L.* 85 (March 1966), 87–8.

Richardson, A. *The Miracle Stories of the Gospels*. London, 1941.

Robinson, J. M. *The Problem of History in Mark*, Studies in Biblica. Theology 21. London, 1957.

Rohde, J. *Rediscovering the Teaching of the Evangelists*, London, 1968. Trans D. M. Barton.

Ropes, J. H. *The Synoptic Gospels*. Oxford, 1960.

Salomonsen, B. 'Some Remarks on the Zealots with special regard to the term "Qannaim" in Rabbinic Literature', *N.T.S.* 12, no. 2 (January 1966), 164–76.

Sanders, E. P. *The Tendencies of the Synoptic Tradition*, Society for New Testament Studies Monograph Series. Cambridge, 1969.

Schmidt, K. L. *Der Rahmen der Geschichte Jesu*. Berlin, 1919.

Schreiber, J. *Theologie des Vertrauens: Eine redaktionsgeschichtliche Untersuchung des Markusevangeliums*. Hamburg, 1967.

Schweizer, E. 'Anmerkungen zur Theologie des Markus' in *Supplements to Novum Testamentum*, vol. 6, 'Neotestamentica et Patristica', pp. 35–46. Leiden, 1962.

'Mark's Contribution to the Quest of the Historical Jesus', *N.T.S.* 10, no. 4 (July 1964), 421–32.

The Good News according to Mark, trans. D. H. Madvig. London, 1971.

Seitz, O. J. F. 'Praeparatio Evangelica in the Markan Prologue', *J.B.L.* 82 (June 1963), 201–6.

Simonsen, H. *Traditionssammenhaeng og forkyndelsessigte i Markusevangeliets fortaellestof*. Copenhagen, 1966.

Simpson, R. T. 'The major agreements of Matthew and Luke against Mark', *N.T.S.* 12 (April, 1966), 273–84.

von Soden, H. P. *Griechisches neues Testament, mit kurzem Apparat*. Göttingen, 1913.

Souter, A. *The Text and Canon of the New Testament*. 2nd ed., rev. C. S. C. Williams. London, 1954.

Stein, R. H. 'The Proper Methodology for ascertaining a Markan Redaction History?', *N.T.* 13 (July 1971), 181–98.

'What is Redaktionsgeschichte?', *J.B.L.*, 88 (March 1969), 45–56.

Stendahl, K. *The School of St. Matthew and its use of the Old Testament*. Lund, 1954.

Stinespring, W. F. 'The Active Infinitive with Passive Meaning in Biblical Aramaic', *J.B.L.* 81 (December 1962), 391–4.

Streeter, B. H. *The Four Gospels: A Study of Origins*. London, 1924.

Sundwall, J. 'Die Zusammensetzung des Markusevangeliums' in *Acta Academiae Aboensis, Humaniora IX*, pp. 1–86. Abo, 1934.

Swete, H. B. *The Gospel according to St Mark*. 2nd ed., London, 1908.

Taylor, V. *The Gospel according to St. Mark*. London, 1952.

Thackeray, H. St. John. *The Septuagint and Jewish Worship*. London, 1921.

Thomas, J. *Le mouvement Baptiste en Palestine et Syrie*. Gembloux, 1935.

Trocmé, E. *La Formation de l'Évangile selon Marc*, Études d'Histoire et de Philosophie Religieuses 57. Paris, 1963.

'L'Expulsion des Marchands du Temple', *N.T.S.* 15 (October 1968), 1–22.

Turner, C. H. Series of articles in *J.T.S.* 25–9 (1924–8): 'Marcan Usage: Notes, Critical and Exegetical, on the Second Gospel'.

I. 'The Impersonal Plural', 25 (July 1924), 378–86.

II. 'φέρειν in St. Mark',
III. 'εἰς and ἐν in Mark', } 26 (October 1924), 12–20.

IV. 'Parenthetical Clauses in Mark', 26 (January 1925), 145–56.

V. 'The movements of Jesus and his disciples and the crowd', 26 (April 1925), 225–8; (i) 'The impersonal plural, followed by the singular', 228–31; (ii) 'The singular followed by mention of the disciples (or the Twelve)', 231–3; (iii) 'The Lord, the disciples, and the multitude', 234–5; (iv) '"His disciples", "the disciples" (οἱ μαθηταὶ αὐτοῦ, οἱ μαθηταί)', 235–7; (v) '"The Crowd" or "The Multitudes"', 237–8; (vi) 'The word "to follow", ἀκολουθεῖν', 238–40.

VI. 'The use of numbers in St. Mark's Gospel', 26 (July 1925), 337–46.

VII. 'Particles': (1) 'ὅτι interrogative', 27 (October 1925), 58–62; (2) 'ὅτι recitative (after λέγειν or similar verbs)', 28 (October 1926), 9–15; (3) 'Asyndeta or absence of particles in Mark', 15–19; (4) 'Particles absent from Mark', 19–22.

VIII. (i) '"The disciples" and "The Twelve"', 22–30; 'Auxiliary and quasi-auxiliary verbs', 28 (July 1927), 349–51. (ii) 'The verb ἄρχομαι (ἤρξατο ἤρξαντο) with present infinitive as auxiliary for the imperfect...', 352–3; (iii) 'The verb δύναμαι as auxiliary...', 354–5; (iv) 'The verb θέλω as auxiliary...', 355–7; (v) 'The verb ἔχω...', 360–2.

IX. (1) 'Miscellaneous', 29 (April 1928), 275–89; (2) 'πυγμῇ', 278–9; 'πάλιν...', 283–7.

IX. (1) 'Titles of address to Christ', 29 (July 1928), 346 9; (2) 'Diminutives in Mark', 349–52; (3) 'The verb at the end of the sentence after noun or personal pronoun', 352–6; (4) 'ἵνα...', 356–9; (5) 'Absence of λέγων (λέγοντες) after verbs introducing a statement or a question...', 359–61.

'Ο ΥΙΟΣ ΜΟΥ Ο ΑΓΑΠΗΤΟΣ', *J.T.S.* 27 (January 1926), 113–29.

'The Gospel according to St. Mark' in Gore, C., Goudge, H. L., and Guillaume, A. (eds.), *New Commentary on Holy Scripture*, pp. 42–124. London, 1928.

Turner, N. *A Grammar of New Testament Greek*, ed. J. H. Moulton, vol. 3, 'Syntax'. Edinburgh, 1963.

Weiss, H. 'History and a Gospel', *N.T.* 10 (April 1968), 81–94.

Wellhausen, J. *Einleitung in die drei ersten Evangelien*. 2nd ed., Berlin, 1911.

Westcott, B. F. and Hort, F. J. A. *The New Testament in the Original Greek*, vol. 2, 'Introduction and Appendix'. 2nd ed., Cambridge and London, 1896.

Wichelhaus, M. 'Am ersten Tage der Woche Mk. i 35–39 und die didaktischen Absichten des Markus-Evangelisten', *N.T.* 11, nos. 1–2 (January/April 1969), 45–66.

Wilder, A. N. 'Form-history and the oldest tradition', in *Supplements to Novum Testamentum*, vol. 6, 'Neotestamentica et Patristica', pp. 3–13. Leiden, 1962.

Williams, C. S. C. *Alterations to the Text of the Synoptic Gospels and Acts*. Oxford, 1951.

Williams, J. G. 'A Critical Note on the Aramaic Indefinite Plural of the Verb', *J.B.L.* 83 (June 1964), 180–2.

Wilson, R. McL. *Gnosis and the New Testament*. Oxford, 1968.

Winter, P. *On the Trial of Jesus*. Berlin, 1961.

'The Marcan account of Jesus' Trial by the Sanhedrin', *J.T.S.* N.S. 14 (1963), 94–102.

Wood, H. G. *Commentary on St. Mark*, Peake commentary (old), pp. 681–99. London, 1919.

Wood, J. E. 'Isaac Typology in the N.T.', *N.T.S.* 14, no. 4 (July 1968), 583–9.

Yates, J. E. *The Spirit and the Kingdom*. London, 1963.

Zerwick, M. *Untersuchungen zum Markus-Stil. Ein Beitrag zur Durcharbeitung des Neuen Testamentes*. Rome, 1937.

INDEX OF PASSAGES QUOTED